THE SILK ROAD TO RICHES

In an increasingly competitive world, it is quality
of thinking that gives an edge—an idea that opens new
doors, a technique that solves a problem, or an insight
that simply helps make sense of it all.

We work with leading authors in the various arenas
of business and finance to bring cutting-edge thinking
and best-learning practices to a global market.

It is our goal to create world-class print publications
and electronic products that give readers
knowledge and understanding that can then be
applied, whether studying or at work.

To find out more about our business
products, you can visit us at www.ft-ph.com.

THE SILK ROAD TO RICHES

HOW YOU CAN PROFIT BY INVESTING IN ASIA'S NEWFOUND PROSPERITY

Yiannis G. Mostrous

Elliott H. Gue

Ivan D. Martchev

An Imprint of PEARSON EDUCATION

Upper Saddle River, NJ • New York • London • San Francisco • Toronto • Sydney
Tokyo • Singapore • Hong Kong • Cape Town • Madrid
Paris • Milan • Munich • Amsterdam

www.ft-ph.com

Library of Congress Cataloging-in-Publication Data
Mostrous, Yiannis G.
  The silk road to riches : how you can profit by investing in Asia's newfound prosperity / Yiannis G. Mostrous, Elliott H. Gue, Ivan D. Martchev.
    p. cm.
  ISBN 0-13-186972-8 (hardback)
  1. Investments, Foreign--Asia. 2. Asia--Economic policy. I. Gue, Elliott H. II. Martchev, Ivan D. III. Title.
  HG5702.M673 2005
  332.67'3095--dc22

                                                        2005033727

Vice President, Editor-in-Chief: Tim Moore
Executive Editor: Jim Boyd
Editorial Assistant: Susie Abraham
Development Editor: Russ Hall
Associate Editor-in-Chief and Director of Marketing: Amy Neidlinger
Cover Designer: Chuti Prasertsith
Managing Editor: Gina Kanouse
Senior Project Editor: Lori Lyons
Copy Editor: Kelli Brooks
Indexer: Lisa Stumpf
Proofreader: Debbie Williams
Compositor: Tolman Creek Designs
Manufacturing Buyer: Dan Uhrig

 © 2006 by Pearson Education, Inc.
Publishing as Financial Times Prentice Hall
Upper Saddle River, New Jersey 07458

Financial Times Prentice Hall offers excellent discounts on this book when ordered in quantity for bulk purchases or special sales. For more information, please contact U.S. Corporate and Government Sales, 1-800-382-3419, corpsales@pearsontech-group.com. For sales outside the U.S., please contact International Sales at international@pearsoned.com.

Company and product names mentioned herein are the trademarks or registered trademarks of their respective owners.

Printed in the United States of America

First Printing, March 2006

ISBN 0-13-186972-8

Pearson Education LTD.
Pearson Education Australia PTY, Limited.
Pearson Education Singapore, Pte. Ltd.
Pearson Education North Asia, Ltd.
Pearson Education Canada, Ltd.
Pearson Educatión de Mexico, S.A. de C.V.
Pearson Education—Japan
Pearson Education Malaysia, Pte. Ltd.

FINANCIAL TIMES PRENTICE HALL BOOKS

For more information, please go to www.ft-ph.com

Business and Society

John Gantz and Jack B. Rochester
> *Pirates of the Digital Millennium: How the Intellectual Property Wars Damage Our Personal Freedoms, Our Jobs, and the World Economy*

Douglas K. Smith
> *On Value and Values: Thinking Differently About We in an Age of Me*

Current Events

Alan Elsner
> *Gates of Injustice: The Crisis in America's Prisons*

John R. Talbott
> *Where America Went Wrong: And How to Regain Her Democratic Ideals*

Economics

David Dranove
> *What's Your Life Worth? Health Care Rationing...Who Lives? Who Dies? Who Decides?*

Entrepreneurship

Dr. Candida Brush, Dr. Nancy M. Carter, Dr. Elizabeth Gatewood, Dr. Patricia G. Greene, and Dr. Myra M. Hart
> *Clearing the Hurdles: Women Building High Growth Businesses*

Oren Fuerst and Uri Geiger
> *From Concept to Wall Street: A Complete Guide to Entrepreneurship and Venture Capital*

David Gladstone and Laura Gladstone
> *Venture Capital Handbook: An Entrepreneur's Guide to Raising Venture Capital, Revised and Updated*

Thomas K. McKnight
> *Will It Fly? How to Know if Your New Business Idea Has Wings... Before You Take the Leap*

Stephen Spinelli, Jr., Robert M. Rosenberg, and Sue Birley
> *Franchising: Pathway to Wealth Creation*

Executive Skills

Cyndi Maxey and Jill Bremer
> *It's Your Move: Dealing Yourself the Best Cards in Life and Work*

Richard W. Paul and Linda Elder
> *Critical Thinking*

John Putzier
> *Weirdos in the Workplace*

Finance

Aswath Damodaran
> *The Dark Side of Valuation: Valuing Old Tech, New Tech, and New Economy Companies*

Kenneth R. Ferris and Barbara S. Pécherot Petitt
Valuation: Avoiding the Winner's Curse

International Business and Globalization

Robert A. Isaak
The Globalization Gap: How the Rich Get Richer and the Poor Get Left Further Behind

Johny K. Johansson
In Your Face: How American Marketing Excess Fuels Anti-Americanism

Peter Marber
Money Changes Everything: How Global Prosperity Is Reshaping Our Needs, Values, and Lifestyles

Fernando Robles, Françoise Simon, and Jerry Haar
Winning Strategies for the New Latin Markets

Investments

Gerald Appel
Technical Analysis

Guy Cohen
The Bible of Options Strategies: The Definitive Guide for Practical Trading Strategies

Guy Cohen
Options Made Easy, Second Edition

Michael Covel
Trend Following: How Great Traders Make Millions in Up or Down Markets

Aswath Damodaran
Investment Fables: Exposing the Myths of "Can't Miss" Investment Strategies

Harry Domash
Fire Your Stock Analyst! Analyzing Stocks on Your Own

David Gladstone and Laura Gladstone
Venture Capital Investing: The Complete Handbook for Investing in Businesses for Outstanding Profits

George Kleinman
Trading Commodities and Financial Futures, Third Edition

Michael J. Panzner
The New Laws of the Stock Market Jungle: An Insider's Guide to Successful Investing in a Changing World

Peter Rosenstreich
Forex Revolution

Michael C. Thomsett
Options Trading for the Conservative Investor

Michael Thomsett
Stock Profits: Getting to the Core—New Fundamentals for a New Age

Leadership

Jim Despain and Jane Bodman Converse
And Dignity for All: Unlocking Greatness through Values-Based Leadership

Marshall Goldsmith, Cathy Greenberg, Alastair Robertson, and Maya Hu-Chan
Global Leadership: The Next Generation

Marshall Goldsmith, Vijay Govindarajan, Beverly Kaye, and Albert A. Vicere
The Many Facets of Leadership

Theodore Kinni and Donna Kinni
No Substitute for Victory

Management

Rob Austin and Lee Devin
Artful Making: What Managers Need to Know About How Artists Work

Thomas L. Barton, WIlliam G. Shenkir, and Paul L. Walker
Making Enterprise Risk Management Pay Off

J. Stewart Black and Hal B. Gregersen
Leading Strategic Change: Breaking Through the Brain Barrier

William C. Byham, Audrey B. Smith, and Matthew J. Paese
Grow Your Own Leaders

Subir Chowdhury
Organization 21C

Nicholas D. Evans
Business Agility

Charles J. Fombrun and Cees B.M. Van Riel
Fame and Fortune: How Successful Companies Build Winning Reputations

Robert B. Handfield and Ernest L. Nichols, Jr.
Supply Chain Redesign

Amir Hartman
Ruthless Execution: What Business Leaders Do When Their Companies Hit the Wall

Faisal Hoque
The Alignment Effect

Kevin Kennedy and Mary Moore
Going the Distance: Why Some Companies Dominate and Others Fail

Steven R. Kursh
Minding the Corporate Checkbook: A Manager's Guide to Executing Successful Business Investments

Roy H. Lubit
Coping with Toxic Managers, Subordinates...and Other Difficult People

Tom Osenton
The Death of Demand: The Search for Growth in a Saturated Global Economy

Stephen P. Robbins
The Truth About Managing People...And Nothing but the Truth

Ronald Snee and Roger Hoerl
Leading Six Sigma: A Step-by-Step Guide Based on Experience with GE and Other Six Sigma Companies

Susan E. Squires, Cynthia J. Smith, Lorna McDougall, and William R. Yeack
Inside Arthur Andersen: Shifting Values, Unexpected Consequences

Jerry Weissman
Presenting to Win: The Art of Telling Your Story

Marketing

David Arnold
The Mirage of Global Markets: How Globalizing Companies Can Succeed as Markets Localize

Michael Basch
CustomerCulture: How FedEx and Other Great Companies Put the Customer First Every Day

Deirdre Breakenridge and Thomas J. DeLoughry
The New PR Toolkit

Jonathan Cagan and Craig M. Vogel
Creating Breakthrough Products: Innovation from Product Planning to Program Approval

Lewis P. Carbone
Clued In: How To Keep Customers Coming Back Again And Again

Bernd H. Schmitt, David L. Rogers, and Karen Vrotsos
There's No Business That's Not Show Business: Marketing in Today's Experience Culture

Yoram J. Wind and Vijay Mahajan, with Robert Gunther
Convergence Marketing: Strategies for Reaching the New Hybrid Consumer

Personal Finance

David Shapiro
Retirement Countdown: Take Action Now to Get the Life You Want

Steve Weisman
A Guide to Elder Planning: Everything You Need to Know to Protect Yourself Legally and Financially

Strategy

Edward W. Davis and Robert E. Spekmam
The Extended Enterprise: Gaining Competitive Advantage through Collaborative Supply Chains

Nicholas D. Evans
Business Innovation and Disruptive Technology

Nicholas D. Evans
Consumer Gadgets

Stacy Perman
Spies, Inc.

Joel M. Shulman, With Thomas T. Stallkamp
Getting Bigger by Growing Smaller: A New Growth Model for Corporate America

For Kornelia, Irina, Bill, and Frances

CONTENTS

ACKNOWLEDGMENTS

The Silk Road to Riches would not have been possible without the assistance of David Dittman. His editorial work, as well as his intellectual curiosity, shaped this book and challenged our thinking.

Thanks are also due to Gregg S. Early for encouraging us to press on to conclusions and for his suggestions regarding the presentation of the material. Thank you to Dr. Robert H. Riemann and Jason R. Koepke for reading the raw manuscript and making many helpful suggestions. Thank you to Devendra Thapar for providing us with a clearer perspective on India. Thank you to Ryan Matherly for supporting us in our quest for a publisher. Thank you, also, to our executive editor Jim Boyd and project editor Lori Lyons at FT Prentice Hall for believing in the project and making the process a smooth one.

Finally, a special thank you to our families for putting up with the distraction of writing.

ABOUT THE AUTHORS

Yiannis G. Mostrous is associate editor of *Wall Street Winners*, a financial newsletter that has been rated #1 by *The Hulbert Financial Digest*, and of *www.GrowthEngines.com*, an online financial journal dedicated to global markets. Formerly an analyst with Finance & Investment Associates and Artemel International, he has worked in international project financing and venture capital financing. He holds an MBA from Marymount University.

Elliott H. Gue is editor of *The Energy Strategist*, the premier financial advisory dedicated solely to covering the complex energy markets, a field he has been covering since 2002. He has been featured as a guest on Bloomberg Television and has been a regular guest in radio shows around the country. He is also an associate editor for Personal Finance. He holds a Masters of Finance degree from the University of London and a Bachelor of Science degree in Economics and Management from the University of London.

Ivan D. Martchev is editor of *Wall Street Winners* and associate editor of *Personal Finance*, which has been recognized by the Newsletter and Electronic Publishers Association as one of the nation's best financial advisory newsletters. He is also editor of the financial weblog www.attheselevels.com and has been a frequent guest in radio shows. He holds an MBA in International Business and Finance from the University of Cincinnati.

The authors' commentaries have been published by *Barron's*, Forbes.com, and Marketwatch.com from Dow Jones.

FOREWORD

For the past 17 years I have traveled the world watching, in true amazement, countries and economies experiencing the agony and the ecstasy of the change process. As the years have passed, with a lot of ups and downs along the way, many of these countries have been able to not only create better futures for their people, but also to take the lead of global economic growth. These emerging economies are changing the way the world does business.

Working with The International Finance Corporation (IFC), the private-sector arm of the World Bank Group, affords me the opportunity to spend a great deal of time observing and participating in the transformation of developing economies. I've also had the chance to meet many investors who recognized the trend and invested in these economies in the early stages. They have profited handsomely.

As I read the first draft of the book you now hold, I was impressed by the level of analysis and struck by the thought that this work could easily become the primary guide for the individual investor. The amount of information and degree of understanding within these pages will help those who read it participate in and profit from the enormous transformation as emerging economies develop their respective capital markets. My position in the field allowed me to experience it first hand.

In the many conversations I've participated in regarding the aforementioned changes, the subject of China invariably commands the discussion. And although China remains the most important and certainly the most visible globalization player, one could make an even stronger case on behalf of India over the long term. After all, India's capital markets and banking system are—as of this writing—far more advanced than China's. I leave it to the authors to explain and will instead share some personal observations based on the two years I spent in India.

In the summer of 2002, I went to New Delhi as IFC's South Asia Director. My years there were two of the most engaging and exciting of my professional life. I was fortunate enough to meet some of the businessmen who are changing India's economy, observing first-hand the change in mindset of the Indian entrepreneur. They now aspire to compete on an international level, and see such competition as a welcome challenge. This has been a rapid departure from the heavily protected and uncompetitive Indian economy of not so many years ago.

That India's economy has undergone a rapid, transforming change is becoming more and more obvious by the day. Indian entrepreneurs, having already created companies that enjoy global leadership positions in their respective industries, are busy buying assets overseas to the tune of more than US$4 billion in 2005 alone. Indians are simultaneously realizing that, for the economy to sustain a high rate of growth, improvements in infrastructure and attention to manufacturing are imperative. Although many eyes are on the infrastructure, where improvements and changes are already underway—as demonstrated in the telecommunication sector—manufacturing could be the big winner. India is still thought of by most in the context of its providing information technology services. But many observers have ignored the fact that India's highly knowledgeable, highly skilled workforce is the basis of robust manufacturing activities. India's emergence as a global hub for the automobile parts sector is just one reflection of this potential.

When it comes to the relationship with the other regional giant, India and China are working toward solving age-old problems in their relationship; one potential outcome of their improved dealings is a symbiotic relationship with increasingly tighter trade and economic ties. As a result, the world might see the rise of a new economic zone of unprecedented size and potential.

When it comes to the Indian story, nothing compares to the transformation of the Indian consumer. I can't help but recall the words of a vice chairman of one of the leading banks in the world during a dinner I attended: "We look at India as a 500-million people market." They are not alone in recognizing this. The world's multinationals have made it a key destination, and India now accounts for a significant percentage of their worldwide sales.

A well-written book on one of the most fascinating topics of our time, *The Silk Road to Riches*, will widen your horizons and open the door to the new realities of a fast-changing world.

Enjoy it.

Dimitris K. Tsitsiragos
Director of Global Manufacturing & Services
The International Finance Corporation
Washington, D.C.
January 2006

INTRODUCTION

Preparing for Change

A vast network of ancient trade routes, the "Silk Road," connected Asia with the West. From the Chinese metropolis of Xian to the shores of the Indian Ocean and the Mediterranean Sea, goods and ideas traveled on this road, enhancing the lives of millions of people.

In May 2005, during the annual meeting of the Asian Development Bank, finance ministers from 13 Asian nations moved a step closer to creating an Asian monetary fund and establishing a Silk Road for a new era. Although building this road is a long process, the fact is that Asian countries (including Japan) are pushing for more regional financial integration.

The reasons for this common desire are twofold. Asian governments were disappointed with the International Monetary Fund's response during the Asian financial crisis of 1997, and the region's emergence as an essential component of global growth is coming to fruition.

This book has at its core an "economic change" premise: Global economic leadership changes over time, and the world is now entering a period of such change. In coming years, Asia will emerge as the leader in global economic growth, whereas the West will enter a more subdued growth cycle.

A big part of the investment community dismisses this argument as nonsense. Very few contemplate imminent change at a time when America's economic and military powers seem boundless. Yet, historically, these are the times when change begins, when expectations are low. As myriad arguments are floated as to why the status quo will persist, those who fall for simplicity will be caught off guard.

Many skeptics will demand more concrete data in support of our conclusions and the underlying assumption upon which our assertions are based. We do not contest the rationality of this point of view, but the reality of structural change is that its evolution begins before hard data becomes available. Far-sighted investors must be ready to explore opportunities before indisputable proof emerges. When it does, everyone will jump at it—or will already have jumped—making it a more difficult, less profitable game. The old axiom that whatever everyone knows is not necessarily worth knowing is another underpinning of this book.

The main challenge, as with any macro-related investment decision, is to assess the impact of Asia's rise on the global economy and the region's role in the new world. Making the right calls regarding India's and China's futures will be critical for successful investing. China's size and rapid development has taken the world by surprise, making it very difficult for people to approach the problem with clear minds.

Large corporations have made Asia the center of their respective production operations. Although lower costs were initially the reason, the use of technology and the introduction of other Western business practices have been instrumental in increasing the productivity of the average employee. True productivity growth started from a lower level and has combined with a low cost base to form an integral part for the multinational corporation's production line. And as long as cutthroat competition remains the name of the game, there is nothing anyone can do to stop the trend.

As the productivity gap between the West and the East has tightened, the wealth gap, too, has begun to disappear, albeit at a much slower pace. In the meantime, expect an array of political moves in America and Europe designed to protect their workers. The process might be slowed, but the outcome is inevitable: the integration of China and India into the capitalistic system and their resulting claim for a bigger piece of the economic pie.

And here is the big question: Does Asia need the West more than the West needs Asia, or vice versa? The answer is that both need each other.

The economic dynamism Asia now projects will eventually lead to a structural rise in domestic demand—this will allow Asia to become more independent. Not long after the British left the Colonies, the New World not only outgrew its reliance on the UK, the Old Country became America's dependant. Asian development will trace the same arc. And as with the young United States, certain parts of Asia will grow not only economically, but politically and militarily as well.

On January 28, 2002, *Barron's* dedicated its cover story to hedge fund manager and legendary short-seller James Chanos because of his famous call on Enron, issued when the now-defunct energy trading giant was still riding high. In that interview, Chanos identified Tyco as the next problem. He was proven right. After the story ran, *Barron's* received letters from angry Tyco stockholders demonizing Chanos in particular and short sellers in general as enemies of America's economy.

Although such actions do, in retrospect, look silly, at the time people believed that the sad arguments put forward by the company and its cheerleaders to defend its actions were not only true but also justified holding Tyco shares.

The foregoing illustrates that investors are notoriously slow in realizing and accepting change. Throughout history, this shortcoming has cost people a lot of money, and will continue to do so. Making an effort to understand and (occasionally) anticipate social, economic, and political changes is one of the most important qualities of a successful long-term investor. Not everyone draws the same conclusions after examining a particular set of data, but different interpretation is a fact of life in the investment world.

This book is best characterized as a guide for the long-term investor. If the ideas and arguments have merit, those who heed them will realize great financial gains. As the story unfolds, fear and hype, booms and busts, and creation and destruction of wealth will mark what will be an explosive transformation altering the global economy—and our lives—forever.

The structure of this book is relatively simple. Part I anticipates and analyzes Asia's rise to global economic prominence. The first chapter discusses why Asia is now at a unique and critical juncture in its history, and how it is positioned to lead the next wave of global economic growth. In Chapter 2, we explore the economic development avenues the region could (and should) follow, and how Asia's decisions will affect the rest of the world. Chapter 3 offers a more detailed analysis of the two leading actors in this drama—India and China—and argues that India is a better destination for long-term investors.

Part II deals with the risks investors may encounter in the future. Risk tolerance—tempered by fear, flamed by greed-is the most basic element of the investment—decisions equation. A book on investing that fails to address this issue cannot be taken seriously. Chapter 4 explains the geopolitical underpinnings as the West is on the verge of ceding strong economic growth to the East. Political challenges facing the global economy at the outset of the 21st century are monumental, and so, too, are the economic risks. This is the focus of Chapter 5, which identifies specific economic imbalances and their potential impacts on world financial markets. Transitioning to risk management, Chapter 6 suggests ways investors can ensure themselves against these risks.

Part III offers investment ideas based on Asia's economic ascent. Chapter 7 deals with the importance of agriculture in the new world. Chapter 8 discusses energy, and Chapter 9 presents the opportunities industrial metals offer. Finally, Chapter 10 touches upon an array of investment opportunities in different industries that should benefit tremendously, and in due time, by the new economic order.

Many companies are identified and recommended for potential investments, but the "under the hood" analysis is not extensive. The purpose of this work is to identify investment trends and representative companies operating in industries that should prosper if the assessment is correct. Readers should use these recommendations as a point of departure.

Although the book is arranged in distinct chapters, it is hoped that the reader will notice the interconnectedness: of a new socioeconomic trend and global growth; of the rise in importance of India and China and the changes in the geopolitical environment; of the precarious state of the global economy and the potential short-term consequences for Asia's emergence; and of the detection of long-term investments trends and an investor's level of future success.

Let us now depart on a journey that in the future a lot more people will make. Let's follow the Silk Road to Asia and see how global economic growth will shift, once again, from the West to the East.

Yiannis G. Mostrous
McLean, Virginia
October 2005

Part I

IT IS ALL ABOUT THE PEOPLE

"Except on matters of detail, there are perhaps no practical questions, even among those which approach nearest to the character of purely economic questions, which admit to being decided on economic premises alone."
—John Stewart Mill

1

A NEW MIDDLE CLASS

That Asia can become the engine of global economic growth is a recurring concept in the relevant literature, a theory floated variously throughout the centuries without yielding tangible results. Based on a perceived inability of the region to deliver on its potential, many people—professional investors included—resist the idea that Asia can develop a sustainable, consumer-based economic growth model. Such resistance is rooted in the region's well-documented dependence on exports to the developed Western economies. Asia, in this construct, will remain a volatile investment proxy to global economic growth, stuck in a perpetual boom-and-bust cycle.

But consider the following set of circumstances: a large population in a demographic "sweet spot,"[1] a high savings rate, an increasing bias toward consumption, and the fact that the world needs a new growth engine for the 21st century. These elements portend a rise of the Asian consumer that will transform the global economy. Although this transformation is still in its early stages, marked by periods of rapid advancement as well as periods of relative stagnation, Asia is steadily becoming the main growth game in town.

Due to the region's internal strengths, the knowledge gained during its boom-and-bust cycles, and the current state of the global economy, Asia's time is upon us.

The firmly entrenched belief that the world cannot grow without the American consumer being the sole dominant force will cost shortsighted investors the opportunity to identify and capitalize on an emerging, gigantic trend.

Because humans are creatures of habit, it is difficult to alter our ideas and identify change. The inability to see the transition to Latin American and Japanese growth in the 1970s after everyone had become extremely comfortable playing the U.S. growth stocks of the 1960s is an example of this stasis. A more recent manifestation of this resistance to change is characterized by the fear sparked by the 1996 collapse of the Japanese consumer that the world would have great difficulty finding a new consumption archetype.

History demonstrates that change in world economic leadership is constant. Consider the great European powers that used to hold the economic reigns of the world. When one city-state was at the height of its influence, neither the city's inhabitants nor people abroad were able to contemplate a change of the status quo.

In the 1300s and 1400s, the Italian powerhouses of Venice, Genoa, and Florence dominated, followed by Spain and Portugal. In the 1500s Antwerp, and then Amsterdam, took over as centers of world banking and trade. In the 18th century, the power shifted to London, with the start of the Industrial Revolution. Eventually, the U.S. took over the lead.

Today, those claiming things will stay the same sound even more naïve than those who grew comfortable in their respective dominant city-states. Given the already significant effects of globalization on the world's economy, change in the current context is a lot closer at hand than many people are willing to accept.[2]

Asia's road is a difficult one, perhaps more difficult than those faced by other fast-growing economic regions. Asia is coming of age during a period of explosive globalization and technological change. Access to technology and capital offers a lot of opportunities, but such access is also restrictive as the region is a member of an extremely complex and interconnected world. Complicated relationships make decision-making especially difficult.

In the past, developing economies did not have outsiders looking over their shoulders. As the road to prosperity is not always clearly defined and "fair," this relative solitude worked to these economies' advantage. Today, though, the rapidly emerging economies operate under the microscope of countless worldwide organizations and governmental agencies—all administrated by the economically developed nations (EDNs). Developing economies must find ways to grow and integrate into the global economic system, while answering the questions and satisfying the demands of the great economic powers.

What would have happened to the Industrial Revolution in England, or what would have been the rate of progress in the American colonies, if they had to play by the rules that developing countries in Asia are required to follow today?

To suggest that now is not the 18th century and that the world has come a long way in civility, freedom, and the like ignores the fact that developing Asia is today at the same position (relative to the progress that the world has made) as the emerging economies of more than 200 years ago. After all, 45 percent of China's total workforce is still employed in the farm sector, a clear indication that China is still at a relatively early stage in the industrialization process.[3]

Looking Back

Asia, especially China because of its size, has long excited the imagination of the Western world. Marco Polo talked about the great wonders of China, and Christopher Columbus—although he never reached China—spoke of an "incalculable amount of trade." In the 1800s, British merchants tried, unsuccessfully, to "conquer" China.

It is beyond the scope of this book to examine the details of these failures, but some brief points are warranted. Few people appreciate (mainly because of Britain's and, later, continental Europe's industrialization boom) the fact that parts of Asia, especially parts of China, Japan, and India, were on the same economic level as Europe until the end of the 18th century. As Kenneth Pomeranz noted, "In sum, core regions in China and Japan circa 1750 seem to resemble the most advanced parts of Western Europe, combining sophisticated agriculture, commerce, and non-mechanized industry in similar, arguably even more fully realized, ways."[4]

This lack of appreciation, coupled with Europe's spectacular economic growth in the 19th century, led to unshakable misunderstandings when the West did business with China in particular. Carl Crow put the problem into perspective in 1937. "Every now and then," he wrote, "we are visited in Shanghai by an export manager, usually a new one, who appears to be spending his company's money on an expensive trip around the world for the sole purpose of discovering how many points of superiority he and others of his nationality enjoy over the people of the country he is visiting."[5] This shallow sense of superiority and a lack of sensitivity to the region's idiosyncrasies has led to myriad mistakes by and financial losses for Western investors.

Of course, this is a two-way street; Asia's own attitudes harmed Asia numerous times. In the 1990s, the region's leaders and businessmen accepted the theory that there was something unique about Asia that made its economies thrive. But the work ethic of its people notwithstanding, a careful look reveals that the region's success was more the result of good timing than anything else. At the time, Southeast Asia was the only part of the world not enmeshed in crisis, and it had fairly open markets facilitating an economic and stock market boom. With Latin America beaten down, Africa facing its chronic problems, and Japan at the end of its run, the "tigers" (for example, South Korea, Taiwan, Singapore, and so on) were the world's only growth investment choice.

The only rational explanation for this "special status" misconception is the vanity of human beings and the conviction that, for whatever reason, their situation—economic or otherwise—is of a special kind that deserves special treatment, and above all is almost certainly irreversible.

One Trick Pony

Asia has become an indispensable part of a complex global economy. It satisfies the world financial system's demand for a source of cheap labor for the developed economies. This is the basis of the East Asia Economic Model (EAEM) that has created huge surpluses in Asian countries while suppressing demand and limiting domestic growth to the amount of foreign direct investment (FDI) it receives and exports. As the Western economies condition themselves to low-priced products, Asia's role in this system is becoming more important by the day.

Both parties—Asian producers and Western consumers—have accepted their respective roles. The EAEM is based on export volume (that is, no pricing power) and depends on foreign demand and foreign direct investment by multinational corporations. This giant export machine helps the Asian countries grow, while the accumulation of savings by the Asian people (and their conversion to U.S. Treasuries and other foreign assets) allows consumers in the developed countries (particularly the U.S.) to expand their seemingly insatiable consumerism to unprecedented levels.

One school of thought characterizes this dynamic as a mutually beneficial arrangement and the result of the superb returns the U.S. and other Western economies offer the world. Asia will always remain on the giving end of the equation, this school maintains, because of its inability to develop the necessary conditions for a consumer-based economy. Although such an observation might seem outrageous to some, Asian governments have failed to foster consumption as a way of economic growth. Even after the crisis of 1997, the region's leaders refused to facilitate domestic demand as a means of reviving the respective economies. Growth became the first priority and, conveniently, the easy path—exports—was chosen again. The opportunity to balance investment and consumption was once again lost. Worse, many of the Asian countries neglected the non-mass manufacturing parts of their economies, although these sectors remain extremely vital to the long-term well being of their economic development and social balance.

On the other hand, there is no concrete proof that the great U.S. consumption machine would have been able to reach such high levels

(72 percent of gross domestic product (GDP) in 2005) if Wal-Mart, which has turned benefiting from low-cost Chinese production into an art form, had not entered the picture. In other words, it is easier to consume more if one can buy a shirt for $10 when, without Asian production, the same shirt would cost $30. At $30, consuming becomes more difficult, especially during times of economic weakness.

For the time being, Asia gladly serves as the facilitator of Western economic growth. Its economies are growing and modernizing. Yet, the moment will arrive when average Asians will demand more for themselves and governments will be forced to spend more resources supporting their own domestic economies as opposed to buying U.S. Treasuries.

Early indications of this change can also be found within the circles of Asian monetary policy making. Rakesh Mohan, deputy governor of the Reserve Bank of India, has noted: "The central banks of Asia are financing roughly 3 to 3.5 percent of the current account deficit of the U.S. and most of its fiscal deficit, as compared to the earlier situation where it was private sector flows that were funding these deficits. In view of the difficulties in monetary management that the situation entails, this situation is clearly not sustainable indefinitely."[6]

Time Is on Their Side

Asia (East, Southeast, and South) is home to 3.5 billion people, 57.5 percent of the world's population. Beyond the raw numbers, Asia's demographics are extremely impressive and important. When it comes to what researchers call demographic advantage, Asia is the spot. The region's dependency ratio[7] is still decreasing and, as Figure 1-1 shows, it is not expected to stop or reverse its decline for at least 10 years.

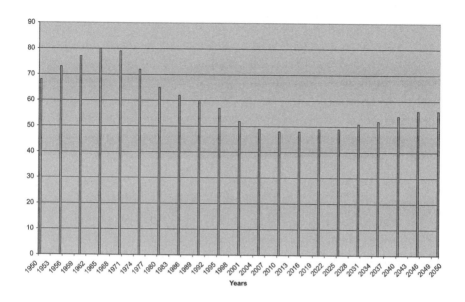

Figure 1-1 Asia's age dependency ratio. (Source: Population division of the department of economic and social affairs of the UN.)

Furthermore, the segment of its population in its 30s to 50s (the high earners and spenders) is expected to grow dramatically in the next five to 10 years, as Figure 1-2 indicates.

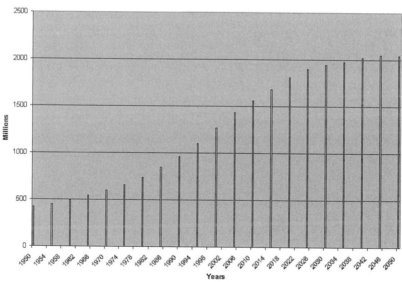

Figure 1-2 Growth of Asia's population age 30s to 50s. (Source: Population division of the department of economic and social affairs of the UN.)

Many young people in their 20s and 30s have chosen a career-oriented singles lifestyle, as opposed to the tradition of getting married early and having children. A lot of those who do marry are not in a hurry to have children. In Thailand, for example, about 34 percent of households today have no "economically dependent" children. New families are choosing (or are forced, as was the case in China) to have just one child, freeing up more disposable income with which to spoil themselves and their young.

As a result of these trends, women are emerging as a major consumption force. A greater number are entering the workforce while opting for fewer children. Not surprisingly, it is in the most affluent economies of the region where these changes are most evident. According to the Asian Development Bank, in Hong Kong, Singapore, and South Korea, the average number of births per woman in 2004 was 1, 1.4, and 1.4, respectively. In contrast, in Pakistan, Bangladesh, and the Philippines the numbers were 4.9, 3.3, and 3.1. But even in the latter countries the number of births has been decreasing.

Consumption is a major part of young people's lives—they dine out, travel, spend money on clothing and personal accessories, and save less. As the urbanization of Asia continues, this trend should persist and become the norm rather than the exception.

India's profile is a particularly important aspect of the Asian demographic advantage. More than half of Indians are under the age of 25, with 181 million people added to the population in the last decade. Population growth projections are still robust, and researchers expect the proportion of working-age people to increase well into the 2020s. Nine million new workers enter its huge work force (470 million) every year. India needs solid growth rates to support this population growth. Emigration will also play a role, especially as the rest of the world is aging.

The fact that demographics favor Asia does not alone mean that it will become the engine of world economic growth. As Stephen King, chief global economist for HSBC, has said, "...even if we had absolute certainty over demographic trends, we might still reach the wrong conclusions. This is particularly so in a situation where expected changes in the demographic profile might lead to unanticipated changes in human behavior. Give someone a tax cut when they are fully confident about the value of their future pension income and there is a good chance that the tax cut will be spent. Give someone a tax cut when there is tremendous uncertainty about future pension income, and there is a good chance that the tax cut will be saved."[8]

Nevertheless, many years of pent-up demand (over a half-century in the case of China) and growing urbanization will be more than enough to nourish the shift toward consumption. In 1990, a typical Chinese household spent almost 80 percent of its income on food, clothing, and other household items. This proportion has since come down to 55 percent and continues to fall.

A look at Asian ownership of commercial goods (see Tables 1-1 and 1-2) provides a snapshot of the continuing changes in income use, and allows for fair assumptions for the future.

Table 1-1 Television Sets per 1,000 People

Country/Region	1970	2003
China	1	350
Hong Kong	113	504
India	0	83
Indonesia	1	153
S. Korea	19	458
Malaysia	12	210
Pakistan	2	150
Philippines	11	182
Singapore	97	303
Sri Lanka	0	117
Thailand	7	300
Vietnam	23	197
Japan	337	785
Latin America	60	289
U.S.	395	938

Source: World Bank World Development Indicators, 2005

Table 1-2 Personal Computers per 1,000 People

Country/Region	1988	2003
China	0.3	27.6
Hong Kong	25.7	422
India	0.2	7.2
Indonesia	0.6	11.9
S. Korea	11.2	558
Malaysia	4.1	166.9
Pakistan	1.3	4.2
Philippines	2.1	27.7
Singapore	42.2	622
Sri Lanka	0.2	13.2
Thailand	1.9	39.8
Vietnam	0.1	9.8
Japan	41.6	382.2
U.S.	184	658.9

Source: World Bank World Development Indicators, 2005

A good comparison for certain basic consumer products can be made between the developed and less-developed economies in Asia, as well as between Asia and the developed Western economies. The most developed economies are enjoying bigger numbers, which is true in Asia, too. But a cursory look at Tables 1-1 and 1-2 reveals that growth in developing Asia has been robust. And as consumer goods become more affordable, these countries will lead future growth.

One Last Time

It is true that the Asian consumer will take time replacing the American as the primary global consumption driver, and that it will take a lot in absolute terms for Asia's middle class to catch up to Western standards.

In relative terms, however, the results are impressive and are improving rapidly. Domestic consumption is a relative term around the world—relative in the sense that prices are different and one cannot compare absolute prices when it comes to consumer goods.

For example, an upper middle-class family in India that owns a Honda Accord has the same, if not higher, status as a family that owns an Audi A6 in the U.S. Therefore, one should focus on the fact that both families have bought an automobile—what matters is consumption not relative prices.

Keep in mind that a lot of the auto companies have factories in Asia. They produce cars that are exported to the West at much higher prices. At the same time, similar or smaller cars are sold in Asia at lower prices, but still produce good profits because the cars are made in places where costs are still extremely low. Profit margins are not as high but they are solid, and can rise more as the region grows. As more people are able to afford to buy cars (or any other product or service), profits will increase because costs will remain low relative to the West.

Consider the case of General Motors. In 2003, GM made a profit of $437 million in China, selling 386,000 cars. In all of North America, the company sold 5.6 million cars for a profit of $811 million.[9] No one expects car sales in China to continue to grow by more than 50 percent per year, but the fact that producers do not have to spend money in incentives to lure buyers shows that there is real money to be made, perhaps "more real" than what GM is making in the U.S.

A crucial assumption about the region's future spending potential is that, as economies in Asia continue to grow, the income for distribution will also increase, expanding the region's middle class.

Asian income distribution is already improving, a good sign for future consumption as well as for social stability. As Table 1-3 reveals, Asia fares much better than not just other developing economic regions (for example, Latin America). One could argue that Asia as a whole has a more favorable income distribution than the U.S., given that on average 45.48 percent of income in Asia is held by the top 20 percent of the population while 7 percent of income is held by the lowest 20 percent.

Table 1-3 Income Distribution: Highest and Lowest 20% of Population

Country/Region	Year	Highest	Lowest
Bangladesh	2000	41.3	9
China	2001	46.6	5.9
Hong Kong	1996	50.7	5.3
India	2000	43.3	8.9
Indonesia	2002	43.3	8.4
S. Korea	1998	37.5	7.9
Malaysia	1997	54.3	4.4
Nepal	1996	44.8	7.6
Pakistan	1999	42.3	8.8
Philippines	2000	52.3	5.4
Singapore	1998	49	5
Sri Lanka	2000	42.2	8.3
Thailand	2000	50	6.1
Vietnam	2002	45.4	7.5
Japan	1993	35.7	10.6
Latin America	2000	56.8	3.55
Europe*	2000	40.8	7.1
U.S.	2000	45.4	5.2

*UK, Germany, France, Italy. Source: World Bank, 2005

As a general rule, Dr. Yuwa Hedrick-Wong of MasterCard International has said a per capita annual income of $5,000 is the threshold level at which a person in Asia becomes a discretionary spender. After reaching this income level, more than 50 percent of every extra dollar earned goes to discretionary spending.[10] According to national statistics, more than 250 million people in Asia qualify right now—and the number is expected to surpass 500 million by 2010. These numbers probably understate the actual situation, as they do not take into account Asia's substantial black-market economy income.[11]

The rise of Asia's middle class is becoming extremely important to the local economies. In China, for example, middle class families include about 130 million people, and their purchasing power is close to that of the more developed Asian economies. The household income for these families surpasses $24,000 (far ahead of the $5,000 mentioned previously) and economists expect that another 40 million people will join this group in the next decade.[12]

The most important development in the Asia story has been the transformation of the financial sector. Credit cards, auto loans, and—most importantly—home loans are unlocking the region's consumerist spirit and driving domestic demand. During the last five years, Asian banks have begun to realize the advantages of consumer lending, and have moved aggressively to secure retail business. This is extremely important. Asian households are notorious for their high rate of savings: close to 33 percent of GDP as of 2003. This attitude was the outcome of a long practice that postponed consumption for a later date. But a new generation is emerging in Asia, one that is looking more toward consumption than their parents did.

Mortgages are by far the most significant tool for Asian governments to push people toward consumption. People gain a great sense of economic and social security after they have a roof over their head. Growth in this credit market will be strongest in the less developed economies of the region (for example, India, China, Thailand). In most developed Asian economies, home ownership already is at high levels. In Singapore, for example, home ownership is at 94 percent.

The same holds true for credit cards. The more advanced economies (for example, South Korea, Hong Kong, Singapore) have greater penetration levels than those of less developed ones. Credit cards are a spectacle in India because few people, relative to population size, have them.

Given years of inaction, banks and consumers are eager to explore the possibilities. Growth is robust and is taking root from extremely low levels, something that will prove to be of immense importance. To understand the magnitude of the potential change, consider that in India, for example, household loans represent a little over 10 percent of total bank loans—a small amount by any measure.[13]

As the attitude toward credit is changing, the potential for domestic demand is growing. Credit can increase consumption under the most difficult circumstances. Between 2001 and 2005, the U.S. consumer was able to spend not because income increased, but because prices of goods decreased and credit was readily available. Even the rise in housing prices, which allowed consumers to borrow against their house value in order to spend, was the consequence of the Federal Reserve's extremely loose monetary policy; even the almighty American consumer machine needed help in order to remain robust.

The U.S. has in place the political and economic institutions that, theoretically, guarantee stability. Americans are willing to go out and spend money because they believe that the system will eventually work out a solution to its problems. It is this conviction that allows Americans to spend even during times of economic slowdowns. The majority of Asian governments have not been able to instill in their people the same confidence. Asia's huge pool of savings is the outcome of a malfunctioning financial system, and the resulting uncertainty regarding the future. When Asian governments successfully establish mechanisms to ensure that rule of law is the prevailing social organizing concept, financial security and respect for institutions will eventually decrease household insecurity and encourage consumption.

China's growth, in particular, has become substantial enough to highlight the critical need for major institutional changes for economic growth and development to continue. Facilitating domestic demand—which, after a point, becomes more important than investment—is the only path to sustainable economic growth. The difference between investment and demand is that the former requires a loan, whereas the latter requires complete trust in the system and the future of the economy.

According to Rudi Dornbusch and Givazzi Francesco, "A sound financial system is also a first-order issue for sound investment and sustained growth. The case of Japan manifests dramatically that neglect of financial regulation and supervision leads to awful balance sheets and a serious credit deterioration and credit crunch. The politics is decidedly difficult when a government has to own up to the fact that the population has worked hard and saved for years only to find that their accumulated assets are seriously impaired...China has a great interest in avoiding that its high saving ratio ultimately shows a payoff for savers in the form of productive capital accumulation rather than high taxes to bail out depositors and investors."[14]

The situation in China is dramatic, given the fact that banks are the main source of lending in the system, accounting for 70 percent of loans outstanding. Improvements that address (and eradicate) the political pressure in the credit allocation process will make the system more commercial.[15]

When the current economic cycle peaks, it is reasonable to expect that China will experience its first real banking crisis. But given the scope of the improvements underway, the crisis will not be the end of the reforms. Barring a domestic uprising or revolution, China should emerge from such a crisis in a sounder position.

Since 1997, Asia has made great progress in improving its financial system, but the region's sustainable growth requires nothing less than total banking reform. Although Asia needs money for development, it still cannot properly exploit its huge surpluses given the financial system's functional problems. A regional liquidity system must be established so that Asia can use its savings and other funds for investments without the interference of others. Only if Asian governments succeed in this respect will Asian countries and their citizens attain steady economic growth through sustainable domestic demand.

Eventually, Asian governments will be forced—either by social pressure or by economic circumstances—to structurally boost domestic demand. The current model of economic growth will lead to prolonged economic slumps, and will create social problems notoriously more difficult to solve than anything else. At a later stage, a structural rise in Asian wages relative to the U.S. and the developed world may take place. Domestic institutional and individual investors could provide the next level of support for the Asian countries. If governments and people work together, the next investment/consumption boom in Asia can be domestically driven, relative to the real economic situation of each country and be more sustainable. Investors worrying about the region's panic-prone characteristics should look beyond the surface. As Paul Krugman has said, "...there is no relationship between good long-run economic performance and vulnerability to crises—that the United States before World War II was both the most productive and the most panic-prone of advanced nations. Well, that cuts both ways: Asia's economic momentum didn't save it from crisis, but its crisis does not mean that it has lost its economic potential."[16]

Asia really needs domestic demand. Despite its progress in becoming a vital component of the global economic system, the region has been completely unable to project an independent voice in the world. The reason is that Asian manufacturers are price takers. Volume remains their main consideration. A huge surplus capacity forces Asian manufacturers to sell even more when demand in developed economies declines, leading to lower prices (good for consumers) while worsening Asia's terms of trade (bad for producers). Only when the region's mercantilist approach toward growth ends will Asia have a chance to become a true player in the global economic and political arena.

Traditionally, mercantilism has been defined as economic nationalism for the purpose of building a wealthy and powerful state. Adam Smith coined the term "mercantile system" to describe the system of political economy that sought to enrich the country by restraining imports and encouraging exports. This system dominated Western European economic thought and policies from the 16th to the late 18th century. The goal of these policies was, supposedly, to achieve a "favorable" balance of trade that would bring gold and silver into the country.

The Asian version has refined the system to include financing the most important customers; one tactic is to buy U.S. dollars, thus keeping their currencies artificially low and consequently helping U.S. consumers maintain strong consumption patterns. A significant motivating factor behind this effort is the psychological impact of the Asian financial crisis.

It is a long road that emerging Asia must take if its leaders are serious about helping their people benefit more from their labor, and if they are serious about making a real difference in the new world financial order. The alternative is to continue scraping at the bottom of the financial pyramid, excited and happy when the economic developed world throws a bone their direction. The rest of the world would not mind such an arrangement; the bet here is that Asians will.

Endnotes

1. We first came across the term in CLSA Asia Pacific Markets equity strategist Christopher Wood's influential September 2002 research report, "Asia's Billion Boomers." Mr. Wood's work set the stage for the research that followed, and brought the "real Pacific century" theme to the forefront of economic and investment discussion. His thoughts and conclusions planted the seed for this book.
2. For our purposes, "Globalization is defined in what follows as integration of economic activities, via markets. The driving forces are technological and policy changes—falling cost of transport and communications and greater reliance on market forces." Wolf, Martin. *Why Globalization Works* (New Haven: Yale University Press, 2004), p. 19.
3. Nolan, Peter. *China at the Crossroads* (Cambridge: Polity Press, 2004), p. 69.
4. Pomeranz, Kenneth. *The Great Divergence* (New Jersey: Princeton University Press, 2000), p. 17.
5. Crow, Carl. *400 Million Customers* (London: Hamilton, 1937), From 2003 edition, p. 137.
6. Mohan, Rakesh. "Challenges to Monetary Policy in a Globalising Context" (Reserve Bank of India Bulletin: January 2004), p. 82.
7. A measure of the portion of a population composed of dependents (people who are too young or too old to work). The dependency ratio is equal to the number of individuals below age 15 or above 64, divided by the number of individuals aged 15 to 64, expressed as a percentage. A rising dependency ratio is a concern in many countries that are facing an aging population, because it becomes difficult for pension and social security systems to provide for a significantly older, non-working population.
8. King, Stephen. "The Lucky and the Losers" (HSBC: October 2004), p. 11.
9. Welch, David. "GM: Gunning It in China" (*BusinessWeek*: June 21, 2004).
10. This rule applies to China, Hong Kong, India, Indonesia, South Korea, Malaysia, Pakistan, Philippines, Singapore, Taiwan, and Thailand. Ziegler, Dominic. "The Weakest Link" (*The Economist*: February 6, 2003).
11. Economist Dr. Jim Walker has long argued that "Asia's black-market economy is as much as half the size of the official economy. This increases dramatically the official numbers since it is a better engine of consumption because it is not taxed at the source." Ziegler, Dominic. "The Weakest Link" (*The Economist*: February 6, 2003).
12. Qu, Hongbin. "China: Middle Class, Center Stage" (HSBC: March 2005).

13. Hobson, John and Robert N. McCauley. "The Future of Banking in East Asia" (Ente Luigi Einaudi Quaderni di Ricerche no. 59: Bank for International Settlements, 2004).

14. Dornbusch, Rudi and Givazzi Francesco. "Heading off China's Financial Crisis" (1999).

15. Because these banks are controlled by the state, lending is often based in political connections.

16. Krugman, Paul. "Will Asia Bounce Back?" (Speech for CSFB, Hong Kong: March 1998).

2

ASIA'S PATH TO PROSPERITY

T he world is changing dramatically. Those who fail to realize this will pay a heavy price.

Consider the U.S., arguably the most agile economy in history. Americans—after experiencing a great economic and financial run from 1982 to 2000 and a housing bubble after that—have come to view their privileged position in the global economic stage as a divine right of some sort, ignoring that the U.S. acquired its global hegemonic position through hard work and sacrifice, not extreme complacency from leaders and citizens. If this attitude persists—and signs of change are difficult to see—it is conceivable that the great U.S. economic machine will fail to adequately adjust to the unfolding new economic order.

A potential result of this failure: The 21st century may well be known as the Asian Century. People in Asia have the drive and the potential to succeed, and the region learned the lessons of the 1997 financial debacle. India will emerge as one of the leaders in the region, and eventually become the most profitable destination for long-term investors.

Coming of Age

The collapse of the Asian economic "miracle" in 1997 was a devastating economic and social shock for the region. "I had never read about, or seen," wrote Marc Faber, "the kind of total economic breakdown and wealth destruction—on such a massive scale, in such a short period of time, and against all expectations—as we saw in Asia in the six months following the onset of the crisis."[1] Investors all over the world felt the consequences.

Theories abound as to why the Asian miracle ended in such spectacular fashion. The most discussed are panic, crony capitalism, and moral hazard in lending. Panic seems to be the weakest explanation. A combination of crony capitalism and moral hazard in lending is the most credible.

Paul Krugman has advocated the moral hazard theory. "It has long been known," said the Princeton economist and *New York Times* columnist, "that financial intermediaries whose liabilities are guaranteed by the government pose a serious problem of moral hazard.... The Asian situation was more murky. In general, creditors of financial institutions did not receive explicit guarantees from governments. However, press reports do suggest that most of those who provided Thai finance companies, South Korea banks, and so on with funds believed that they would be protected from risk—an impression reinforced by the strong political connections of the owners of most such institutions."[2]

Krugman's last sentence underscores the theory that crony capitalism was a prerequisite. Asian governments played the crony capitalism game for years, without serious criticism from either domestic or international critics. As Amy Chua noted, "[C]rony capitalism: the corrupt, symbiotic alliances between indigenous leaders and a market-dominant minority. For a global market place, this is a cozy solution....In the short run, the result is a boom in foreign investment, economic growth, and riches for the rulers and their cronies. At the same time, however, the country's inner furies begin to boil. Sooner or later—and it is usually sooner—the situation explodes."[3]

And explode it did.

In Indonesia, the nepotistic and autocratic model of the government Suharto established after he seized power militarily in 1965 was for a long time supported by the international financial community. Given Indonesia's solid economic growth, no one was paying attention to the fact that no institutions were put in place to sustain growth. The main argument was that, although institutions were absent, Suharto was doing the right things under the guidance of Western-educated technocrats.

He did listen to the technocrats for some time, but Suharto followed the path every autocrat follows: He involved the family in business and politics, and set the table for crony capitalism. Suharto's children were incompetent, but maintained a suffocating grip around Indonesia's resources and economic activity. His Chinese billionaire cronies, like Bob Hasan and Liem Sioe Liong, made sure that Suharto's financial needs were always met. Through much of the 1980s and '90s, no one outside of his family—not even high ranking cabinet ministers—was closer to Suharto than these two men, who spent hours every week golfing with the president, planning their joint ventures.[4]

In May of 1998, the Asian crisis was in full scale and Suharto's 32-year reign was breaking down. It is no surprise that when violent riots broke out in Jakarta, they were aimed mainly at the Chinese and at the city's very expensive private neighborhood of Lippo Karawaci. "That deadly day in Java shattered what remained of a long-held illusion—the illusion that Indonesia and much of the rest of East Asia would move in a more or less straight line along a road of increasing economic prosperity and political development," wrote Mark L. Clifford and Pete Engardio.[5]

The aim here is not to address the ethical aspects of the problem. Of critical importance, though, is the fact that very few technocrats were willing to acknowledge—as Krugman and precious few others did—that Indonesia's economic miracle was being built on shaky ground, the same shaky ground upon which other Asian nations built.

On December 10, 1996, Michael Camdessuss, then president of the International Monetary Fund, assured investors that Thailand's economic fundamentals were sound. Oddly enough, in January 1997,

Thailand deposited its approximately $1 billion of gold reserves with the IMF in order to "optimize income," surely a euphemism.[6]

Now, the question is whether Asia established the necessary conditions for sustainable economic growth, even in the event of a U.S.-led economic slowdown. The quick answer is yes.

As a threshold issue, it is our contention that free trade is a positive-sum game that allows people to prosper and, consequently, consume. Trade has been one of the main powers behind the world's economic growth, especially since the early 1970s, and as globalization forces grew stronger, expansion in trade contributed even more to the increase in the global gross domestic product (GDP)—38 percent between 1997 and 2004. The expansion of trade and Asia's growing role in it will prove to be the main force in establishing the region as an important part of the world's economy.

It's difficult to talk about trade and economic growth without mentioning Adam Smith and David Ricardo, whose works have been a tremendous influence on how we view the world. Without delving into a full-scale analysis, a few points warrant our attention.

In his seminal 1776 work, *An Inquiry into the Nature and Causes of the Wealth of Nations*, Adam Smith talked about division of labor and its importance to economic progress. He wrote,

> To give the monopoly of the home-market to the produce of domestic industry, in any particular art or manufacture, is in some measure to direct private people in what manner they ought to employ their capitals, and must, in almost all cases, be either a useless or a hurtful regulation...

> It is the maxim of every prudent master of a family, never to attempt to make at home what it will cost him more to make than to buy. The tailor does not attempt to make his own shoes, but buys them of the shoemaker. The shoemaker does not attempt to make his own clothes, but employs a tailor. The farmer attempts to make neither the one nor the other, but employs those different artificers. All of them find it for their interest to employ their whole industry in a way in which they have some advantage over their neighbors, and to purchase with a part of its produce, or what is the same thing, with the price of a part of it, whatever else they have occasion for.

What is prudence in the conduct of every private family can scarce be folly in that of a great kingdom. If a foreign country can supply us with a commodity cheaper than we ourselves can make it, better buy it of them with some part of the produce of our own industry, employed in a way in which we have some advantage.[7]

Forty years later, Ricardo, in *The Principles of Political Economy and Taxation*, presented the theory of comparative advantage, an idea that's endured to this day as a central tenet of trade theory.

What Ricardo said was fairly simple. Every country will devote its resources (labor, capital, natural resources, and skills) to the production of the goods in which it has a relative advantage. This is distinct from an absolute competitive advantage.

Ricardo used an example of two commodities, cloth and wine, and two countries, England and Portugal. To summarize, if it takes 100 men to produce a given quantity of cloth in England and 120 men to produce wine, England will produce cloth and export it to buy wine from abroad because that's the most efficient way for England to use her labor resources. This fact holds even if it costs less labor to make both cloth and wine in Portugal. In Portugal, if it takes 90 men to produce the cloth and 80 to produce the wine, Portugal has an absolute advantage in both products—it's cheaper in labor terms to make both products in Portugal. Because it's cheaper to make wine than cloth in Portugal, that nation would focus on the production of wine—the most efficient way to use labor. Portugal will use its wine exports to pay for the import of cloth from Britain—the importance is relative, not absolute, prices.

Although Ricardo's idea has passed the test of time, it is to this day fairly controversial. "At a deeper level," notes Paul Krugman, "comparative advantage is a harder concept than it seems, because like any scientific idea it is actually part of a dense web of linked ideas."[8]

Outsourcing and Offshoring

Outsourcing—an appalling word to millions of people in developed economies—is nothing more than an effort by a company to produce part of its products (in which it has no comparative advantage) elsewhere. Because outsourcing can also take place within the same country, it is offshore outsourcing that is viewed as the biggest threat to job security by affected workers around the world.

Offshore outsourcing is not new. U.S. manufacturing has been offshored in Asia, excluding Japan, since the 1970s, but the recent and dramatic technological transformation of the global economy has allowed companies to use offshore outsourcing on a much larger, wider scale. *Nontradable* service jobs are now sent overseas, and a lot of white-collar workers are finding out that their jobs are no longer safe. As the public outcry is growing louder by the day, politicians are being forced to take action, and as always their initial reaction is to revert to protectionist measures. But this is not a rational way to address the trend. Protectionism never did and will not stop the changes that are taking place around the world.

A real effort to stop the trend would involve the U.S. closing down its borders and reopening the factories that were closed down as jobs were shipped overseas. Although this possibility should not be ruled out, it is an unlikely scenario. Such a move would change the corporate cost structure overnight, dealing a huge shock to the U.S. economy with excruciating consequences for an economic model built around strong growth.

Financial markets would also suffer. The assumption market participants usually make is that companies are free to make choices regarding outsourcing or other business decisions to enhance the company's position and, therefore, its shareholder's returns. This freedom is incorporated when earnings expectations are being formed. If these expectations fail to materialize or go into reverse—because of governmental interference—the stock market will experience a collapse of epic proportions. Perhaps governments prefer financial market crises to economic ones, but in an asset-based economy, where a greater number of people tend to base consumption decisions on rising asset prices (that is, stocks, housing, and so on), such a big shock to one of the pillars of the system will damage the confidence of the people and ferociously shake the economy.

Given that consumers have been conditioned to expect lower goods prices while developing an increasingly lower threshold for pain, they will not be able to tolerate such a change. Offshoring will continue despite occasional cries over lost jobs and "inferior service" from abroad. Think of Wal-Mart. Many have accused Wal-Mart of destroying America's towns and small businesses, yet these are the same people who search for the "lowest price," something individual businesses will never be able to provide.

In a capitalist and democratic system, people make the decisions—at least in goods-and-services matters—and the people have decided that Wal-Mart is the way to go. Sometimes, they get a little sentimental, voicing their support for small stores that cannot offer the big discounts everyone has become accustomed to, but this sentimentalism evaporates the minute Wal-Mart offers the next big bargain.

The level of outsourcing described previously is just one parameter of the phenomenon. Consider that outsourcing has reached such levels in Asia that companies there outsource among each other, based on relative position in the production chain. This outsourcing takes place not only among companies located in the same country, but in different countries as well. The region has created a multicountry supply chain that is not only a vital part of global trade but also of a continuously growing intraregional Asian trade.

A dramatic reduction in tariffs is the driving force behind Asia's intraregional trade growth. More than 90 percent of trade among Asian countries is conducted in a context of tariffs between 0 and 5 percent. This liberalization policy has begun to make a difference in the numbers. According to the IMF, Asia-Pacific (including India) intraregional trade grew from $384 billion in 1992 to $982 billion in 2003. During the same period, trade with the U.S. grew from $377 billion to $949 billion.

Another factor in strong intraregional numbers is the steady incorporation of China into the global economic system. Although exports are China's main engine for rapid economic growth, its needs for domestic economic development comprise another substantial force. These needs include improvements in its public infrastructure and industrial base, support for its rapid pace of urbanization, and strong growth in retail sales. Its domestic needs are as important as exports to the continuous growth of its economy.

Because of its domestic needs, China has been trading feverishly with the rest of the world. China is running surpluses with some of its trading partners (for example, the U.S.), while running trade deficits with its Asian partners. At the bottom line, China's trade is balanced, and net exports account for just 1 to 2 percent of GDP.[9]

China's domestic growth allowed U.S., Japanese, and European Union companies to increase their exports during the 2000-01 global economic slump. This made companies around the world realize that there is more to China than cheap production. China's rise has become of paramount importance to the rest of the Asia-Pacific region, including Japan and Australia. China's gradual integration in the world economy will be beneficial to everyone.

Despite the benefits China's rise has brought to the rest of Asia, many observers worry that Asia's other economies will be wiped out as China continues to take away its manufacturing base. Changes are indeed necessary if the rest of Asia is to participate in the new economic century, but manufacturing has remained a strong part of other Asian economies, despite China's growth.

The Association of South Eastern Asian Nations (ASEAN 5)[10] have been able to preserve their global manufacturing share at 4.4 percent, while increasing their manufacturing output to $216 billion in 2004 from $133.8 billion in 1994 (see Table 2-1).

Table 2-1 Manufacturing Share

	Global % Share of Manufactured Exports		Manufactured Final Output $bn	
	1994	2004	1994	2004
ASEAN 5	4.4	4.4	133.8	216
Taiwan	2.5	1.9	70.8	78
Hong Kong	3.3	2.8	11.4	6.3
China	2.2	5.9	224.6	759
South Korea	2.1	2.6	117	173.5
India	0.5	0.6	N/AV	97

Source: Morgan Stanley

The main reason for this strength is comparative advantage. Many Asian economies maintain strong positions in a lot of manufacturing sectors; China has become a competitor in some sectors (clothing, electronic components, textiles, leather products, consumer electronics, and transport equipment), whereas it is still on the sidelines in others (some basic manufacturing, minerals, processed food, and wood products).

It is often said that Asia and China are still extremely dependent on the American consumer and their respective economic futures are tied to that of the U.S. Although there is a lot of truth in this observation, it is not as bad as it sounds.

Given the continuing integration of the world's economies, almost all depend on each other. Singling out Asia and China as "dependent junkies" is naïve. It's clear that the U.S. and the rest of the developed economies depend on Asia for a big part of their manufacturing needs—Asia has assumed a role that no one else is able or willing to accept. After all, someone has to make the goods. Manufacturing is extremely beneficial to Asia, especially if the region expands its spectrum of economic growth so it can cope better with economic cycles. This is particularly important for China to realize because it did not suffer the trauma of 1997.

Exports and China are the two strongest forces in the Asian growth arsenal, whereas consumption is slowly and steadily growing in importance. It will eventually become the main pillar of the region's economic growth.

Asia is gradually finding itself in a favorable position in the world economy.

A Changing World

The argument that Asia (China, more specifically) aims to "take over the world" is nothing more than a base appeal to emotion, sensationalism in place of logic.

One of the main tenets of this position is that "imports from countries where labor is cheap cause unemployment in the United States." Murray N. Rothbard answered this question:

> One of the many problems with this doctrine is that it ignores the question: why are wages low in a foreign country and high in the United States? It starts with these wage rates as ultimate givens, and doesn't pursue the question why they are what they are. Basically, they are high in the United States because labor productivity is high—because workers here are aided by large amounts of technologically advanced capital equipment. Wage rates are low in many foreign countries because capital equipment is small and technologically primitive. Unaided by much capital, worker productivity is far lower than in the United States. Wage rates in every country are determined by the productivity of the workers in that country. Hence, high wages in the United States are not a standing threat to American prosperity; they are the result of that prosperity.[11]

If developing economies are able to raise productivity to Western standards, wages will rise too—Japan proved this. Constant change—or, as the great Austrian economist Joseph Schumpeter termed it, *creative destruction*—is what capitalism is all about. According to Schumpeter:

> Capitalism, then, is by nature a form or method of economic change and not only never is but never can be stationary.... The fundamental impulse that sets and keeps the capitalist engine in motion comes from the new consumers' goods, the new methods of production or transportation, the new markets, the new forms of industrial organization that capitalist enterprise creates....The opening up of new markets, foreign or domestic, and the organizational development from the craft shop and factory to such concerns as U.S. Steel illustrate the same process of industrial mutation—if I may use that biological term—that incessantly revolutionizes the economic structure from within, incessantly destroying the old one, incessantly creating a new one. This process of Creative Destruction is the essential fact about capitalism.[12]

This is what the "sensationalists" fail to understand: The world will not come to an end, but rather will adjust to the new economic order, much like it did when the U.S. was the new up-and-coming economic power. The world, said Marc Faber, had to cope with a tremendous force back then. "By 1885, the U.S.—which had hardly any industries at the beginning of the century—now approached 60 million people and led the world in industry, producing 28.9 percent of global manufactured goods.... America's rise to global economic dominance is unique from an economic-historical point of view—and today it is the dream of every emerging-market investor to find another 19th Century American growth story."[13]

One of the most important changes that will take place is the adjustment in world wages. The Western world will experience decreasing wages, whereas the East will enjoy the opposite. This shift will take place at a relatively slow pace—China, for example, has a huge labor force and will therefore require more time to reach full employment and achieve substantial wage gains.

In an effort to keep some outsourced jobs "home," Citigroup reportedly hired 100 American college students to do computer programming work, paying them $17 an hour. The bank reckoned that this was about half what it would have to pay comparable programmers in India.[14] This can be viewed as a first step to keep jobs home, but more importantly as a mechanism for lowering the wage expectations of these college students when it comes time for them to accept a full-time job. With the lingering outsourcing threat, young workers may feel pressure to accept a lower salary.

As once nontradable jobs become tradable, a new set of nontradable jobs will emerge. With the evolution of the employment picture, wages will inevitably drop, even in the new nontradable jobs. New workers in the developed countries will try to pursue these new nontradable jobs in larger numbers, increasing competition while decreasing the level of wages. Given the flexible U.S. social contract, change will start there.

Stephen S. Roach, chief economist for Morgan Stanley and one of the most respected and independent thinkers in the business, has for some time argued on behalf of what he has called the Global Labor Arbitrage, a combination of matured offshore outsourcing platforms, e-based connectivity, and the new imperatives of cost control that allow corporations to seamlessly move around the world in an effort to stay competitive and profitable.[15]

These changes will coincide with a decrease in asset prices in the West and a corresponding increase in the East because of changing income levels. The benefits will be universal, as consumption will increase due to rising incomes and the integration in the global economy of China and India.

Signs of a changing employment environment in the U.S. manifest in jobs statistics: In the majority of states, jobs in higher-paying industries have given way to jobs in lower-paying industries, with industries that are gaining jobs relative to industries that are losing jobs paying 21 percent less annually.[16]

Integration into the Global Economy

For Asia to be able to take advantage of the current global economic situation, governments must find ways to create the environment to foster sustainable domestic demand. Asian countries need—among other things—to take advantage of their particular indigenous characteristics while focusing their efforts toward domestic investments.

This is particularly true for the economies of Malaysia, Thailand, Indonesia, and the Philippines. These countries must be prepared in the event China takes on an even bigger role as a low-cost producer of goods. India's rise as the preferred destination for services outsourced by multinationals could also be at the expense of Southeast Asia (although to a lesser degree).

These countries have held their own in manufacturing, but need to move up the chain from low value-added mass manufacturing products to a higher pricing-power export industry. They must also take advantage of domestic natural resources and spend money on domestic-related investments.[17] The ultimate goal is to create the necessary conditions for domestically driven economic growth.

It remains to be seen whether the respective governments have the capacity, first, to develop this strategy and, second, to execute it. Thailand, under the guidance of Prime Minister Thaksin Shinawatra, has shown capability in these respects; and though the final outcome of his efforts is still to be determined, Thailand has a substantial head start. If successful, Thailand will join the global economy on terms that will benefit its citizens as well as multinational corporations. The same is true for other Southeast Asian economies that follow a similar strategy.

Wealth distribution is improving in Asia, but financial security remains a privilege of the few. Of course, if the improving wealth distribution trends discussed in the previous chapter stop, it will be virtually impossible for our scenario to unfold. But it will also be impossible for governments to continue ignoring their people, given the easy access to mass media the majority now enjoys. In other words, the people—knowing exactly what is going on in other places—will demand that governments devote more attention to them.

Domestic investment in infrastructure is of paramount importance. Thailand, Indonesia, and the Philippines have not done enough to improve their aging infrastructure, not only in the agricultural sector but also in the service sectors of their economies. This is the only avenue by which these economies will achieve sustainable economic growth.

The status of agriculture provides a case in point. Development has been ignored for the past 30 years. Governments must shift attention from urban centers to developing the rural areas of their countries. Rural areas are not only home to the largest portion of their respective populations, they are also best positioned to exploit natural resources, providing a new, sustainable growth alternative to the countries of Southeast Asia.

The conditions under which these people operate are absurd. In Thailand, for example, many farmers have *de facto* but incomplete *de jure* rights over their land. Under a distribution program in place for decades, they are given state land without land title deeds, and they are not allowed to sell it, pledge it to the bank, or use it for purposes other than farming.[18] Until these people and others like them are given access to capital, credit, and allowed real property rights, the economies of Southeast Asia will remain prisoners to the whims of multinational corporations.

It is beyond comprehension how a farmer in Thailand can do little better than subsist when the biggest economies on earth do whatever they can to help their farmers (in the form of subsidies). To understand how important agriculture is for developed and developing economies alike, consider the following. The World Bank and the IMF estimate that removal of U.S. subsidies in cotton could lead to a fall in production, a subsequent rise in global price, and a revenue increase of $250 million annually for the countries of West and Central Africa (this is one of the few sectors of world trade in which Africa is internationally competitive). But subsidies for U.S. cotton farmers are likely to increase by 16 percent—this for a total of 25,000 farmers whose net household worth averages about $800,000.[19] This is only one minor example of the manner in which governments in developed economies aid their farmers.

Absurd as it is that developing countries can be penalized for the benefit of a handful (relatively speaking) of high-end farmers, it is also quite naïve to expect that these farmers or their governments would do otherwise. This is why it is extremely important for developing economies to create the foundation for a system that is responsible for facilitating economic and social growth. The difference between rich and poor states is the result of differences in the quality of their economic institutions.[20]

Agricultural subsidies remain an issue where developed economies still dictate the rules of the game and how new members (that is, China) are joining the system. Although developing economies are currently under pressure to reduce subsidies, Western economies—the U.S. and the EU—subsidize at extremely high rates. Most of their subsidies take the form of direct payments to farmers rather than price subsidies. According to the latest rules promulgated by the World Trade Organization (WTO), these payments are not subject to any limitations. These rules were written by the developed economies during the so-called Uruguay Round of WTO negotiations. China cannot adopt such an approach—it still has 240 million farm families and lacks sufficient government staff at the village level to determine the direct subsidy to each household.[21]

The field will level as new members familiarize themselves with WTO procedures. Such members will then demand changes to establish ever more equal footing. Global trade has already provided developing economies the opportunity to create groups in an effort to promote their interests. One of these is the G-20, whose sole purpose is to unite the developing nations and enhance their negotiating power in global trade issues. The G-20 has been urging the U.S. and the EU to cut farm subsidies, which "tend to depress world markets."[22]

Returning to the cotton example, in July of 2005 the U.S. agreed to change a cotton subsidy scheme to comply with a WTO ruling, which followed a legal challenge by Brazil. At issue was an export-credit guarantee program for cotton farmers worth $4 billion a year. Although the U.S. promised to change the subsidy, its representative neglected to reveal the administration's Step 2 program to compensate American cotton millers for using more expensive U.S. cotton.[23]

Institutions like the WTO, though limited in authority over national sovereignty, provide developing economies a platform to more easily operate on a global scale. Although the WTO is still dominated—with regard to many issues—by developed economies, negotiations have led to better results for developing economies. Globalization has also furthered this process, as the level of global economic interdependence has increased dramatically, allowing smaller players to demand and receive more than they would otherwise.

Lessons Learned

Taking a look at Asia today, there is a sense that many things have changed for the better. Current account balances have gone to surplus, foreign exchange reserves have been rebuilt, and dependence on short-term capital inflows has diminished.

At the same time, Asian companies—notoriously cash flow negative until 1997—have changed course. Positive cash flows have become the name of the game and Asian companies are expected to stay on this course for years to come. Debt-to-equity ratios have been declining and it will come as no surprise if the majority of Asian corporations are nearly debt free by the end of 2006.[24]

These factors have allowed Asian companies to become more share-holder friendly by increasing dividend-payout ratios. Dividends have grown substantially since the mid-90s and investors can expect dividend growth of at least 7 percent per year in the future. Asian companies now realize that making money is more important than increasing sales at any cost.[25]

Asia's current economic cycle is of a higher quality than those of the past, and is showing strong signs of long-term sustainability. The reforms since the crisis of 1997, the rise of China and India, and the economic and other changes distinguish this period from the past. That said, the prospect of a crisis of some sort must not be ignored. Booms end with busts, for the simple reason that euphoria brings bad investment choices and, eventually, recessions. This time, for Asia in general and China and India in particular, the inevitable downturn should be viewed as a small detour on the way to joining—on an equal footing—the capitalist economic system.

Endnotes

1. Faber, Marc. *Tomorrow's Gold: Asia's Age of Discovery* (Hong Kong: CLSA BOOKS, 2002), p. 199.
2. Krugman Paul. "What Happened to Asia?" (Conference in Japan, 1998).
3. Chua, Amy. *World on Fire* (New York: Doubleday, 2003), p. 147.
4. Ibid. p. 152.
5. Clifford, Mark L. and Pete Engardio. *Meltdown: Asia's Boom, Bust, and Beyond* (New Jersey: Prentice Hall, 2000), p. 2.
6. Condor Advisers. "What the IMF Doesn't Want You to Know About Thailand" (June 2, 1997).
7. *Glasgow Edition of the Works and Correspondence of Adam Smith* (1981-87) Vol. I., p. 480. Colloquial spellings have been corrected.
8. Krugman, Paul. "Ricardo's Difficult Idea" (Manchester Conference of Free Trade, March 1996).
9. MasterCard International. *MasterCard Insights Report* (Second Quarter 2005).
10. The Association of South Eastern Asian Nations (ASEAN) includes Brunei Darussalam, Cambodia, **Indonesia**, Laos, **Malaysia**, Myanmar, **Philippines**, **Singapore**, **Thailand**, and Vietnam. The term ASEAN 5 refers to the biggest economies (in bold) among them.
11. Rothbard, Murray N. *Making Economic Sense* (Athens, AL: Mises Institute, 1995), p. 21.
12. Schumpeter, Joseph A. *Capitalism, Socialism and Democracy* (New York: Harper Perennial, 1956), p. 82-83.

13. Faber, Marc. *Tomorrow's Gold: Asia's Age of Discovery* (Hong Kong: CLSA BOOKS, 2002), p. 49.
14. *The Economist.* "Relocating the Back Office" (December 13, 2003).
15. Roach, Stephen S. "Outsourcing, Protectionism, and the Global Labor Arbitrage" (Morgan Stanley, November 11, 2003).
16. The Economic Policy Institute. "Economic Snapshots" (January 21, 2004).
17. These could include services, agriculture, agro-businesses, and Small and Medium Enterprises. Emphasis on education and economic infrastructure to help these businesses will also be needed.
18. Lian, Daniel. "Capital Creation—The Next Step Up?" (Morgan Stanley, January 16, 2003).
19. Moore, Mike. *A World Without Walls* (Cambridge: Cambridge University Press, 2003), p. 48.
20. Kay, John. *Culture and Prosperity* (New York: Harper-Collins, 2004), pp. 354-355.
21. Lardy, Nicholas R. *Integrating China into the Global Economy* (Washington D.C.: Brookings Institution Press, 2002), pp. 156-157.
22. The G-20 comprises **Argentina**, **Brazil**, Bolivia, Chile, **China**, Cuba, Egypt, Guatemala, **India**, **Indonesia**, Mexico, **Nigeria**, Pakistan, Paraguay, The Philippines, South Africa, Tanzania, **Thailand**, **Venezuela**, and Zimbabwe.
23. Beattie, Alan. "US Bows to Pressure over Cotton Support" (*Financial Times:* July 1, 2005).
24. Net debt to equity peaked at 81.8 percent in 1998 and decreased to 20 percent in 2004.
25. Chinese companies are an exception given the peculiarities of the economy and China's place in the development cycle.

3

THE GREAT COMPARISON

One of the most important international events of 2003 was India's Prime Minister Atal Bihari Vajpayee's state visit to China. During that visit, Vajpayee and Chinese Premier Wen Jiabao signed a Declaration of Cooperation and nine protocols on bilateral cooperation, normalizing Sino-Indian relations. Two years later, in April 2005, the Chinese Premier visited India and signed more agreements on trade, border issues, and the development of new energy sources.

Given their bitter past, and a border dispute that has been going on since 1962, China's and India's willingness to put their differences aside and concentrate on their mutual economic growth is viewed here as one of the most important global developments of the 21st century thus far.

Together, the two countries represent 40 percent of the world's population and 8 percent of its economy; thus, their success will define not only Asia's role in the world economy, but also trigger a strong reaction from the developed economies of the world.[1] Their level of cooperation and the West's reaction to it will set the course for the global economic and political developments of this century.

Given that India is closer to Western institutions and ideas than China, it could become a more desirable investment destination. China may come to be viewed as an adversary rather than an ally by Western powers. Such an outcome—together with the country's democratic values—could help India ultimately become the main engine of economic growth in Asia and the world.

India: A Powerful Force

In 1991, India endured its biggest economic crisis. Foreign exchange reserves were almost depleted. Down to three weeks worth of imports, the government had to fly part of India's gold to London to satisfy would-be guarantors, the Bank of England and the Bank of Japan, and facilitate a loan from the International Monetary Fund (IMF). With the country on the brink of collapse, drastic change was needed.

Manmohan Singh and Palaniappan Chidambaram[2] executed the most radical reforms in India's recent economic history, including a devaluation of the rupee, dismantling of import control, slashing of duties, liberalization of industrial licensing, and opening of the capital markets. These pivotal moves allowed India to emerge as a deregulated economy in the global market. In the four years after the crisis, India's economy grew by 6.7 percent per year.

India has steadily progressed over the last 45 years. As Martin Wolf, chief economic commentator for the *Financial Times* and one of the most astute observers of the global economy, noted, "Between 1960 and 1980 a moving average of the previous 10 years of economic growth oscillated between 3 percent and 4 percent a year. Since the early 1980s, however, these 10-year moving averages have been on a rising trend. In the most recent period (the 10 years that includes fiscal year 2003-04, April to March), growth of net national product per head has reached 4.4 percent a year. At that rate, incomes per head will double every 16 years."[3]

India's progress is not in question. Inevitably, India's economic achievement and future prospects invite comparisons to China. Although this is a legitimate comparison, India possesses certain characteristics that make its long-term investment story much more interesting and desirable than any other in Asia.

While India has never exhibited the strong growth characteristics the rest of Asia did and cannot match China's reported growth rates, it also avoided the boom-and-bust cycles so prevalent in the region's developing economies. For an investor interested in achieving serious long-term returns, this fact is of paramount importance. India (home to 17 percent of the world's people) still accounts for a small fraction of the global economy, 2 percent of global GDP, and 1 percent of world trade.[4] Because of this relatively minor impact, India has been less important to investors and economists alike.

But India has several characteristics that are of extreme importance if it is to sustain economic development. Banks in India have been fairly conservative, maintaining the rate of nonperforming loans at a low 8.8 percent of total lending (as of March 2003). Its capital markets are among the most developed of the emerging economies, and they operate with greater efficiency and transparency than China's.

The country also has a fairly independent legal system—the main problem lies in its lack of efficiency, not its integrity. This characteristic is particularly important in regards to property rights, an essential foundation for sustainable economic and domestic demand growth. Property rights in India are protected and the rule of law, albeit with a time lag, usually prevails.

The entrepreneurial spirit of its people is India's most important quality, evidenced by their building world-class companies despite an arteriosclerotic bureaucracy. This is the fine point that astute investors have long understood: Contrary to China's, the India story is a microeconomic one. This was a good enough observation for some very profitable investments to be made.

Problems Abound

A broad consensus has formed around the idea that although India is in much better shape now, more change is needed. Otherwise, the country risks its economic future and, with that, its social stability.

As we write, the newly elected leaders of India seem to have the right reform plan in place. And in India's case, "Reform is about removing the obstacles to it."

The main obstacle is corruption and inefficiencies, especially in the state and lower levels of government.[5] These inefficiencies can sometimes reach incomprehensible levels, as the following anecdote illustrates.

India has a grain procurement system, whereby the central government sets minimum price supports for rice and wheat and purchases large quantities from farmers in prosperous areas like Punjab. This form of subsidy exists so that more than 220 million poor people all over the country can receive cheap grain.

The central government stores the grain but the states are responsible for transportation and distribution. Due to poor management by the states, the government's stocks reach such huge amounts that sometimes it's actually impossible to distribute. According to *The Economist*, one-fifth of the food produced in India, including one-tenth of grain reserves, is wasted.[6]

Politicians and government employees, both in the state and central governments, are considered the most corrupt. On the other hand, the judiciary system is viewed as less corrupt and more independent. Many believe the status of the judiciary, particularly that of the Supreme Court, has prevented the collapse of the country.

Labor laws (namely, the inability to dismiss a worker without the permission of the state government) remain the focus of complaints by many domestic and foreign investors. Furthermore, extremely powerful, almost always negative oriented, and often destructive unions, whose only reason for existence is to make their leaders rich, also frustrate businesses. Often, the choice for business comes down to paying extensive bribes to the union leaders or moving to another city or state. No matter what the outcome, the average worker pays the price.

Poor infrastructure is another major problem India needs to solve. As things are now, it will be impossible for India to achieve double-digit growth for the simple reason that infrastructure at almost every level of the economy remains weak. Power and water top the list. The country is in need of new power stations and must charge proper, unsubsidized fees for water and electricity usage. Extreme subsidization has encouraged unreasonable use, especially in the agricultural sector.

Acknowledging that urgent improvements are needed, India decided to use a part of its foreign exchange reserves to fund domestic infrastructure projects, a government action without precedent in the world. The idea is to use India's money to serve the Indian economy instead of just buying U.S. Treasury bonds. As one official put it at the time, "We are subsidizing the American economy; these are scarce resources that can be put to better use."[7]

This decision seems unassailable in light of statistics showing that most infrastructure services costs are 50 to 100 percent higher in India than in China. A highway expenditure program due for completion by the end of 2006 has already positively impacted the economy. More effort is required, particularly for railway transport and for ports, areas where overall efficiency remains low.

More than 70 percent of the population lives in rural areas, making agriculture one of the main pillars of the Indian economy. Although the agriculture sector represents close to 60 percent of employment, its GDP share is only 22 percent. The service sector represents 51 percent of GDP.

Because of the sheer number of people living and working in rural areas, improving agricultural infrastructure is as important as building new roads. India has a lot of water and fertile land, and one of the long-term bets for India remains the improvement of its irrigation and other agricultural techniques so that the monsoons are not the only factor determining a good crop.

Until recently, India's tax system was extremely complicated and tax collection was fairly inefficient, accounting for only 14 percent of GDP in 2002. On April 1, 2005, India introduced a value-added tax (VAT) system that states were asked to adopt. The intention was to simplify the indirect tax systems, thus providing a more reliable source of funds for the government. The process of simplification was slowed because several states did not implement the system immediately.

The budget deficit (10 percent of GDP) is the most important financial weakness of India. The overall public debt-to-GDP ratio is above 80 percent, but 90 percent of India's public debt is domestic. Because of this peculiarity, and the country's fairly strong growth, India has been able to manage it fairly well.

A crisis is not imminent, but the current status prohibits the government from wisely spending its money for infrastructure, energy, education, and health care. Almost all revenue goes to interest payments, civil servants' wages and pensions, defense, and subsidies. Combine these with tax inefficiencies, and the idea of turning to the private sector to take the lead in infrastructure projects (as was done before with telecommunications) becomes a more viable alternative by the day.

Democracy and Growth

Indians, in general, are extremely proud of their democracy. When it comes to economic development, however, opinions diverge. Some believe that the democratic procedures have prevented India from realizing its full potential, pointing toward China's achievements to illustrate relative lack of growth. Others believe that slow growth is the price that one must pay if freedom is to be enjoyed and democracy is to blossom.

As noted here, democracy is not a necessary condition to stimulate an economy, but it is essential to sustainability. India, by having to grow through an admittedly turbulent democratic process, has already accomplished what China will eventually need to do in order to solidify its extraordinary achievements. Having a working democracy is much harder than instigating economic growth. In this respect, India is ahead.

For investing purposes, a democratic environment, even one as noisy as India's, is preferable because a lot of domestic problems can be more easily identified and then discounted by investors as they make capital allocation decisions. Corruption cannot be blamed on democracy, as some would like us to believe. Chinese officials—on almost every level—are equally as corrupt and inefficient as their Indian counterparts.

Entrepreneurial spirit and freedom has allowed Indians to create successful, internationally recognized companies, the majority of them in the information technology (IT) arena. India's software and IT-enabled services industry currently employs more than 1 million people, a jump of more than 50 percent in just three years.

India's IT companies are moving beyond the easily commoditized data processing and call center operations. Right at the time that a lot of workers in the developed economies (especially in the U.S.) are starting to realize what is going on, the world has moved much further ahead.

For years, the manufacturing sector in the developed economies was losing jobs, but the majority of people did not care because their jobs were in the service sector and, as everyone knew, services had to be delivered on site, or so a lot of prominent academics maintained. Those lost were blue-collar jobs, workers living paycheck to paycheck, which many argued was not important. Now though, that manufacturing is becoming an industry of the past in the U.S.; those holding service jobs will need to go through a change exercise.

The best-known IT applications that Indian companies and subsidiaries of U.S.-based corporations have been developing in India run from software programming and multimedia platforms to systems support and network management. In addition, Indian firms have been moving up the chain into business process outsourcing (BPO), which includes procurement, accounting, insurance management, human resource and benefit management, as well as internal corporate control functions. The latest applications are in the more specialized medical, actuarial, and legal areas.

India has also rapidly progressed in pharmaceutical and other health-related industries. India is now home to the largest number of FDA-approved pharmaceutical plants outside the U.S., and the United Nations buys more than half of its vaccines for its inoculation programs from a private company in India. In contrast, much of China's vaccine production is considered substandard.[8]

As India develops, the rest of the world gets a well-educated, English-speaking work force at discount prices, and it seems that both sides of the economic development spectrum will have to adjust. As long as

India keeps its standards high when it comes to research and development, one of the pillars of its future economic growth is secure.

When it comes to manufacturing growth, India is far behind China. There are reasons for this underperformance and they are reversible. Yet, there is a tendency among researchers and economic observers to maintain the view that India should concentrate on the IT and other high-end industries and ignore manufacturing. We respectfully disagree.

No matter how good India is in the technology arena, the country is so big and its needs are so huge that one cannot solve them by turning the country into a giant computer. If India is serious about improving its infrastructure, there is no reason why manufacturing cannot become another important part of the Indian economy.

Poor infrastructure, high taxes, labor costs, and low productivity are usually the reasons cited for India's weakness in the manufacturing area. A closer look at the sector reveals some positive changes. Average labor cost as a percentage of total costs, for example, is only around 5.5 percent, not enough to hurt performance. On the productivity front, improvements are visible, especially in industries where foreign involvement is high (that is, telecommunications, electronics, and software). In the more protected domestic-controlled businesses like textiles, productivity remains quite low.

A very interesting test of the states' capability to improve their infrastructures is taking place in the extremely poor and infrastructure-starved state of Orissa. Orissa, situated on the eastern coastline of India, is extremely rich in mineral resources. The state accounts for 40 percent of India's proven reserves of bauxite, 27 percent of iron ore, 16 percent of coal, and 98 percent of chromite.

Because of Orissa's proximity to East Asia and its natural resources advantage, a lot of companies, domestic and foreign, have been investing. The poor infrastructure means that they have to make additional investments in electricity facilities, port infrastructure, and roads.

The big question is whether the state and the central government will be able to cooperate to improve the business environment and attract huge amounts of foreign direct investment (FDI), and in the process improve the life of the state's people.

As progress is being made in India, it is the country's middle class—more than 150 million strong—that is most affected by the changes taking place. This is a huge consumption market that is opening up, but one must always be aware of the potential for social unrest.

The big challenge is to extend the benefits of progress to the lower levels of Indian society. If politicians and civil servants fail—something that cannot be ruled out—the country could enter a period of economic destruction and social unrest as India's younger generation tries to enter the work force. Unemployment could lead to an unraveling. As long as some of the prosperity finds its way down to the poorest strata of society, and infrastructure development progresses, the path of economic growth will be fairly smooth.

India, like China, is extremely large. Unlike China, it has deep, though noisy, democratic traditions. These traditions, however, make it a more difficult ship to turn. Provided India's forward progress remains visible—even at a pace slower than its regional rivals—investors should continue exploring opportunities as they arise.

India has followed the correct path toward economic development, one charted by monetary targets (for example, inflation and a balanced budget). This approach, the results of which are less obvious in the short term, is a long-term creator of economic stability and growth. Contrary to the ideas of the usually extremely negative domestic intelligentsia (who have retained and perfected the British talent of cultivated cynicism), India's journey is just starting.

China: Waking Up

Andy Xie, Morgan Stanley's Asia economist, once said that China is big and opaque. In other words, explaining China's present and forecasting its future are among the most difficult tasks one can undertake.

Despite the magnitude of the challenge, China is the topic *du jour*. From politicians to money managers and academics to folks on the street, everyone seems to have something to say about China. And yet there is still much to be learned about the world's most populous country, and this lack of clarity, curiously, renders all assessments right and wrong at the same time. As always, readers and listeners need to evaluate the information.

The approach here is fairly simple: We have assessed where China is coming from and where it may be going. This analysis, though ultimately subjective, is based more on historical facts and Chinese actions rather than only on government statistics and short-term hype; it is drawn from reliable local observers, notable researchers, and global development agencies.

One who understands that long-term growth is not a straight line phenomenon would not question China's economic prospects. Charts of economic growth in developing nations depict what appear to be straight lines, but such long-term straight lines are comprised of many periods of ups and downs, booms and busts, consolidations and breakouts, and policy errors and reinventions.

This is China's path.

Despite current overconfidence and crude extrapolation regarding China's future, the Chinese have a different understanding regarding their homeland. Although they realize the big changes that are taking place, they still think China is too small to affect the global economy. Unsurprisingly, their understanding of what is going on in their own back yard differs wildly from the positions of politicians and labor union leaders around the world. If one pays attention to the latter, one will come away with the impression that China is ready to take over the world and destroy the well being of millions of people.

But China's is indeed a small economy. It accounts for about 4 percent of the U.S.'s $32 trillion world economy, and 5 percent of the world's total manufacturing exports. Although economic growth has been impressive, China is far from threatening a major global economic shakeout.

As with almost every other Asian country, China has followed a model of growth based on manufacturing. Given the country's unique characteristics, it has been able to record extremely strong growth since 1980, but China is still playing a catch-up game in the industrialization process. It took more than a hundred years for the country to start moving forward and, huge challenges and indigenous shortcomings notwithstanding, this is the only road China can follow.

China's immediate economic future is tied to a high degree to global demand and the relentless cost-cutting actions of corporations around the world. The country's low-cost production setup makes it conceivable that manufacturing-related industries can all eventually be relocated to China.

Such a move makes economic sense, but not many are willing to discuss the viability of this development given the socio-economic distortions and attendant political costs involved. Two things are certain: The trend is continuing; and there are no signs when it will stop. And China is doing everything in its power to steer the global economy in that direction.

The developed world, led by the Board of Governors of the United States Federal Reserve System (the Fed), is also doing its part. Since the Asian financial crisis of 1997, the Fed has maintained a loose monetary policy, creating one bubble after the other in its quest for constant growth. And Chinese exports have grown dramatically during that period.

Export growth has led to huge amounts of money coming into China. These flows have been redeployed to support infrastructure projects, like roads, power plants, housing, and so on. In addition, FDI has become an important pillar of China's growth.

At the same time FDI has increased, Nicholas R. Lardy, a senior fellow at the Brookings Institution, has noted, "While foreign domestic investment is very substantial and has risen to around US$500 billion, it remains a relatively small proportion of overall capital formation. Only around 10 percent of overall capital formation in China comes in the form of foreign direct investment...Chinese capital investment comes overwhelmingly from domestic savings. The savings rate is close to 40 percent. China has the highest saving rate of any significant economy anywhere in the world."[9]

If the current trade environment persists, China will probably out-compete most export players in basic manufacturing in the future. Naturally, a lot of producers will be late in accepting China's superiority and prefer to lose out in the marketplace rather than try to change through identifying new competencies. Although it is admittedly easier to speak of developing and marketing new technologies or processes than to actually develop and market them, it seems that this will be the only road to survival and prosperity in the new world economy.

Solving Problems

China, on almost every level of its economy and its society, has many daunting problems to solve. The challenges faced by Chinese leadership are of monumental proportions and require extreme flexibility and creativity in order to overcome them.

China's main problems are relatively well known: the sorry state of the banking system; the disastrous status quo of the state-owned enterprises (SOE); the policy mistakes the government is prone to commit; the always-suspect official Chinese data (even economically stagnant regions report "greater than target" output growth rates); the neglect of the rural areas; entrenched corruption. Many respectable analysts have pointed out and analyzed these failings.

The system's shortcomings engendered a terrible allocation of funds, which led to bad loans for the banking system, a buildup of worthless capacity, and pathetic investment returns. These factors damaged the economic change envisioned by Mao Tse-tung's successor, Deng Xiaoping, and burdened China with huge liabilities.

The main issues for investors, though, are a little different in nature, and can be reduced to two questions. Have the leaders of the Communist Party understood the problems and decided on a proper course of action to solve them? And will they be successful?

One can answer the first one satisfactorily and then make a fairly legitimate guesstimate on the second. But for investing purposes, direction is far more important, and China is heading in the right direction.

It is easy to forget that China was growing steadily throughout the 1920s and 1930s until Japan's full-scale invasion in 1937 halted the process. After that period, Communist rule completely distracted the country and it was not until the mid-1980s that China started becoming a part of the global economy again.

A closer look at policy decisions, and tangible results, reveals that China is, indeed, making progress again and has achieved a lot in the last 25 years. It has grown into the fourth-largest trading nation after the U.S., Germany, and Japan, while steadily removing protectionist barriers. In 1980, import tariffs were as high as 50 percent, but by 2004, they dropped to 10 percent. China also fared quite well during the 1997 Asian financial crisis and the 2001 global recession.

On the domestic front, the government has been dismantling protectionist measures that made trading among provinces difficult in the past and contributed substantially to the rise in prices of goods. So stiff were the domestic protectionist trade barriers that agricultural and commodity prices in China were often much higher than in the rest of the world.

China's leaders also encouraged private sector development as a means to increase the number of jobs. According to credible estimates, more than two million private enterprises employing more than 30 million people exist in China. Although there is a lot to be done, the government is trying to improve the legal and investing framework in order to attract more investing capital, and has worked to dismantle existing monopolies. Some of the sectors where change has occurred are telecommunications, aviation, energy, and banking. After 50 years of extreme economic and social mismanagement, the progress toward privatization in China is now clearly evident.

It is important to bear in mind that even in developed economies privatization occurred neither quickly nor early. It was not until 1979 that the British government began to privatize and listed British Petroleum in the stock market; not until the early 1980s were state companies like

British Aerospace, British Telecom, and British Gas listed. Even in the U.S., competition in long-distance telephony was finally allowed in the 1970s, and it was not until 1978 that the airline business really opened up to competition. In Asian countries that enjoy prosperous capitalistic economic systems, privatization took time too. Japan had a state monopoly in tobacco and telephone services until the mid-1980s. Taiwan dropped its tobacco and alcohol monopolies in 2001 when it joined the World Trade Organization (WTO).

Another positive development has been allowing ownership of property. In 2001, then-President Jiang Zemin declared, in a tacit recognition of ownership rights, "It is not advisable to judge a person's political integrity by whether he owns property and how much property he or she owns."[10] By then, the state had already started selling (at deeply discounted prices) to state-sector workers the apartments they lived in, which previously belonged to the state. This helped workers feel a little more secure in their futures, and led to increased spending and improved investing habits.

Historically, property rights have been instrumental in furthering social and economic development by strengthening the political and economic institutions of a society. As Nobel Laureate Douglass C. North pointed out, "Institutions form the incentive structure of a society and the political and economic institutions, in consequence, are the underlying determinant of economic performance."[11]

Deng Xiaoping also recognized the importance of property. When he started the reform process in the late 1970s, his initial efforts were concentrated in improving the rural sector. The House Responsibility Law allowed the allocation of land among farmers and permitted them to own and sell for their own benefit what they produced above a set quota. The land, however, was still the property of the state.

Given the Chinese economy's condition when Mao died, the changes were quite substantial and impacted agricultural growth; rural consumption from 1978 to 1985 grew faster than that of urban areas. Consequently, farmers' support for the changes Beijing was trying to implement increased.

Gradually, Beijing's attention moved toward the faster track to economic growth, namely manufacturing and exporting. In the process,

China changed the manufacturing process of the world. This change in focus, of a scale never seen before in history, created enormous inequalities between rural residents and their urban counterparts.

Decisions to decentralize health, education, and welfare provisions to local areas added to the problems. A large number of rural hospitals were left without funding and had to charge locals for treatment at prices much higher than what their incomes could support. The SARS epidemic was a stark reminder of the perils of the Chinese healthcare system.

Indicating an ability to diagnose and treat existing weaknesses, the current leadership in Beijing has come to power with the idea that a strong rural foundation is extremely important for the future growth of the economy. The agriculture tax is being abolished and certain fees farmers used to pay are being reduced. Chinese farmers now have 30-year leasehold rights on their properties, which—under certain circumstances—can be traded. The central government's next step is to increase its contributions to rural areas.

Another drastic change is the reformation of the hukou system. Hukous are internal passports distributed on the basis of urban or rural residence. Not so long ago, it was extremely difficult for people to change their hukou. But a desire to increase its urban population and to help its citizens climb the income ladder has led the Chinese to allow rural migrants seeking jobs in cities to transfer from a rural hukou to an urban one. This government-supported employment migration to urban centers has made the improvement of education and healthcare in rural areas a priority. The reason is that rural areas need to become more attractive so people will choose to stay, because given the size of China's population massive immigration is not sustainable. On the other hand, people that decide to immigrate should have the basic qualifications needed in order to survive in the antagonistic city environment.

Progress is slow, but top leadership seems committed to helping rural areas. If the good intentions do not evolve into measurable results, the country will be damaged on several fronts. The potential investment and consumption growth in rural areas could be lost. Social unrest could become extreme, pressuring the central government into a choice between suppressing it by force or losing control, choices unwelcome by the Chinese as well as international investors.

It is very easy for critics to identify China's missteps as the country moves toward change. The tendency to compare everything to the established practices of the Western world leads to negative judgments. China will make mistakes and will often mislead the rest of the world, but progress can be made. History shows that the trajectories of very few, if any, developing nations followed the rules of any particular business rule book. As those nations once were so enabled, China needs some slack.

The Time Factor

When Deng started down the path of change, Chinese households had zero wealth, hardly surprising in a strict socialist system where the state is expected to take care of its citizens' needs. But as the Chinese economy evolved, its people tried to accumulate wealth to care for their children and to tend to themselves in their later years.

The explosive growth of the so-called *gray economy* is one consequence of this accumulation. Studies have shown that the black economy in China represents 50 to 60 percent of gross domestic product. In theory, this is a loss of revenue for the government. In China, however, where state-owned enterprises (SOE) previously suffocated the business spirit of the Chinese people, it also indicates that a great number of individuals have started their own (usually small) businesses rather than wait for the central government to deal the final blow to the SOE monstrosity. This development could not have taken place without the changes instigated by Chinese leadership.

The art of tax evasion is one reason the gray economy has become so big. It is not clear whether the central government can, if it wishes, collect a bigger portion of taxes. At this juncture, it may not be in Chinese authorities' best interests to do so. The capitalist spirit of the Chinese people is evident based on their business success in other parts of the world. A government trying to overhaul an economy as big as China's should view this vibrant business activity as a good thing. Ultimately, this activity increases the pressure to completely dissolve SOEs and increases the options for workers seeking employment once released by SOEs.

This is not to say that China should avoid fixing its tax collection system. But the high rate of corruption and the complications of the tax law, combined with the preceding, lead us to believe that there is some time before the authorities get a better grip on the situation, thus extending the time until total reforms prevail.

The complex problems of the tax system illustrate the broader arguments of critics. It is said that China will be incapable of transforming itself and will eventually collapse under the weight of its internal dysfunctions. Academics aside, Gordon G. Chang is the most vocal of critics. In his book *The Coming Collapse of China*, Chang writes, "The issue, however, is not whether China is doing the right things these days. Look at the country, and you will find evidence of solutions that, with time and political will, could work. If China had, say, thirty years, everything might come out right. But whether China is on the right road is not the matter at hand. When historians write the final chapter on the People's Republic, they will say that there wasn't enough time."[12]

Chang's approach centers on the "moral collapse" of the Chinese society, and the lack of political reform. Our purpose is not to judge Chang's approach. In fact, his point that corruption remains the biggest problem the Chinese leadership has to solve is valid. We are not prepared, however, to write off China on the basis of time; an unfortunate fall can happen tomorrow or in ten or twenty years. Many analysts, particularly those based in the U.S., believe political reform should be the first step in a reform effort. However, a look into the history of the world demonstrates that economic development usually precedes democratic rule, because it is only after incomes rise that the masses demand representation.

Democratic institutions, of course, foster sustainable economic growth, but are not necessary to beginning the process. As D.C. North has noted, "economic growth and the development of freedom are complementary processes of societal development. Economic growth provides the resources (and leisure) to support more complex societies; and it is unlikely to persist in the long run without the development of political and civil liberties. A world of specialization and division of labor—the roots of economic growth—is going to nurture democratic polities and individual freedoms."[13]

Investing in an emerging market environment has always entailed danger. And there are ways—as we will show in later chapters—for investors to profit from the changes that are taking place in China even if the current reforms fail and total chaos prevails, as Mr. Chang expects. No matter which predictions come to pass, Napoleon will still be the most prophetic: "Let China sleep, for when she wakes, she will shake the world."

Endnotes

1. In terms of purchasing power parity (PPP), China and India represent 25 percent of the world's economy.
2. In 1991, Manmohan Singh was the Finance Minister while Palaniappan Chidambaram, the other main architect of the reforms, was the Commerce Minister. In the 2004 election, the former became Prime Minister and the latter the Finance Minister.
3. Martin Wolf. "Promoting India's Inexorable Ascent" (*Financial Times*, March 1, 2005).
4. In purchasing power parity terms, a way to compare living standards across countries, India's share of the world economy is at 5.8 percent. To compare, Japan's share stands at 7 percent and China at 12.6 percent.
5. India has 28 states and seven centrally administered union territories.
6. *The Economist*, June 12, 2004.
7. Luce, Edward. "India to Dip into Forex Reserves to Build Roads" (*Financial Times*, October 16, 2004).
8. Kynge, James and Edward Luce. "India Starts to See China as a Land of Business Opportunity" (*Financial Times*, September 23, 2003).
9. Presentation at Merrill Lynch, September 17, 2003.
10. Jiang Zemin's speech at the meeting celebrating the 80th anniversary of the founding of Communist Party of China, July 1, 2001.
11. North, Douglass C. (Nobel Prize lecture, December 9, 1993).
12. Chang, Gordon G. *The Coming Collapse of China* (New York: Random House, 2001), p. xx.
13. Douglass C. North. "The Paradox of the West" (Working paper, Washington University, St. Louis, 1993).

Part II

RISKY
BUSINESS

*"Dread Achilles, we will indeed save you now, but the day
of your death is near, and the blame will not be ours, for
it will be heaven and stern fate that will destroy you."*
—Xanthus to Achilles; Homer, The Iliad

4

POWER GAMES

"Hegemonic empires," observed Henry Kissinger, "almost automatically elicit universal resistance, which is why all such claimants sooner or later exhausted themselves."[1]

As the U.S. is currently the world's sole superpower, its reaction to new cooperation between and among old enemies (for example, China and India) in the quest for economic growth will shape the geopolitical and investment climate for the 21st century. The U.S. must accept new relationships it might have previously frowned upon given its deep dependence on foreign capital to finance its needs. The current global instability brought about by this realignment of relationships is augmented by a new arms race.[2]

Global and regional geostrategic developments are of immense importance when making long-term investment decisions. Investors and policy makers are similarly situated: Those who understand the purely economic reasons for the new relationships will prosper, serving their portfolios and their countries well.

Regarding Asia, the resolution or clarification of the following issues will have global consequences:

- China's political ambitions and military capabilities

- India's desire for first-world power status
- The outcome of the U.S.-Russia-China race for influence in central Asia
- Russia's role as a vital source of energy
- The potential Korean unification
- Iran's importance to Asia
- Japan's future security needs
- U.S. involvement in Asia and how it affects the changing geopolitical landscape in the region

These issues are interrelated and therefore extremely complicated, but one central conclusion can be drawn: The post-World War II status quo in Asia is unwinding.

This process will take time and will not dramatically affect our economic and investment projections for the next 10 years. Over the next decade, the U.S. must gradually disengage itself from certain security obligations (for example, Korea, Japan, and Taiwan) in a smooth manner. But there is no guarantee that a mindless move by any of the major players will not derail a peaceful transition. This is a variable that could threaten stability in Asia and the world.

The Russia-Iran-India-China axis is a potential force with which the U.S. will either compete or cooperate (see Figure 4-1). A competition would involve a division of economic spheres along multipolar lines as opposed to the current unipolar arrangement. Japan's response to the rise of such an axis is also critical; it could be economically beneficial but strategically unacceptable. Based on its history, Japan will most likely develop strong ties with the axis, given the profound economic impact such cooperation will have in Asia.

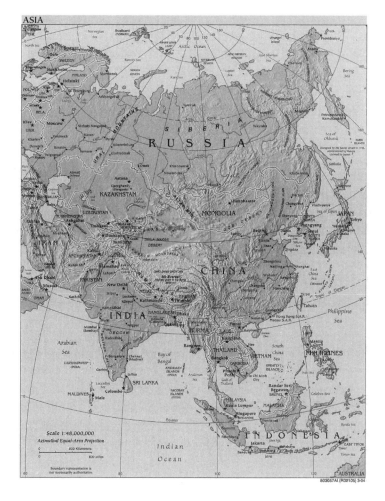

Figure 4-1 The Asian axis of Russia-Iran-India-China.
(Source: Perry—Castaneda Library Map Collection.)

The West will soon have to alter its foreign policy model to produce results that further stability. The current approach seems to emphasize the adoption by the emerging world of particularly Western ideological values. "It is sheer hubris," Samuel Huntington has written, "to think that because Soviet Communism has collapsed, the West has won the world for all time and that Muslims, Chinese, Indians, and others are going to rush to embrace Western liberalism as the only alternative."[3]

Mark Mazower, writing in the *Financial Times*, expressed similar concerns. "States that believe promotion of their interests depends on export of their culture and values are doomed to fail...of course China's rise does not portend the downfall of the U.S. or Europe but it does challenge the West's self-perception as the civilizational hegemon in global affairs...the world before 1800 was one of multiple power-centers and value systems: let us adjust to the fact that it is starting to look like that again."[4]

It may be difficult for many to accept Mazower's conclusion, let alone imagine a situation where the U.S. is confronted directly. A rising state must first catch up with and then challenge the world's sole super-power. Rather than resting on the ambitions of a single nation, the threat to U.S. hegemony lies in the possibility that it exercises its power-projection capability through military action in a number of asymmetric conflicts. This could push the U.S. into selecting the parts of the world where it concentrates its influence and power.[5]

The question is this: How far can the U.S. stretch itself militarily, diplomatically, and economically? The prolonged occupation of Iraq demonstrates that once a large-scale conflict arises, the majority of resources and intellectual capacity are concentrated on that particular conflict. Other issues in different regions are ignored. East Asia is a clear example of this dynamic, and exposes the previously unthinkable possibility that the U.S. may still dominate the balance of power, but not the balance of influence.

Investors who fail to consider or, worse, treat lightly the geopolitical changes taking place substantially increase the risk to their domestic and international investments.

Ambiguous Relationships

"India is now a nuclear weapons state...we have the capacity for a big bomb now. Ours will never be weapons of aggression," asserted then Prime Minister Atal Behari Vajpayee on May 14, 1998, after India's nuclear test.[6]

The Prime Minister's statement betrayed India's knowledge that the ways of the 1970s, when the U.S. would send the Seventh Fleet to the Bay of Bengal to intimidate India during its war with Pakistan, were over. Although the Clinton Administration adopted harsh measures toward India after the test, one year later, during the Kargil War, U.S. diplomatic efforts favored India, marking a shift in U.S. policy.

Serious observers knew that it was only a matter of time before India demonstrated its nuclear capabilities—a large part of India's ruling class has always believed that possession of an independent nuclear capability is a prerequisite for achieving major-power status.

As professors Baldev Raj Nayar and T.V. Paul have noted, India's vision for major-power status has been alive for a long time. "Although Nehru often spoke against great-power politics, underneath his idealism lay a submerged realism about the potential of India to become a major power in the international system. Such a desire was evident in his pursuit of nonalignment, in his autarkic economic development strategy, which placed heavy emphasis on the public sector and heavy industry, and in the prominence he gave to science and technology. The building up of the nuclear and space program by Nehru and his successors has also been driven largely by the desire to become a major power."[7]

India never signed the Treaty on the Non-Proliferation of Nuclear Weapons because, as K. Subrahmanyam has noted, "India has a far more realistic view of the game of 'non-proliferation' and therefore refused to accept a regime conceived by a few nations violating the basic international norms that all nations are entitled to the same category of weapons for their defense. Nor was India taken in by the concept of a 'nuclear-weapon-free zone,' which legitimized nuclear weapons in the hands of a few powers."[8]

India's obsession with security is understandable in light of its turbulent relationship with the U.S. in the period after World War II. The Cold War years proved to be difficult for India. Its nonalignment policy was viciously rejected by the U.S., and India was considered a satellite of the Soviet Union. This misapprehension caused a delay in cooperation that could have begun years ago. It must be noted that "India turned to the Soviets for arms in the 1960s only after the United

States had started its military aid to Pakistan and only after New Delhi had made an unsuccessful bid for large-scale U.S. military aid."[9]

U.S.-India relations began to improve after 2000, a rapprochement that gathered momentum in the wake of the September 11, 2001 terrorist attacks. Though the central focus of their respective foreign policies has not changed, the U.S. has come to realize that India can be a major ally in Asia. The new relationship is founded on an understanding that "[India] is bound to emerge as a major market, it is a reservoir of readily tappable brainpower which will be required by the U.S. if it is to maintain its position as a technological hyperpower. There are no inherent conflicts of national interests between the U.S. and India. And in the light of uncertainties regarding China and the Islamic world, India could be a convenient and friendly countervailer."[10]

Relations are improving not only in economic terms, but also in strategic and military ones. The U.S. views India as a potentially strong ally in its global war on terrorism. The technologies offered by the U.S. and Israel are important to India, with the transfer of military technology from the U.S. holding special significance.

India is slowly gaining support in domestic U.S. political circles. Many opinions that would have been characterized as reckless or anti-American five or 10 years ago are now freely expressed and accepted. Former U.S. Ambassador to India Robert D. Blackwill said in the summer of 2005, "In my view, the United States should now integrate India into the evolving global non-proliferation regime as a friendly nuclear weapons state. We should end constraints on assistance to and cooperation with India's nuclear industry and high-tech trade, changing laws and policy when necessary."[11]

President George W. Bush acknowledged in July 2005 that India is "a responsible state" and said that he would seek agreement from Congress to end more than four decades of sanctions that have barred full U.S. cooperation with India on civilian nuclear energy programs, perhaps hinting at a desire to positively influence the process of change in Asia. But the president's proposals require the blessing of a Congress that, as of this writing, may be loath to give it.

The end of the Cold War has given rise to cooperation that once would have been deemed impossible between other states, at the same time further complicating the geopolitical game. In January 2005, India and Iran signed a multibillion dollar deal under which Iran will supply India with 7.5 million tons of liquefied natural gas (LNG) annually for 25 years starting in 2009. India will participate in the development of oilfields in Iran in cooperation with Iran's state oil company, Petropars. The two countries have also conducted joint military exercises, and it is believed that Indian personnel have helped Iran modernize its Soviet-made weapons systems. Cooperation also extends to improvements in ports, roads, and rail systems.

The problems are obvious. Iran has been identified as a part of President Bush's "axis of evil," and is not trusted by Israel. India's position is, at times, very difficult. The U.S. knows that India's importance grows by the day, and that a constructive relationship is in everyone's best interest. The evolving view of India by U.S. opinion leaders lowers the political costs of advocating a closer relationship, as does the realization that Pakistan can compete with India neither in commerce nor in arms purchases, both essential components of the U.S. economic growth. The U.S. has been lenient with India and its dealings with Iran—given the 1996 U.S. Iran-Libya Sanctions Act, which penalizes foreign companies for investing more than $20 million in either of the countries. Obviously, the money being invested by India (and China) in Iran exceeds the limit by a wide margin.

India's position on the subject has been clear. Its Ministry of External Affairs spokesperson explained, "The United States has its relationship with Pakistan, which is separate from our own relationship with them. Our relationship with Iran is peaceful and largely economic. We do not expect it to affect our continuing good relations with the United States."[12]

Israeli Prime Minister Ariel Sharon raised concerns regarding the Iran relationship, particularly the possibility that India might transfer Israeli military technology to Iran, on a visit to India in September 2003. As Sudha Ramachandran reported, "Sharon is said to have demanded explicit guarantees from India that it would not transfer any technology acquired from Israel to a third country, especially Iran. India, while assuring Israel that such 'leaking' would not happen rejected Israeli calls to shun Iran."[13]

"A continuation of sophisticated military aid [to Pakistan] at the levels that have prevailed since 1980," wrote Selig S. Harrison in 1989, "would place the United States on a collision course with India—a course that would become increasingly damaging to American security interests as New Delhi achieves regional power and importance in the decades ahead."[14] Up until 2000, many U.S. political analysts and power players refused to face this reality, advocating instead confrontational and paternalistic policies.

As in the investment side of the story, few people are paying attention to India. But the country will surprise in the geopolitical arena as it will in the investment one. The main story for the next 20 years is whether India can realize its economic and geostrategic potential.

The Dragon and the Eagle

Paul Kennedy's classic *The Rise and Fall of the Great Powers* is said to have significantly influenced Chinese strategists. Kennedy's thesis fits China extremely well: "...wealth and power, or economic strength and military strength, are always relative and should be seen as such. Since they are relative, and since all societies are subject to the inexorable tendency to change, then the international balances can *never* be still, and it is a folly of statesmanship to assume that they ever would be."[15] American leaders have not, one can safely assume, taken Kennedy's book seriously.

The Sino-American relationship operates on two levels: economic and geopolitical. The former can be easily defined: China produces and the U.S. consumes. The latter is more complicated. The two countries share many delicate and complex issues of mutual concern. And on several critical matters, the U.S. and China hold conflicting views, further complicating the relationship.

Major conflicts between the two countries stem more from commitments the U.S. has in Asia than from any direct territorial or economic disagreement. U.S. security commitments to Japan, South Korea, and Taiwan form the point from which problems develop. The avenue for U.S.-China cooperation would broaden if the U.S. gradually disengaged itself from these commitments. This will happen in the next 10 years because the U.S. is the "inheritor of a vast array of strategic commitments, which had been made decades earlier, when the nation's political, economic, and military capacity to influence world affairs seemed so much more assured. In consequence, the United States now runs the risk, so familiar to historians of the rise and fall of previous Great Powers, of what might roughly be called 'imperial overstretch'—that is to say, decision makers in Washington must face the awkward and enduring fact that the sum total of the United States' global interests and obligations is nowadays far larger than the country's power to defend them all simultaneously."[16]

If the U.S. and China can find common ground, or at least avoid unnecessary confrontation, Asia and the world will be better served. Vigorous and sustainable long-term economic growth will become more viable.

To expand its world presence, China has been changing its ways. Chinese international affairs experts and government officials reached the conclusion in 1999 that "China needed to stabilize and improve its relationship with the United States, as the single most important country for China's national interests."[17]

China is also doing its best to become a more approachable regional player. As David Shambaugh noted, "Beijing's diplomacy has been remarkably adept and nuanced, earning praise around the region...most nations in the region now see China as a good neighbor, a constructive partner, a careful listener, and a nonthreatening regional power...just a few years ago, many of China's neighbors voiced growing concerns about the possibility of China becoming a domineering regional hegemon and powerful military threat."[18] Changes in approach to the U.S. and to its regional neighbors have allowed China to strike new economic deals all over the world.

This new profile has, however, inspired concern throughout the ranks of U.S. policy makers, economic analysts, and foreign policy strategists. The dominant view predicts waning U.S. influence and power in Asia, and even the world. Many political analysts and scholars have called for a containment strategy to prevent China from challenging the U.S. position in the region.

The European Union (EU) has also cooperated with China via a vast array of economic and policy projects. The situation is easier for the EU because, unlike the U.S., it has no real military or strategic interest in East Asia. No European military forces are based in the region, and no security alliances or other commitments exist that would cause either side to view the other as a potential threat.[19]

The U.S. is the only country whose interests span the globe, and it will have to be extremely agile when designing its foreign policy. The U.S. will be faced with the grand strategic dilemma of allocating resources in the regions most important to its interests.

The current tumult in Central Asia and the Middle East currently demands more U.S. blood and treasure than does East Asia, but China is uncomfortable with the increased U.S. military presence in Afghanistan, Kyrgyzstan, Uzbekistan, and Georgia. This extension of U.S. power—on top of its presence in South and East Asia—exacerbates Chinese anxiety. Chinese military capability is—contrary to popular belief—extremely limited. Credible assessments of the Chinese military power have concluded that "the balance between the United States and China, both globally and in Asia, is likely to remain decisively in America's favor beyond the next twenty years."[20] Furthermore, "there is scant, if any, evidence of the PLA [Chinese army] developing capabilities to project power beyond China's immediate periphery."[21]

The U.S. presence in Central Asia is in its early stages (see Figure 4-2). However, since 2001, the Pentagon has established military bases in Afghanistan, Uzbekistan, and Kyrgystan, and is now trying to attain access to Tajikistan and Kazakhstan. Kazakhstan is the most important Central Asian state for Russia, due to a shared border 6,846 kilometers long and the fact that 30 percent of the population there is Russian. China, in cooperation with Russia, has been trying to increase its influence in the region through the Shanghai Cooperation Organization (SCO).[22] The U.S. commitment to the region may lead to an increase in tensions and a strengthening in the relationships between China, Russia, and Iran.[23] One hopes the competition for Central Asia dominance will not lead to a resurgence of the antagonism of the late 19th and early 20th centuries, when the Russian and British empires stood at the brink of war for regional hegemony.

Ironically, such a war was averted then with the coming of World War I as "British and Russian difficulties in Central Asia were set aside while the Great Powers addressed the far more urgent crises of world war... Had war not intervened, the Anglo-Russian accord, which has persisted in the face of adversity through seven years of Persian revolutionary unrest, Afghan obstructionism and the Tibetan geostrategic void, would have faced the challenge of re-evaluation and revision—a challenge it might not have survived."[24]

Figure 4-2   Central Asia's proximity to the world's hot spot.
(Source: Perry-Castaneda Library Map Collection.)

The Sino-Russian relationship is rooted in economic and security concerns. China is a critical oil and weapons systems customer of Russia, and both are trying to contain Washington's strategic moves in Central Asia. Since the mid-1990s, the two countries have worked on a plan for a pipeline to deliver oil to China. In 2004, Japan interfered and initially persuaded Russia to terminate the pipeline at Nakhodka, closer to Japan on Russia's Pacific coast, and not in China. Japan persuaded Russia to change plans by offering to invest $7 billion in the project.

In a dramatic turn in September of 2005, Mr. Putin said that the multi-billion dollar oil pipeline would first go to China and only later to the Pacific Coast. Russia's decision was a clear indication that relations with China have improved considerably. Japan's "intransigence over the Kurile Islands territorial dispute that has held up the signing of a peace treaty between the two countries since World War II"[25] has been cited as one reason for the change. The resolution is uncertain, but this issue illustrates not only Asia's pressing need for energy, but also the trend emerging across the globe to the formation of new alliances. Such alliances will eventually alter the global political and economic status quo.

Japan and China have had a very chaotic past, and distrust and bitterness still characterize the relationship. The modern era of this centuries-old antagonism dates to Japan's defeat of China in 1895 and the subsequent treaty that required China to cede South Manchuria and Taiwan to Japan. Japan enhanced its global position. (It later participated in Great Britain's first 20th century alliance in 1902. This arrangement alleviated much of Great Britain's Far East security responsibility.[26]) China's sense of cultural superiority over Japan made this defeat even more excruciating. Japan's victory in the Russo-Japanese war two years later further stoked its confidence, something that played a great role in its successful invasion of northeastern China in 1931. By 1937, the fighting had spread, and by 1940 Japan's occupation of China was a grim reality.

China and Japan continue to spar over the interpretation of certain historical incidents and claims to many islands in the East China Sea, but they have become very close economically. China now accounts for one-fifth of Japan's trade and is on pace to become Japan's largest trading partner by 2020. There are more than 700 Japanese manufacturing facilities in China. Given China's growth and Japan's quest to spark its economy, this is shaping up as one of most important bilateral relationships of the 21st century.

The U.S. has more than 40,000 troops stationed in Japan, with more than half of them based in Okinawa, which is closer to Shanghai than to Tokyo. These troops do not really serve U.S. interests. They do consume U.S. resources to defend Japanese territory and trade routes. The trade-route defense is becoming increasingly unnecessary as the perceived threat to sea-lanes—China—lives and dies on the flow of imports and exports.

The only potential problem will be Sino-Japanese competition for oil. Both countries depend on others for the commodity; Japan imports all of its oil, whereas China is expected to import 50 percent of its needs by 2010. But even this potential trouble spot does not justify such a massive U.S. military presence.

If China establishes a firm foothold in Taiwan, it will control the South China Sea through the Taiwan and Luzon Straights (see Figure 4-3). But this should increasingly become a Japanese and/or Korean problem. Japan (given its usually pragmatic view on geopolitical issues that has produced its strong alliance with the U.S.) "may have to choose between 'balancing' against or 'bandwagoning' with China."[27]

The U.S. has been encouraging the Japanese to become more involved with issues of their own security. During the last 30 years, Japan has consistently spent one percent of GDP on defense, making its military budget the fourth largest in the world in absolute terms. In late 2004, the Japan Defense Agency (JDA) issued the National Defense program guidelines, which stated: "China, which has a strong influence on the security in this region, has been modernizing its nuclear and missile capabilities as well as naval and air forces, and expanding its area of operation at sea. We have to remain attentive to its future course."[28] This was the first mention of China as a potential threat. The document also addressed the North Korea and Taiwan Straits "situations." A few months later, after a meeting in Washington, the U.S. Department of State issued a joint statement of the U.S.-Japan security consulting committee identifying a common Asia-Pacific strategic objective to "encourage the peaceful resolution of issues concerning the Taiwan Strait through dialogue."[29] This was the first time in the last 50 years the two governments issued a joint statement concerning the Taiwan Straits.

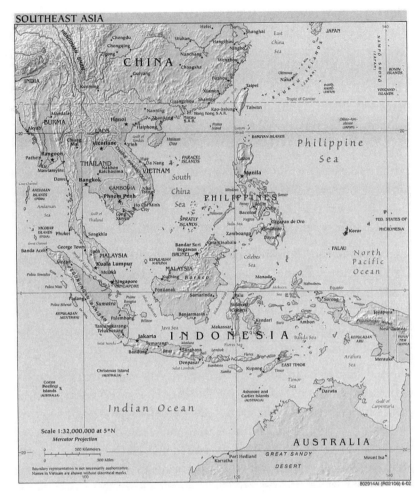

Figure 4-3 Taiwan's strategic location is very important to China's security plans. (Source: Perry-Castaneda Library Map Collection.)

Preventing Taiwan from declaring independence remains China's most sensitive security concern. The U.S. has "recognized that Taiwan is a Chinese province, not an independent state,"[30] and does not want a military conflict over the issue, but it is an issue the U.S. could exploit to gain concessions on matters more crucial to its own interests. If the Chinese handle it elegantly, Taiwan will no longer be an obstacle to expansion of U.S.-China relations.

The other potential flashpoint in the region is the Korean peninsula. Though the timing is impossible to pinpoint, North and South Korea will eventually reunify. The U.S. would then be able to withdraw the more than 35,000 troops it has stationed on the peninsula. Currently, U.S. presence in South Korea has more political than military significance.

Though a unified Korea will most probably possess nuclear weapons, this is a positive given its proximity to China and indications that it would follow a fairly independent or slightly pro-U.S. policy rather than a pro-Chinese or a pro-Russian line.

Japan, however, would not welcome a nuclear Korea. Koreans harbor deep animosity over Japan's brutal colonial rule. Japanese likewise look upon Korea with disdain. As Selig Harrison has observed, "Japanese cultural contempt for Korea and Koreans makes the idea of a militarily superior Korea psychologically intolerable, apart from the security threat involved."[31]

China will eventually emerge as a big player in the world. To ensure a peaceful transition, existing powers, especially the U.S., must ensure that the Chinese do not sense an effort by the developed power to block its ascent. Including China in world affairs on an equal basis is the best strategy. The U.S. will eventually opt for a multilateral approach in "which the U.S. leads but does not attempt to dictate," allowing China to assume the responsibilities and enjoy the benefits as all great powers are expected to do. Because economic development is the top priority for existing and emerging powers, most political questions will be resolved in favor of global trade.

This optimistic view is tempered by U.S. President Bush's doctrine of preemptive war and the profound change in U.S. foreign policy since 2001. "The United States has long maintained the option of preemptive actions to counter a sufficient threat to our national security," stated Bush. "The greater the threat, the greater is the risk of inaction—and the more compelling the case for taking anticipatory action to defend ourselves, even if uncertainty remains as to the time and place of the enemy's attack. To forestall or prevent such hostile acts by our adversaries, the United States will, if necessary, act preemptively."[32] U.S. foreign policy since the turn of the century leaves the impression that "among modern international history's great powers, only the United States seems unable to accept the fact that great powers must live in a world with others who neither like them nor share their values."[33] And yet the "secret of the United States' long brilliant run as the world's leading state was its ability and willingness to exercise power within alliance and multinational frameworks, which made its power and agenda more acceptable to allies and other key states around the world."[34]

Political leaders will realize that sustainability of the U.S. position in the world system requires more than simplistic, brute force. "Because it has so much power for good or evil, because it is the linchpin of the western alliance system and the center of the existing global economy," suggested Paul Kennedy, "what it does, or does not do, is so much more important than what any of the other Powers decides to do."[35]

Endnotes

1. Kissinger, Henry A. "The Long Shadow of Vietnam" (*Newsweek*, May 1, 2000).
2. *Stockholm International Peace Research Institute 2005 Yearbook*. Arms spending increased for the sixth successive year in 2004. The global total exceeded $1 trillion, with the U.S. accounting for $455 billion.
3. Huntington, Samuel P. *The Clash of Civilizations and the Remaking of World Order* (New York: Touchstone, 1996), p. 66.
4. Mazower, Mark. "The West Needs a New Sense of Self" (*Financial Times*, March 30, 2005).
5. There are many analytical levels to which the term *asymmetric conflicts* can be used. For our purposes, it is used in the sense that a smaller power can count on the conflict being more important to it than the stronger power (the U.S., in this case), thus limiting the amount of resources the stronger power is willing to spend in order to defeat the weaker power.
6. On May 11 and 13, 1998, India had a five-shot nuclear test series as a response to Pakistan's missile test in April of the same year. India first tested a nuclear explosive in 1974.
7. Nayar, Baldev Raj and T.V. Paul. *India in the World Order* (Cambridge: Cambridge University Press, 2003), p. 27.
8. Harrison, Selig S. and K. Subrahmanyam. *Superpower Rivalry in the Indian Ocean*, ed. Selig S. Harrison, K. Subrahmanyam (New York: Oxford University Press, 1989), p. 228.
9. Ibid., p. 269.
10. Subrahmanyam, K. "Indian Autumn on Capitol Hill" (*The Indian Express*, November 6, 2004).

11. Blackwill, Robert D. "The India Imperative" (*The National Interest*, Summer 2005), p. 10.
12. Ramachandran, Sudha. "The Glue That Bonds India, Iran" (*Asian Times*, January 12, 2005).
13. Ibid.
14. Harrison and Subrahmanyam. *Superpower Rivalry in the Indian Ocean*, p. 283.
15. Kennedy, Paul. *The Rise and Fall of the Great Powers*, 1989 edition (New York: Random House, 1987), p. 536.
16. Ibid., p. 515.
17. Shambaugh, David. "China Engages Asia" (*International Security*, Winter 2004/05) p. 71.
18. Ibid., p. 64.
19. Shambaugh, David. "China and Europe: The Emerging Axis" (*Current History*, September 2004), p. 246.
20. Brown, Harold, Joseph Prueher, and Adam W. Segal. "Independent Task Force Report: Chinese Military Power" (*Council on Foreign Relations Press*, June 12, 2003), p. 2.
21. Shambaugh. "China Engages Asia," p. 86.
22. The SCO was established on June 15, 2001 and includes China, Russia, Kazakhstan, Kyrgystan, Tadzhikistan, and Uzbekistan.
23. Sinopec, a Chinese state-controlled oil company, has struck a $70 billion deal to buy Iranian crude oil and LNG over three decades.
24. Siegel, Jennifer. *Endgame* (London: I.B. Tauris, 2002), p. 201.
25. Chazan, Guy. "Russia Confirms China-Pipeline Plan" (*Wall Street Journal Online*, September 7, 2005).
26. Siegel. *Endgame*, p. xvi.
27. "Mapping the Global Future" (*Report of the National Intelligence Council's 2020 Project*, December 2004).
28. "National Defense Program Guidelines for FY 2005 and After" (Japan Defense Agency, December 10, 2004).
29. Joint Statement of the U.S.—Japan Security Consultative Committee (Washington, D.C., February 19, 2005). The committee included the U.S. Secretary of State, the U.S. Secretary of Defense, Japan's Minister for Foreign Affairs, Japan's Minister of State for Defense, and Japan's Director General of the Defense Agency.
30. Layne, Christopher. "China's Role in American Grand Strategy: Partner, regional power, or great rival?" P. 77. Contribution to "The Asia Pacific: A region in transition" (ed. Jim Rolfe). Honolulu: Asia Pacific Center for security studies. 2004.
31. Harrison, Selig. *Korean Endgame*. (New Jersey: Princeton, 2002), p. 290.
32. "The National Security Strategy of the United States of America" (The White House, September 2002), p. 15.
33. Layne, op. cit., p. 79.
34. Ikenberry, John G. "America's Imperial Ambition" (*Foreign Affairs*, September/October 2002, Volume 81, No. 5), p. 56.
35. Kennedy, *Rise and Fall of the Great Powers*, p. 535.

5

STRAWS IN THE WIND

R ichard Russell of Dow Theory fame once said, "I believe stocks in bull markets advance to the point where they are seriously overvalued. I believe bull markets end—after which stocks make the long trip down to the area where stocks become seriously undervalued."

If big bull markets spawn big bear markets, investors must ask if the bear market of 2000-02 was *the* spawn, or if there is more pain down the road. If stocks did indeed become more overvalued at the 2000 top than at any other point in history, have they made the trip to the bottom that now makes them seriously undervalued?

The answer to this quintessential question is the basis for formulating a long-term investment strategy as it can alter the assumed rate of return on investments to a degree that would render an investment strategy useless.

Before we answer that question, we have to clarify a few misconceptions.

Our objective is to identify the many challenges on the horizon in the most developed stock markets, detail a roadmap for investors to follow to their desired financial destinations. This is not a "doom-and-gloom" story, although one could write an entire book from such a perspective. The failure of the many negative critiques of the current financial and economic system appearing in recent years is a lack of direction on what investors can do to cope with the problems. Few have provided actionable advice. Nonetheless, it is necessary to dispel some myths about investing before we detail our roadmap.

How Long Is the Long Run?

The discussion of stock markets begins with two main categories: developed and emerging. Among the developed markets, one—the United States—comprises about half of world stock market value, and the American economy accounts for about a third of the global economy.[1] Due to its sheer size, in the end, everything comes down to America. If cracks appear in the U.S. stock market or economy, the world's major markets shake.

The most common misconception about stocks is that their long-term average return is "guaranteed." The average investor has been brainwashed into believing that one cannot lose money in the long term in the U.S. or any other stock market. The most widely advertised long-term annualized return for stocks is the 10.7 percent (usually quoted as 11 percent) derived from a study by *Ibbotson Associates* of stock market returns from 1926 to 2000.[2]

Based on the belief that 11 percent describes a pretty good place to park your money for 20 or 30 years, the average investor is willing to wait out any financial storm. But in light of the collective experience since the top in the stock market in 2000, investors should question whether that 11 percent is a reliable performance indicator. If the market is flat for a decade or two, any substantial deviation from the 11 percent return assumption can be devastating.

Ten thousand dollars compounded at 11 percent over a 20-year period is $80,623; assuming a rate of return of 7 percent halves the end figure to $38, 697; and at 3 percent, the disappointment is just too much: $18, 061 (see Figure 5-1).[3]

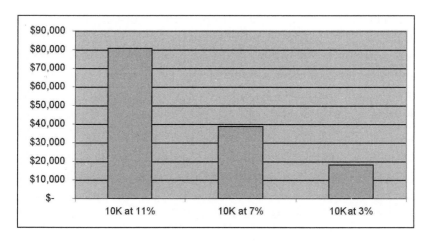

Figure 5-1 Investment returns under different rate of return assumptions. (Source: Ivan Martchev)

Many commissioned financial professionals fail to share with their unsuspecting clients that there have been long periods in U.S. financial history when stocks have produced no positive returns. The indexes can languish for many years in very wide, sideways trading ranges with big rallies and big selloffs that ultimately take them nowhere. There have been three periods in the last 100 years when the market has been flat for 15 or more years at a time. Those periods could sometimes comprise the whole investment horizon of an individual investor. If you happen to have invested near the beginning of one of those cycles, you pretty much got swindled by the phrase "stocks always go up in the long run."

Driven by the 11 percent rule, in the 1980s, and especially in the 1990s, public participation in the stock market dramatically increased. According to a recent study by the Investment Company Institute, assets held in mutual funds increased from under $300 billion in 1984 to $7.6 trillion by the end of June 2004. During the same time frame, the number of U.S. households owning mutual funds increased from 10.2 million (about 12 percent) to 53.9 million, or one out of every two U.S. households in 2004. That translates to 92.3 million individual fund shareholders.[4]

The Wall Street selling machine has managed to quadruple the size of its mutual fund shareholder base in only two decades, while providing them with an inferior product. The product is inferior because most mutual fund managers have underperformed their benchmark indexes over those two decades and, due to the structure of the mutual fund industry, are likely to do so in the future. We explain why shortly.

Due to that underperformance, it has recently become very popular to buy index products and not individual stocks. Exchange-traded funds (ETFs)—baskets of stocks representing a particular index that trade like individual securities—are among the most prominent of these vehicles. The sales pitch is irresistible: ETFs have much lower expenses than mutual funds due to their passive management, and because the majority of mutual fund managers underperform over the long haul, why bother with mutual funds?

Assets in ETFs have seen remarkable growth, increasing by 48 percent to $222.9 billion in 2004 from $151 billion in 2003.[5] More and more money is being allocated to index mutual funds (funds that specifically try to mimic the performance of a particular index), and many actively managed mutual funds are stealthily designed to mimic the performance of their major benchmark indexes. You might be paying for active management, and you might think you're getting it; in practice, the fund actively benchmarks against the S&P 500 by buying mainly the biggest stocks in the index. Because the S&P 500 is a market capitalization-weighted index (the biggest stocks in the index by market value have the biggest impact), being long the 50 largest names allows "active" fund managers to closely match the performance of the benchmark index. Most actively managed funds employing such a strategy would never explicitly tell you what they're doing. If you knew it, there would be no reason for you to pay them to "manage" your money.

Your chances to beat the market over long periods of time with such funds are very slim and not worth taking.

Mutual fund companies are in the business of managing money for a profit, a goal they achieve through fees and expenses. The larger those fees, the greater the chance that the mutual fund you are paying to beat the market will actually underperform over long periods of time. Due to those expenses, the average mutual fund is already starting from behind if it employs a strategy that tries to mimic an index.

Add to that the 5 percent (and sometimes higher) sales charge that you usually see on a front-load mutual fund (a type of fund sold through commissioned sales representatives; the load represents that commission) and you are almost guaranteed to trail the averages. We will never understand why you have to pay for a service before it is performed in a competent manner, much less paying those front loads in return for mediocre performance.

Not every mutual fund manager is incompetent, and there are good front-load funds. But the majority of loaded funds will prove to be so expensive in a market environment that is likely to be hostile over the next 10 years that most are simply not worth buying.

Only long periods of subdued or negative returns are likely to change the practice, but by the time the majority of individual investors figure it out, it will be too late for many of them to do anything but sell out. In fact, there is well-documented evidence that individual investors are the ultimate contrarian indicator when it comes to major exits and entries in the market. Also, the evidence suggests that this is true not only for the stock market, but also for the bond market (see Figure 5-2).

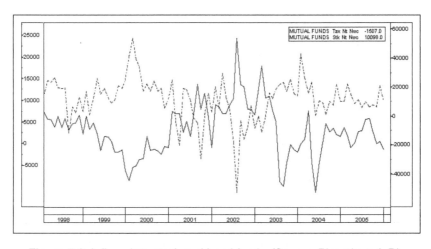

Figure 5-2 Inflows into stock and bond funds. (Source: Bloomberg L.P.)

Monthly mutual fund inflows stood at their highest levels—$53.7 billion—near the February 2000 top (as in Figure 5-2). The market topped out on March 10. In retrospect, that was the time to sell the market (i.e. get out of stocks), and not to be jumping into the buying frenzy with the crowd. The summer of 2002 mirrored the 2000 top. In July, monthly outflows, after steadily rising in the previous several months, spiked to the all-time record of $52.6 billion. The market bottomed out in the late morning July 24 to flush out the last poor souls after dropping like a stone at the open.

The same tale is true when it comes to bond funds. Mutual fund investors were selling out of their bond holdings, probably selling bond funds in order to get into stock funds near the top in the stock market. They should have been doing the opposite. Later, near the stock market low in July 2002 as individual investors were throwing in the towel on stock funds, they were piling into bonds at exactly the wrong time. Major outflow of funds in August of 2003 and May 2004 again proved to be bottoms for bonds—exactly the wrong time to be throwing in the towel.

Because that type of individual investor behavior is unlikely to change, a multiyear trading-range market is the worst type of environment for the average investor. If they are buying at the top and selling at the bottom for 15 years, eventually disgust with the stock market will be so high that most will end up missing the ultimate bottom. Despite all the advantages, not even ETFs will help if the market stays flat for 20 years. That may sound a little extreme, but world financial history is peppered with such examples.

At its 1903 low, the Dow stood at 42. If you were smart enough to buy at those levels, you probably felt pretty good for the next 25 years. But failure to sell out brought you back to that same level as the Dow declined 89 percent to 41.22 after the 1929 crash and the ensuing selloff that carried to 1932. Three decades of long-term gains evaporated in three years (see Figure 5-3).

Some may point out that those are extreme examples with no application to the current environment. This is simply not true. You must remember The New Economy and the way its proponents rationalized the Nasdaq 5000 mania. The collapse of the Nasdaq is very similar to

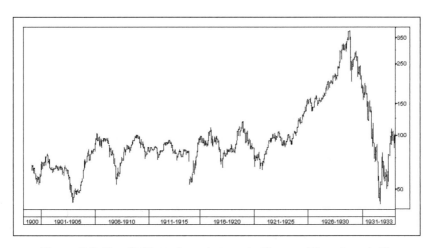

Figure 5-3 The 1929 stock market crash. (Source: Bloomberg L.P.)

the collapse of the Dow in the 1930s (though by some measures many aspects of the bubble economy have not even begun to unwind like they did in the 1930s).

Investors in Thailand, Indonesia, and many other markets in that region experienced a similar wipeout during the Asian Crisis in 1997-98. Another wipeout occurred in Japan, but in slow motion. The Japanese Nikkei 225 index topped out in December 1989 at just below 40,000, but declined to 7,600 in May 2003. Financial history is riddled with burst bubbles, which have popped up reliably for hundreds of years, and, due to human nature, will most likely continue to appear. Greed unchecked by fear is a recipe for disaster and there is little anyone can do to stop it.

Returning to our Dow example, let's say that you were not around to buy near the 1903 low, but you got in the market near the 1929 top (just as so many did in the late 1990s before the 2000 top). You heard that there was a smart Ivy League professor who had calculated that you could make 11 percent in the market if you hold "for the long term." You followed that seasoned advice and you held on. It took 25 years for the Dow to better its 1929 high, until 1954.

That is as long as many individuals' investment horizon.

Then again, you could have assumed that your predecessors in the U.S. had bad luck and the 1930s experience was an outlier unlikely to be repeated very often. You happened to live in the 1960s when the economy was great; you started making a lot of money and began piling into the stock market in 1966 with the Dow near 1,000. After enduring several 20, 30, and one 40 percent decline in 1974, you were ready to retire in 1982 just as the Dow was crossing 1,000 to the upside (see Figure 5-4). True, a lot of stocks made fortunes in those unfortunate periods, but most of those were not in the major indexes. The 1990s idea of indexing would not have worked very well.

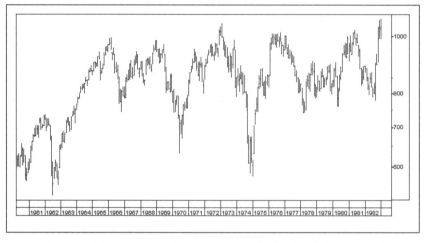

Figure 5-4 The Dow made little progress in the 1966-1982 period.
(Source: Bloomberg L.P.)

Although they say lightning rarely strikes in the same place twice, when it comes to U.S. financial history, it appears that lightning strikes at the same place with every new generation. In the 1930s, it was the Dow Industrials and radio stocks, whereas in the 1990s, it was the Nasdaq and semiconductor stocks. The names are different, but investor behavior and hype in both cases are identical.

So where is the market right now if we have established that the 11 percent rule is not a sure thing?

The Dow Industrials topped out in January 2000, the rest of the major indexes a couple of months later. The market has spent the time since the 2000 top in a sideways trading range with very substantial selloffs in the meantime, very much like any of our previous examples. If history is any guide, stocks can continue this pattern for another 10 years or longer.

Ultimately, stock prices reflect the earnings power behind the companies that issue the underlying shares. Warren E. Buffet, one of the most successful stock investors of all time, has a favorite expression: "In the short run, the market is a voting machine, but in the long run it is a weighing machine." Clearly, stock prices can deviate substantially from the earnings power they represent, but over the long term—five years, 10 years, or longer—that is not likely to be the case.

The long-term returns for stocks come in two forms: price appreciation and dividends. In the 1990s, no one really cared about dividends, but many individual investors who entered the market in those hay days will be surprised to find out that a large part of the long-term appreciation for stocks has come from dividends.

Of course, to enjoy this type of appreciation, you have to own stocks that actually pay meaningful dividends. Interested in a look at how dividends at present compare to what investors have been able to receive in the past?

The current dividend yield of the S&P 500 is 2 percent. At the 2000 market highs, when no one wanted to hear about dividends, it was 1.1 percent. Marginal improvement can be attributed to new tax legislation that encourages corporations to pay dividends, but by historical norms, today's dividend yield can only be characterized as measly (see Figure 5-5).

Major bull markets end with stocks wildly overvalued. We saw that with the S&P 500 yielding 1.1 percent and selling at 29.3 times earnings in 2000 (actually, the P/E ratio climbed as the market declined into the 2001 recession as the earnings part of the calculation declined faster than the price). Compared to the last major stock market peak in 1966, the stock market in 2000 was much more overvalued. Stocks in 1966 sold at 17 times earnings and had a 3 percent dividend yield.

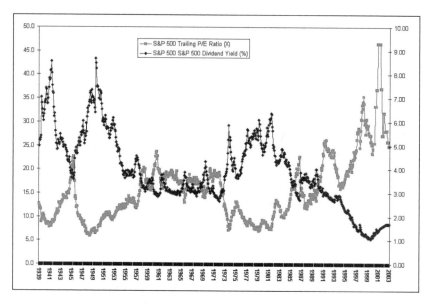

Figure 5-5 Dividend yields and P/E ratios do not suggest a market bottom. (Source: American Association of Individual Investors, Bloomberg L.P.)

How about comparing the market today with the market in 1974, at the lows of the 1966-1982 trading range, a time that is likely to be very similar to what we experience over the next 10 years? The S&P 500 sold at a P/E multiple of 7.6 and was yielding 5.3 percent. The same is true for valuation lows prior to that. At one point in 1949, the S&P 500 P/E ratio was equal to its dividend yield; they were both at 7. In some instances in that period, the earnings multiple actually declined below the level of the dividend yield, as unbelievable as that may sound.

The valuation cycles are very clear: The market moves from grossly overvalued to grossly undervalued and back to grossly overvalued. Those cycles repeat over the decades and there is no evidence yet that they are about to stop working.

There are only two ways that stocks can become cheap compared to previous bear market bottoms. Either prices will decline precipitously, on the order of 50 to 70 percent, or earnings and dividends will double or triple in the next 10 years. Because such wide-eyed growth in earnings and dividends is simply impossible, a probable development in the market cycle is a substantial decline in prices in the next five to 10 years.

Right now, most investors would appreciate a reassuring word that the worst is over, and they can have back their 11 percent dream. They are hearing that from many investment-community professionals who have vested interests in the perpetuation of that dream.

Unsustainable Macroeconomic Imbalances

The world has seen many economic systems, and history has proven that none is perfect, but capitalism and free markets have established themselves as the most successful way of allocating scarce resources. Problems arise when gatekeepers abuse a capitalist system. In the U.S., those gatekeepers are the monetary authority (the Federal Reserve) and the fiscal authority (local, state, and federal governments). In a perfect world, a free market without intervention would take care of most imbalances in an economy. But when vested interests cross swords, the story changes dramatically.

The federal government's policies over the years have resulted in the accumulation of the largest budget and current account deficits (in absolute terms) of any economy on the planet in history. The combination of the two deficits was over $1 trillion dollars in 2005 and is now widely recognized by the popular nickname, the Twin Deficits. It is true that, in terms of percentage of gross domestic product (GDP), or the total value of goods and services produced, other countries have accumulated more absurdly higher numbers. Those who want to spin the numbers positively often mention that fact, but that is just an intellectually dishonest and a very irresponsible way of looking at the situation because the size of the U.S. problem threatens the world financial system.

The large budget deficit is a direct result of the choice of the U.S. government to lend fiscal support to a faltering economy in 2001-02 with numerous tax cuts and increased defense and homeland security spending. The budget deficit is more easily controllable than the current account deficit as it is the result of the direct decisions the government makes on spending and taxation. Although there is no question that tax cuts have fostered economic activity, what is swept under the rug is the substantial long-term cost of entrenched deficit spending and its effect on inflation and interest rates. Neglected, too, is the inefficient allocation of resources resulting from a larger government.

We do not underestimate the importance of the federal budget deficit; of greater relevance for our purposes are the long-term implications of the current account balance (or more accurately, *lack* of balance), which is the most complete definition of the trade balance.[6] The trade deficit is certainly a creature of both Republican and Democrat administrations fed over many years. It is likely that at its current proportion and growth rate there will be a crisis by the year 2010, which, provided the current political climate persists, would most likely fall in the lap of a Republican administration. This is not a political statement, merely an observation that no matter who occupies the White House the outcome will be similar.

As of this writing, the current account deficit stands at $669.5 billion, which also happens to be about 5 percent of the U.S.'s $12 trillion GDP.[7] Every month, the U.S. imports $50 billion more worth of goods than it exports, or just under $2 billion a day. By the time you read this, based on current growth rates, the daily number is likely to be above $2 billion.

Think of it in terms of an individual, average American. If you were making an annual salary of $70,000, but were consuming $75,000 worth of goods and services a year, you would need a lender for that extra $5,000. You wouldn't be doing it otherwise. Year after year, that debt piles up. Your creditor thinks that you can pay, so when you ask for $10,000, you get the money. You may even be able to go as high as $15,000, or even $20,000. But at what point does your creditor say, "Enough is enough."

At present, the U.S. requires close to $2 billion net inflow of capital every day to finance the trade deficit. No one can say definitively that creditors will stop the financing binge if that figure grows to $3 billion, but it is our belief that the rejection notice on the loan application will come before that number is reached. At $3 billion a day, the current account deficit projects to more than $1 trillion annually, which even the U.S. is unlikely to sustain.

Basic economic theory suggests that when the trade deficit is very large a weakening currency can help the problem. It sounds rather simple that a cheaper U.S. dollar will make exports more competitive and make imports more expensive, therefore the situation *should* be self-correcting. In practice, though, the reverse has happened; the trade deficit has ballooned as the dollar has declined.

The reasons for that bizarre development are quite intriguing and suggest that this ballooning will continue. The decline in the dollar has come predominantly against major developed hard currencies like the euro, the Swiss frank, and the British pound, among others. Recently, some Asian currencies have begun to appreciate moderately against the dollar. This is important because the U.S. runs the majority of its trade deficit with Asia, but most Asian central banks follow mercantilist policies, intervening on the foreign exchange market to keep their currencies artificially subdued.

Because China, with its inflexible currency, is the U.S.'s major Asian trading partner, most blame naturally falls on the Chinese peg to the dollar. It is more acceptable politically to say that the U.S. is running a large deficit because of the peg, but the truth lies elsewhere.

Of the $669.5 billion current account deficit in 2004, $161.9 billion came from trade with China (see Figure 5-6). But few report that U.S. and foreign companies' trade with Chinese subsidiaries accounts for a

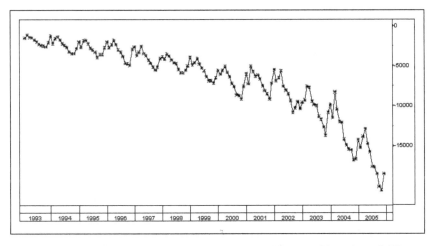

Figure 5-6 U.S.-China monthly trade balance. (Source: Bloomberg L.P.)

large part of the deficit. The July 2005 decision by the Chinese to revalue their currency marginally, thus moving the currency to a managed float against a basket of currencies, will not materially alter the status quo. The move gave China a more flexible currency regime that should allow for a greater variety of choices when planning domestic monetary policy.

A big part of the problem is that American companies are exporting back to the U.S. to realize the vast cost savings that come from operating in China, India, or elsewhere in Asia. The competitive advantage gained by paying a factory worker in the Guangdong province of China $1 an hour versus paying an American worker $15 an hour is self-evident. Eliminating the peg will not eliminate that cost advantage, and politicians in both countries know it.

Globalization, like it or not, has resulted in a massive shift of production facilities to low-cost countries, and it is likely to cause a financial crisis as the U.S. current account deficit reaches extremes (see Figure 5-7). To prevent the current account deficit from spiraling out of control, major trade policy changes are necessary. There is, however, no political will to effect the necessary changes. It is a question of when—not if—the current account ticking time bomb detonates, because the pressure on the U.S. currency is mounting.

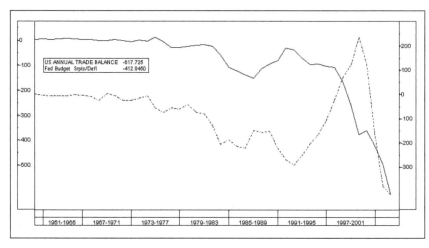

Figure 5-7 America's financial imbalances: current account and Federal budget deficit.
(Source: Bloomberg L.P.)

THE SILK ROAD TO RICHES

In 2004 and 2005, when the current account deficit began to spiral out of control, it became popular to blame the deficit on the speed of U.S. economic growth. The spin was that the U.S. was developing faster than any other developed economy, was consuming more, and therefore the deficit was ballooning to an unsustainable degree.

Dr. Marc Faber, a well-known economic contrarian, explains the ridiculousness of this spin. "I am a director of a company," wrote Dr. Faber. "When I ask questions at board meetings the chairman of the company occasionally responds by saying first that my question is the stupidest he has ever heard in his life. I am greatly relieved, therefore, that the chief economic advisor to the U.S. president also makes really bizarre (to put it politely) statements, since it should be obvious to anyone that Asia excluding Japan, a region that has economic rates that are around twice that of the U.S. (and not driven by debt and asset inflation), actually has rising trade and current account surpluses with the U.S."[8]

The large and growing current account deficit can put tremendous pressure on the dollar, which still serves as the reserve currency of the world. If foreign central banks and large institutional investors decide to diversify away from dollar assets—a process that has already stealthily started in our view—that will accelerate the currency decline to crisis proportions. And nothing is worse than a sinking currency to a heavily indebted economy like the U.S.

It has to be noted that the U.S. is the only country that can pay its rising debts with its own currency, currency it prints at its own discretion (or whim). No other country is allowed that luxury. Absent this luxury, the run rate of the trade deficit would not have been approaching such grotesque levels. Because of this luxury, the macroeconomic imbalances the U.S. faces will likely become a lot larger, thus making the unwinding of those imbalances more painful when it happens.

And it must happen.

Bubble All the Way

When trying to define a bubble, being economic or stock market related, there is always one common ingredient: the extension of too much credit. Ample credit shifts economic activity into overdrive and ends up pouring a lot of money into too many unproductive uses. Because there is one primary gatekeeper of monetary policy in the U.S. or any other economy—the central bank—the bubble-creating culprit is easily identified.

By extending too much credit into the economy in the late 1990s and early 2000s, the U.S. Federal Reserve facilitated the flow of capital to many unproductive uses and asset prices in the economy (stocks, bonds, real estate, and so on) grew at unsustainable rates. It is not a coincidence that, as total financial leverage in the system began to grow faster than at any rate since the early 1980s, a major rally began to unfold in both the stock and the bond markets.

In the early 1980s, the economy emerged from a period of stagflation, and the decline in inflation rates as well as general economic stabilization allowed for an increase in financial leverage. The resulting economic growth stimulated more borrowing, a mightily rewarding virtuous cycle that produced two decades of enviable prosperity for the American consumer and for U.S. corporations.

Indiscriminate use of financial leverage can only go so far, and in 2000, cracks appeared. As nature took its course and last-gasp buyers bought their shares of the Nasdaq dream at 5,133, share prices began to swing from one extreme to the other as the cracks deepened, the foundation crumbled, and the stock bubble burst.

The Fed realized exactly what was going on—this had happened before in the U.S. in 1929, and on multiple occasions, throughout the world. What is a central bank to do when faced with an unraveling stock market in 2000 threatening the entire economy? It actually injected even more money into the economy and drove short-term interest rates from 6.5 percent in 2000 to 1 percent in 2003—in other words, it did the same things it did that helped create the bubble in the first place.

This massive injection of monetary stimulus created another set of bubbles, the most notable of which, dear to the hearts of Americans, is the real estate bubble that commenced in 2001. With affordability indexes at all-time lows and real estate-to-GDP values at all-time highs, "How high is too high?" is an irrelevant question, asked too many times as the real estate market has defied every expectation.

Many motivated real estate professionals and officers in the home building and mortgage lending industries who have profited handsomely from the meteoric rise of real estate prices have repeatedly stated, publicly, that there is no real estate bubble. They sound like CEOs of Nasdaq companies who, when asked about their stocks and business outlooks in 1999 and 2000, would only answer that the sky is the limit for the New Economy. This is a good place to mention a bubble litmus test often presented by Merrill Lynch Strategist Richard Bernstein on the state of the housing market.

Bernstein lists five main factors that indicate a financial bubble.[9] The *availability of ample liquidity* is defined by easy monetary policy and the willingness of banks to lend excessively. The *increased use of financial leverage* measured as the portion of house prices financed with debt, rather than equity; this measure is currently near all-time highs. *Democratization of the market* is reflected in the highest proportion of homeownership ever—70 percent in 2005.[10]

Bernstein's fourth criterion is *increased turnover* in the real estate market, referring to the shorter timeframe people occupy their houses before they sell them; some buy for the purpose of quickly reselling. Last is the *record new issues*, or new supply of homes on the market, which Bernstein compares to influx of new IPOs in the stock market bubble.

Where will this all end? It is often the case that real estate keeps appreciating even after a major top has been made in the stock market, as people feel more secure putting their money into tangible assets. But when the desire to own a home has been abused beyond oblivion with aggressively loose monetary policy, there is only one possible outcome. The real estate bust, when it happens, is likely to be the final straw. It will end, in an ugly fashion, the biggest credit expansion in U.S. history. The only way it can end is when the credit bubble unravels and debt liquidation suppresses asset prices in the economy, be they stocks, bonds, or real estate.

We're often asked for our target for the major stock indexes as so many individual investors have tied their fortunes (at the wrong time) to these widely followed measures of financial and economic health.

A very basic principle describes the unwinding of bubble markets: full retracement.

Such indexes generally decline to the point where the bubble started; they go down as much as they rose on the unchecked greed and reckless credit expansion that took them out of natural, sustainable trends.

Sometimes, full retracement takes many years (in Japan, it took 13, until 2003); sometimes, it's a lot faster (less than three years for the Dow after 1929, and just a year or two for many Asian markets after the 1997 crisis). It looks to us that the 2000-02 decline in all the major indexes was not full retracement due to the continuation of building of debt excesses and other credit bubbles in the economy, as well as the inadequate valuations for stocks seen at other major bear market bottoms.

Full retracement for the Dow Jones Industrial Average looks like the 4,000 level, which corresponds to roughly 500 on the S&P 500 and 800 on the Nasdaq Composite. There is a high probability this will happen within the next five years, 10 years at the most (see Figure 5-8).

Figure 5-8 A Dow Jones Industrials full retracement can be devastating for the unprepared. (Source: Bloomberg L.P.)

The unorthodox investment opportunities in the U.S. and abroad identified here are capable of doing well regardless of performance of the main stock indexes. By opening new investing avenues, investors will benefit from the great economic shift taking place in the world.

Endnotes

1. In the last two years, U.S. market value as a percentage of world market value has declined as other world stock markets have massively outperformed. In recent history, the U.S. stock market value has been more than 50 percent of world value.
2. Ibbotson Associates. "The Supply of Stock Market Returns."
3. Since 1989, investors in Japan's major benchmark index, the Nikkei 225, are still sitting on better than 60 percent losses 15+ years later. Japan is starting to improve, but we have some other U.S. market examples later in this chapter.
4. Latest periodical data available in June 2005 from the Investment Company Institute (ICI).
5. ICI statistics.
6. Net flow of goods, services, and unilateral transactions.
7. As of year-end 2004.
8. "The Gloom Boom & Doom Report" (February 2005).
9. Bernstein, Richard. "Housing Is Still a Cyclical Industry" (Merrill Lynch, March 29, 2005).
10. A 70 percent home ownership rate is a big positive, but when it comes at any cost, with unreasonable and risky financing that involves little or no equity, the story changes completely.

6

THE LOST GUARANTEE

 Pierpont Morgan's straightforward answer to a question about gold during a Congressional hearing on a financial crisis is probably the best-known expression among precious metal enthusiasts.

"Gold is money."

The legendary financier's retort could have made an excellent title for this chapter, as it has for many essays on gold. Alternative inspiration comes from Aristotle, who wrote more than 2,300 years ago, "Money is a guarantee that we may have what we want in the future. Though we need nothing at the moment, it insures the possibility of satisfying a necessary desire when it arises."

Aristotle clearly believed that the concept of money implied a guarantee of purchasing power, but paper money, as we know it, is anything but that. The U.S. dollar, the most widely held currency in the world and the primary reserve currency, would have disappointed Aristotle deeply in its inability to guarantee purchasing power over time.[1] Today's dollar, adjusted according to the Consumer Price Index, is worth 69.1 cents in 1990 dollars, 44.5 cents in 1980 dollars, 20.5 cents in 1970 dollars, and 15.4 cents in 1960 dollars.[2]

What would Aristotle have thought of the concept of paper money and the pathetic loss of purchasing power over time? By the Greek philosopher's time (384 B.C.-322 B.C.), gold had already been accepted as the major form of money. The first mentions of gold are found in Egyptian hieroglyphics dating to 2600 B.C., and the first coinage of gold currency happened around 650 B.C. in Lydia (now Northwest Turkey), a burgeoning kingdom in Asia Minor.[3]

The Paper Standard

To understand gold, one first has to understand paper money. U.S. dollars and other paper currencies in the world are essentially *fiat* money. The dollar is backed by the "full faith and credit of the U.S. government," but there is nothing tangible behind it. U.S. dollars were once exchangeable for gold at a fixed rate, but that practice ended in 1971 when President Richard Nixon decided to sever all ties of the U.S. currency to gold.

Many European currencies were decoupled from gold much earlier in the 20th century. True paper money has not been around for long, whereas gold and other precious metals have been used as currency or store of value for millennia.

Paper money exists in the first place *because of* precious metals. Because carrying large amounts of any precious metal for payment was inconvenient, banks began to issue paper certificates backed by gold and other precious metals to facilitate exchange of the precious metal.

Prior to 1963, U.S. dollar notes bore the words "will pay to the bearer on demand" or "payable to the bearer on demand," but such phrases were removed and convertibility into gold ended eight years later.

Why end convertibility if it had worked so well for thousands of years in its many forms? Central banks in the 20th century needed more "flexibility" to act upon monetarist economic theories. In other words, central bankers sought to affect the economy more directly by increasing or decreasing the money supply as they deemed necessary.

Many of the U.S. financial system's problems (see Chapter 5, "Straws in the Wind") stem from this "flexible" monetary policy. Aggressive monetary policy can work miracles for many years, but in the end, there is no free lunch; someone has to pay the mountains of debt this monetary policy creates.

The process of monetary policy abuse is like what an athlete goes through when taking steroids. The athlete achieves much better results in the short run, but with time, it takes ever-increasing dosages to achieve the same level of performance. In the end, the toxicity in the athlete's body is so high that it leads to serious side effects and, in most cases, irreparable damage.

The U.S. total debt to GDP ratio is currently the highest on record. At 300 percent and growing, the U.S. has more debt than at any point in its financial history. It is brutally obvious that this is an unsustainable trend. The accumulation of debt will most likely end by 2010, but such financial manias generally carry further than one expects. That's why they are called bubbles.[4]

The widely publicized tech bubble of the 1990s re-inflated somewhat in the 2003-04 period. The view here is that a housing bubble succeeded the tech bubble. However, most people do not realize that those are just sub-bubbles, part of the biggest bubble of them all, the Great Debt Bubble (see Figure 6-1).

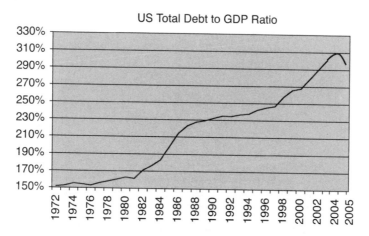

Figure 6-1 U.S. Total Debt to GDP Ratio. (Source: Bloomberg L.P. Federal Reserve.)

A gold standard for paper money does not preclude manias; irresponsible lending practices are the culprit in financial bubbles. But gold provides a safeguard to the financial well being of the innocent bystanders.

Even though the U.S. officially ended the dollar's convertibility into gold in 1971, gold bullion has maintained a very strong correlation to the U.S. currency over the years. In many respects, gold has acted as the anti-dollar in the recent past and as an alternative currency, just like it has for thousands of years. In periods of broad U.S. dollar strength, gold has been weak; and in periods of dollar weakness, gold has been quite strong.

On a weekly basis, that correlation has been predominantly in the range of 65 percent to 95 percent. Between 2001 and 2005 (encompassing the top in the stock market and the top in the dollar), the correlation has consistently hovered over 90 percent.

The U.S. Dollar Index (DXY)[5] is the main market gauge for dollar performance against a basket of major currencies (see Figure 6-2). With the introduction of the euro as a single currency, former European currencies combined their weights in the basket. That resulted in an exorbitantly high weight of the euro currency of 57.6 percent. The second highest rated component, the Japanese yen, the only Asian currency in the index, accounts for 13.6 percent.

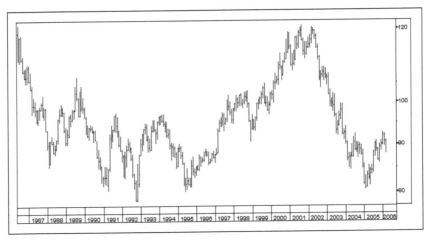

Figure 6-2 Mighty from lower levels. (Source: Bloomberg L.P.)

There is one major representative in the Dollar Index of the so-called "managed currencies" team: the Japanese yen. In a single year, hundreds of billions of dollars can be purchased by the Bank of Japan and then put to work—recycled, as some traders like to say in the U.S. Treasury bond market. One may wonder where U.S. long-term interest rates would be without the Asian central banks' purchases.[6]

That leaves the euro, the largest nonmanipulated currency, to be "the single vent" and to have outsized moves when the dollar has to blow off steam (investors buy euros when they want to diversify away from the dollar). But if the euro is behaving as a hard currency and an "anti-dollar," and gold is behaving as an anti-dollar, gold is therefore positively correlated to the euro vis a vis the U.S. dollar and with a much more stable euro price. Hence, when the euro rises, gold rises, too.

At least that used to be the case until 2005, when Europe was thrown into a political crisis upon the rejections of the European constitution by France and the Netherlands, followed by a contested German election and riots later in the year again in France. Furthermore, the Federal Reserve had pushed U.S. short-term interest rates over 4 percent, which is about double the euro short-term interest rates at 2.25 percent as of the time of this writing.

With political problems and interest rate differentials in favor of the dollar, the euro substantially sold off in 2005, yet gold still rallied in both dollar and euro terms sparking hopes that it had finally decoupled from the dollar. Many precious metals enthusiasts had long stated that when gold started to rally against all paper currencies at the same time—not only against the dollar—the next leg in the gold bull market would start. Based on the action in gold in 2005, that has already happened.

The inflation of the 1970s coincided with the de-linking of the dollar and the Midas metal, leading to the assumption that gold is an inflationary hedge. Gold *is* a hedge against all kinds of political and economic uncertainty, including inflation as well as deflation.

During the last deflationary period in the U.S., in the 1930s, gold was highly sought as a store of value at a time when many financial institutions were unstable. The high demand for the precious metal prompted the U.S. government to adjust the convertibility of the dollar into gold, devaluing the dollar by 68 percent virtually overnight.[7]

The move is not dissimilar to the current market-driven rise in gold prices—bullion rose from $255 per ounce in 2001 to $570 per ounce in early 2006, a 124 percent increase.

But the mysterious appeal of gold bullion lies elsewhere. Many market participants remember its spectacular rise from the day it was freely floated at $35 per ounce in 1971 to the day it hit $850 in 1980. This monstrous nine-year move resulted in a total nominal (not adjusted for inflation) return of roughly 2,300 percent (see Figure 6-3).

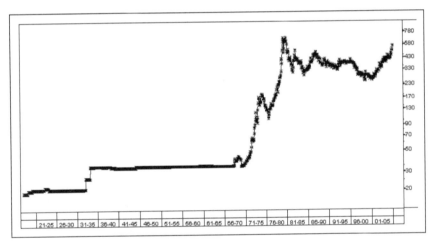

Figure 6-3 Gold's future. (Source: Bloomberg L.P.)

It's understandable that many investors who caught a piece of that move held on through a 20-year bear market. And without endorsing the views of the Gold Bugs, it's easy to understand the current attractiveness of gold bullion not only as a hedge against financial mayhem but as an investment in what is likely to be a significant move in many commodities, much like the 1970s.[8]

Off their lows in November 2000, gold stocks have greatly outperformed the S&P 500, the most widely followed U.S. benchmark stock index. Much has been said and written of the end of the bear market in stocks, but many commentators forget to mention that if this is indeed a new secular bull market for stocks, gold shouldn't outperform. It's understandable that a lot of those who did not spot the end of the 20-year bear market in gold and other commodities cannot now see the new secular bull. And it's also unfortunate that anti-gold rhetoric will keep many people away from an exciting opportunity.

Figure 6-4 depicts the relationship between gold and stocks in terms of a ratio of the Dow Jones Industrial Average to the price of gold and also describes the relationship between hard assets and financial assets. At a San Francisco precious metals conference, Pierre Lassonde, president of major gold producer Newmont Mining, took ownership of the chart; it was first published in the 2002 annual report of his company.[9]

The ratio speaks volumes about the future of gold prices. In every case during the past 100 years when the Dow/gold ratio has turned down, it has moved all the way into the single digits, resulting in very expensive gold and very cheap stock prices. The ratio currently stands at 19. At the lows in 1980, the ratio stood at 1.3. So far, all the empirical evidence suggests that the ratio is headed toward its 1980 lows.

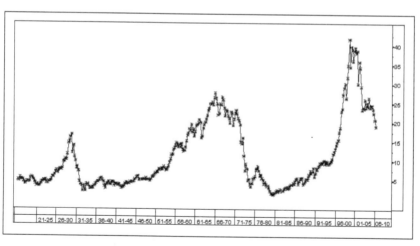

Figure 6-4 Relationship between gold and stocks.
(Source: Newmont Mining, Bloomberg L.P.)

This won't happen overnight. The Dow surged 1,368 percent, from 800 to 11,750, in its 20-year run, with plenty of shakeouts along the way that augured the end of the bull market. If gold behaves similarly, it will reach $3,700 per ounce by the time its bull run is over. This will happen by the end of the current decade.

Not possible, you say?

Few, if any, thought it possible that gold would advance from $35 per ounce at the time its peg to the dollar was removed in 1971 to a high of $850 per ounce. The similarities between the last three bull markets in gold and today's circumstances are striking. The previous three bull markets occurred amid severe shocks to the financial system. The coming multiyear move in gold will be the result of the unwinding of the biggest debt bubble in history, which hasn't yet started. The problem of too much debt cannot be fixed with more debt, U.S. fiscal and monetary policy from 2001 to 2004 notwithstanding.

James E. Turk, a long-time admirer of precious metals and author of several books on the perils of the current financial system, has also come up with a very interesting way to derive a price target for gold after a rally that he believes will unfold in the next five years.

Every paper currency has reserves of precious metals left over from the days when such paper was convertible at a fixed rate. According to Turk, just as you could debase a gold coin in the old days by adding other metals, you can debase paper money by printing too much of it without increasing your gold reserves.

In his 2003 article, "Inflation, Debasement, or Both," Turk studied the monetary balance sheet of the dollar and reflected on the aggregate assets and liabilities of what he calls "the nation's money cartel," the Federal Reserve and the commercial banks.

The term *cartel* is appropriate, wrote Turk, because only the Federal Reserve and the banks have been granted by the U.S. government the special right to have their liabilities circulate as dollar currency.

Turk considered that there are two assets in the dollar's balance sheet: The U.S. Gold Reserve of 261.6 million ounces and government bonds owed to the banks and the Federal Reserve. In the period evaluated in his study, the M3 total money supply has grown nearly fivefold, whereas the value of the gold asset has declined by 35.9 percent (see Table 6-1).

Table 6-1 Golden Dollars (Source: Wall Street Winners, James Turk)

Monetary Balance Sheet of the U.S. $	06/30/03 (billions)	12/31/79
Assets		
Gold @ $347.70/536.50	$91.00	$142.00
IOU's Owed to Banks	8,666.90	1,666.30
	8,757.90	1,808.30
Liabilities		
FED Notes	$646.40	$104.80
Bank Deposits	8,111.50	1,709.50
M3	8,757.90	1,808.30

He identified two factors that have led to this decline. First, the total weight of gold dwindled by 3 million ounces from 264.6 million ounces. Second, the dollar's rate of exchange to gold had dropped by $188.80, or 35.2 percent. Because the quantity of dollars has increased massively while the amount of gold backing those dollars has declined in value, Turk concluded that the dollar has been debased.

Turk found that a 1979 dollar has 7.85 percent gold content, whereas a 2003 dollar only has a gold content of 1.04 percent. This is an 86.8 percent decline in the gold base of the dollar. Turk concluded that to fix the problem, it is not necessary to find more gold—the price of gold must rise in dollar terms. If the dollar achieved the same gold content it held in 1979, 7.85 percent, the gold price would be $2,624 per ounce.

Turk purposefully used 7.85 percent because it is the average monthly gold content of the dollar since the formation of the Federal Reserve in 1913. Although the current gold content is the lowest since then, the highest content, 29.9 percent, was reached during the Great Depression. If that happened again, the price of gold would be $9,996 per ounce. The basic assumption in the preceding study is that that the quantity of dollars remains unchanged, which Turk admits is highly unlikely.

Gold Bullion Versus Gold Stocks

An important distinction between gold bullion and gold stocks must be made. They are not the same thing. It is true that when gold rallies, gold stocks tend to rally, and vice versa. This is quite similar to what happens to copper mine stocks when copper rallies, or what happens to oil company stocks when oil rallies.

Gold stocks are paper assets, whereas gold bullion is still considered one of the most reliable hard assets around. In other words, gold stocks are considered investments—companies try to mine the metal profitably and must constantly look to expand their business. Gold bullion is considered a hedge—in times of great uncertainty, the stocks and the metal can diverge significantly.

A good example is Black Monday, October 1987. Gold stocks sold off dramatically to the tune of 30 to 40 percent, whereas gold bullion rallied (see Figure 6-5). The same thing happened in July 2002 during one of the most vicious stock market selloffs since the top in the major indexes in 2000. Gold bullion didn't decline much, whereas gold stocks sold off 30 percent in just three weeks.

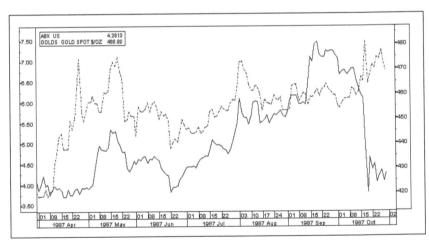

Figure 6-5 Gold and gold stocks on Black Monday. (Source: Bloomberg L.P.)

Many investors who caught a big part of the move in gold stocks off the 2000 lows were puzzled by their sharp decline in the first half of 2005. The early 2005 selloff was caused by a relief rally in the U.S. dollar, borne by rising short-term interest rates and a tightening of monetary policy. Such conditions are dollar bullish, as they decrease temporarily the rate at which extra dollars are being dumped into the economy.[10] Unless there is permanent change to long-term trade policy, or in the behavior of the U.S. central bank, it is unlikely that the 2005 dollar rally will turn out to be anything more than a big upside correction in an ongoing multidecade bear market for the U.S. currency.

Since the U.S. dollar (USD) was floated in 1971 after the end of the Bretton Woods agreement, it has declined against almost all major currencies over the long term. One can still extrapolate the exchange rate of the German mark (DM) through the exchange rate of the euro.[11] By looking at the history of the USD/DM relationship (see Figure 6-6), you can see what a 30-year-plus bear market looks like. Without getting too technical, this is the history of a broad decline in five major waves—in its wake are lower lows and lower highs. Because the dollar declined relentlessly in the 2002-04 period, there is room for a countertrend move, but ultimately, due to current macroeconomic policies, any upside correction is likely to fail.

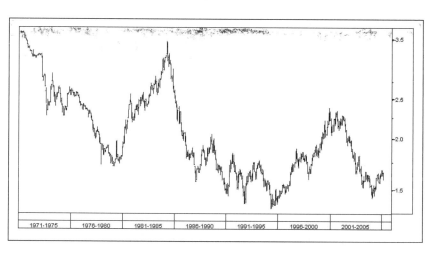

Figure 6-6 History of the USD/DM exchange rate. (Source: Bloomberg L.P.)

Regarding U.S. dollar/Japanese yen trading history (USD/JPY), the moves are even more extreme due to Japan's perennial trade surplus with the U.S. (see Figure 6-7).

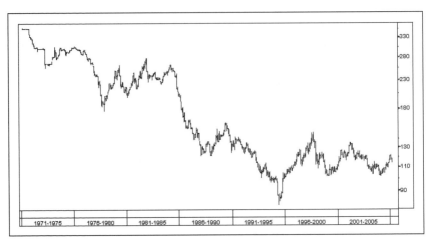

Figure 6-7 History of the USD/JPY exchange rate.
(Source: Bloomberg L.P.)

Some currencies, like the Australian and New Zealand dollars, have not performed as well over the long term against the greenback (save for the all-encompassing comeback in the 2002-04 period). But since 1971, the story of the U.S. dollar is one of substantial decline.

Any correction in gold bullion in the rally off the 2001 lows is a good risk/reward entry point if you want to buy some bullion and if you plan to keep it for the next five or 10 years. Check www.kitco.com for gold and silver bullion quotes and pricing. Kitco can store the gold for a fee, but if you want to go through all the trouble of acquiring physical gold bullion, you're probably better off renting a safe-deposit box in a major bank.

A lot of investors disagree with the concept of storing gold in a safe-deposit box, because the monstrous rally in gold is a question of when, not if, and one must protect against confiscation risk. That confiscation risk is non-existent in the 21st century is a nice thought, but ownership of gold bullion by private individuals has been restricted in the U.S. in the past.[12] Therefore, although storing physical gold may be inconvenient and costly, some will certainly prefer that over having someone else store it. Several exchange-traded trusts, the shares of which can be purchased through a brokerage account, provide a more cost-effective way to hold gold bullion as a hedge without the difficulties of physical storage. These trusts, one in London and two in the U.S., are very similar in their structure. The biggest U.S. exchange-traded trust is the streetTRACKS Gold Trust (NYSE: GLD), whose shares trade at one-tenth the price of gold and represent fractional ownership in the trust. The trust is sponsored by a subsidiary of the World Gold Council, the leading global authority in the gold mining industry. State Street Global Advisors, the largest institutional asset management firm in the world, handles marketing and advisory efforts for the trust.

The much-anticipated November 18, 2004 launch of the streetTRACKS Gold Trust reduced the significant barriers to ownership of gold bullion for many investors. Those once deterred by the large sums of money necessary to buy physical gold bullion, as well as the difficulty of storing and insuring those holdings,[13] now had a simple, convenient investment vehicle. As of this writing, the trust had amassed roughly $2.5 billion in gold bullion stored securely in an HSBC Bank vault in London.

Precedent exists for confiscation of gold bullion held by individual investors in exchange for paper money in the United States, so the case can be made for actual physical ownership. Though it is difficult to imagine a 21st century confiscation scenario, and the trust shares can be used effectively and safely as an alternative to physical gold bullion, it is still understandable why some investors would prefer to have the Midas metal in their own hands, rather than a vault in London.

The Broad Diversification Approach

Due to the operating leverage associated with gold mining stocks, a 50 percent increase in the price of gold bullion could result in a 300 to 500 percent increase in the price of some gold mining stocks. This operating leverage factor is true for all types of mining companies and commodity producers.

Because it costs money to mine gold, the lower your cost basis per ounce, the more money you make per ounce mined. Ironically, in times of rising gold prices, the best-performing gold stocks are generally those with the highest costs of mining as they see the biggest improvement in their bottom line.

For example, well-run company A mines gold for a cost of $200 per ounce. If gold rallies from $300 to $400 per ounce, the amount of profit that A realizes doubles from $100 to $200 per ounce. Bottom-of-the-barrel company X, due to the poor quality of its gold-deposit mines and high costs of its unionized labor force, has a mining cost of $290 per ounce. If gold rallies from $300 to $400, the profit X realizes rises eleven-fold, from $10 to $110 per ounce.

This is an oversimplified way of looking at mining stocks, but it does illustrate the concept of operational leverage. The same dynamic operates in periods of declining gold prices: high-cost producers are more likely to massively underperform their lower-cost brethren.

Plenty of individual investors will likely get burned chasing the most leveraged gold stocks without regard for risk. A more diversified approach that lets professional money managers handle the stock picking limits this risk. As detailed in Chapter 5, the broad mutual fund industry is populated with chameleon-like managers who simply mimic broad benchmarks, but select managers have proven their mettle day-in and day-out. When one deals with specialized sector funds or funds that have an investment objective other than just beating the S&P 500 by a tenth of a percent every quarter, there are some great investment opportunities for the long term. In the case of precious metals, there are some excellent mutual funds that allow individual investors to diversify and avoid taking too many high flyers (of which the precious metals sector is full). Just as with individual stocks, there are several funds that range from more conservative to more aggressive. The choice depends on the individual investor's risk tolerance.

Long-term investors are better off with a more conservative approach to precious metals. The more conservative approach allows investors to reduce the variability of their returns over time, gaining less in bull markets and losing less in selloffs for gold bullion and gold mining stocks. Over time, if regular additions are used to build the position, the low-variability approach is much easier to handle.

Vanguard Precious Metals (VGPMX, 800-662-7447, $10,000 minimum initial investment/$50 thereafter) is undoubtedly the best-run precious metals fund in the industry, and is the best example of the more conservative approach. A good example of the more aggressive approach is American Century Global Gold (BGEIX, 800-345-2021, $2,500 minimum initial investment/$100 thereafter).

These are two very different funds. Vanguard also invests in platinum, palladium, and industrial metals stocks, as well as large, diversified mining companies BHP Billiton and Rio Tinto, to limit volatility. American Century Global Gold invests primarily in pure gold and silver mines, and has some exposure to smaller, up-and-coming producers not typically found in the Vanguard Precious Metals portfolio. Another fund with an excellent track record and a more leveraged strategy similar to American Century Gold is Tocqueville Gold (TGLDX, 800-697-3863, $1,000 minimum initial investment/$100 thereafter).

If you benchmark the three funds' performance since the major bottom in gold stocks in November 2000, the performances are very similar. At different times, one fund may be outperforming the other, but because they all focus on the same sector, the macroeconomic forces behind their approach are the same.[14]

A $10,000 minimum initial investment for Vanguard may be too much for some individual investors, but it is a worthy allocation of resources. Graham French has managed the fund since 1996, through bull and bear markets. The smaller minimum initial investments for American Century Gold and Tocqueville Gold make them much more suitable for the average investor, and a position in either fund is suitable if one wants to achieve long-term diversified exposure to precious metals.

The Stocks

Individual investors have always preferred to venture out into the wild world of precious metals mining companies. Junior mining companies' siren songs of unlimited riches are just too loud. Individual investors should have exposure to junior mining stocks, but the core of many precious metal positions should be in gold bullion (via exchange-traded trusts or the physical commodity), established mining companies, and/or the previously discussed sector funds.

Research all the major and secondary gold mining names based on the criteria that follow. The volatility in the smaller producers will be great—so great that it may not be bearable from a long-term perspective. In many cases, small-cap gold stocks hold only a claim to a deposit and haven't begun mining. This leads to volatility in share prices as the market attempts to discount the value of their future earnings. A reasonable allocation in a diversified portfolio with exposure in precious metals is 5 percent in gold bullion, 10 percent in established mining stocks (or funds), and 5 percent in junior gold mines.

Two primary benchmark indexes focus on the gold sector. The Philadelphia Stock Exchange (PHLX) Gold and Silver Index (XAU) and the American Stock Exchange (AMEX) Gold Bugs Index (HUI). Since its inception in 1979, the XAU has been the leading benchmark for the gold sector. The index is capitalization-weighted; the greater the market value of the stocks, the greater the weight in the index (see Table 6-2).

Table 6-2 PHLX Gold & Silver Index (XAU) (Source: Bloomberg L.P.)

Company	Symbol	% of MV	Country Based
Newmont Mining Corporation	NEM	24.2%	U.S.
Barrick Gold Corporation	ABX	17.7%	Canada
AngloGold Ashanti Limited	AU	13.0%	South Africa
Freeport-McMoRan Copper & Gold Inc.	FCX	9.4%	U.S.
Placer Dome, Inc.	PDG	8.8%	Canada
Gold Fields Ltd.	GFI	7.5%	South Africa
Harmony Gold Mining Co. Ltd.	HMY	4.4%	South Africa
Goldcorp, Inc.	GG	3.9%	Canada

Company	Symbol	% of MV	Country Based
Glamis Gold Ltd.	GLG	2.9%	Canada
Kinross Gold Corporation	KGC	2.8%	Canada
Meridian Gold Inc.	MDG	2.4%	Canada
Agnico-Eagle Mines Limited	AEM	1.5%	Canada
Pan American Silver Corporation	PAAS	1.4%	Canada
Totals		100.0%	

The HUI index has been around since 1996 and has a little different purpose. The index uses a different weighting system and includes only stocks of companies that do not hedge their production past one-and-a-half years (see Table 6-3). This is important as the lack of hedging allows individual investors to focus on more leveraged stocks when gold prices are trending higher.[15]

Table 6-3 AMEX Gold BUGS Index (Source: Bloomberg L.P.)

Company	Ticker HUI	% Weight in the Index	Country Based
Gold Fields Ltd.	GFI	15.2	South Africa
Newmont Mining Corporation	NEM	14.8	U.S.
Freeport-McMoRan Copper & Gold Inc.	FCX	10.1	U.S.
Goldcorp, Inc.	GG	5.8	Canada
Kinross Gold Corporation	KGC	5.7	Canada
Glamis Gold Ltd.	GLG	5.7	Canada
Eldorado Gold Corporation	EGO	5.6	Canada

(continues)

Table 6-3 AMEX Gold BUGS Index (Source: Bloomberg L.P.) (Continued)

Company	Ticker HUI	% Weight in the Index	Country Based
Meridian Gold Inc.	MDG	5.3	Canada
Agnico-Eagle Mines Limited	AEM	5.0	Canada
Iamgold Corporation	IAG	4.9	Canada
Harmony Gold Mining Co. Ltd.	HMY	4.8	South Africa
Golden Star Resources Ltd.	GSS	4.6	Canada
Randgold Resources	GOLD	4.5	Channel Islands
Coeur d'Alene Mines Corporation	CDE	4.5	U.S.
Hecla Mining Company	HL	3.6	U.S.

The lack of hedging works both ways. In falling markets, companies that sell forward their production tend to outperform as they realize higher prices for their output than their nonhedging competitors. This is illustrated by the HUI/XAU ratio, which fell precipitously from 1997 to November 2000.[16] Since the bottom, the HUI index has outperformed on all meaningful rallies.

The HUI index has more than doubled XAU's performance since the new bull market in gold stocks started in 2000 (see Figure 6-8), but that assumes that many investors caught the low in 2000 (not a likely scenario). For the majority of investors who are just entering the sector, sticking with established, low volatility companies is essential. This way, on one of the notorious 30-percent corrections, positions can be affordably maintained.

In an environment where the more conservative XAU index declines by 25 to 30 percent, stocks of junior gold mines can decline 50 to 60 percent. This has happened on several occasions since the rally started in 2000. Junior gold stocks can be great fun to trade actively on both the long and short side, but buying and holding larger positions requires nerves of steel. The most leveraged stocks should command no more than 5 percent of available portfolio funds.

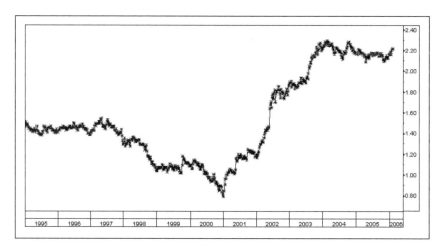

Figure 6-8 HUI/XAU ratio. (Source: Bloomberg L.P.)

With that caveat, let's look at some prime candidates for long-term holdings. As evidenced by the composition of the two major indexes that cover the precious metals sector, most index components are based in Canada. The largest weighting in both indexes is Newmont Mining (NYSE: NEM). Newmont is truly a "best in class" company; as the largest component of both the XAU and HUI indexes, it has served as a good proxy for the whole sector for most of the last four years. It is also the only gold mine stock represented in the S&P 500. When institutional investors think about gold, they think of Newmont Mining.

Newmont had in 2004 a mining cost of about $231 per ounce, up from $189 per ounce in 2002 in absolute terms. This rate has actually declined in relative terms as the average cost per ounce has risen across the industry. But Newmont's costs have risen less than that average. Mining costs have risen because 25 percent is allocated to energy, and energy prices have spiked since 2002. To hedge against rising energy costs, Newmont has taken a 6.6 percent position in Canadian Oil Sands Trust, which has 40 years of oil reserves at current production levels. Other considerations include the age of the mines and the quality of certain deposits.[17]

Though based in the U.S., Newmont is a multinational mining conglomerate with operations in Australia, New Zealand, Asia, North and South America, as well as exploration projects in new and promising areas across the globe. It remains the largest gold producer in the world and will be a prime beneficiary of the bull market in precious metals that will unfold in the next decade. Newmont has no meaningful hedging strategy, increasing the appeal of the stock in an environment of rising prices for precious metals. The lack of hedging has been a big plus for the stock.

Due to hedging strategies, Barrick Gold (NYSE: ABX) has actually been a great stock to own over the long-term. Over the last 20 years, management has been able to "sell forward" gold at times when they perceived gold bullion to be expensive. Barrick stock has racked up a 19 percent annual return.[18] That strategy can succeed when gold prices spend 20 years trading between $300 and $500 per ounce, selling forward near the top of the range. But the strategy will undoubtedly backfire in a sustained uptrend for gold prices. Barrick's management undoubtedly understands that, and has scaled back its hedging strategy over the past couple of years.

At a conference in late 2004, some long-term Barrick shareholders expressed concern that the stock, after many years of good returns, had begun to underperform the rest of the gold sector. "Should we sell?" they asked.

"Absolutely not," we replied. "It's a great idea to buy some junior gold mines in addition to, but not in lieu of, your Barrick holdings."

As previously discussed, lower quality stocks tend to do much better in an environment of rising gold prices relative to the operational leverage involved. But if you have been so lucky as to pick the best managed gold mine, why would a long-term shareholder sell?

Just like larger Newmont, Canada-based Barrick is a multinational company. Its operations and exploration span the U.S., Canada, Australia, Peru, Chile, Argentina, and Tanzania. Barrick receives 60 percent of its production from North America, but, curiously, only 27 percent of the company's reserves are located there (see Figure 6-9). The largest reserve base is in South America (47%), whereas only 13 percent of current production is derived from there. This indicates where Barrick's future growth will be based.

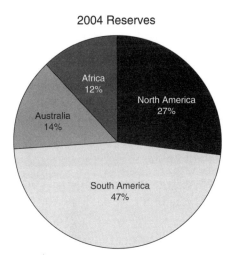

Figure 6-9 Barrick Gold reserve base. (Source: Barrick Gold.)

Future success will be judged on Barrick's two main projects: the Veladero operations in Argentina and the Alto Chicama area in Peru. If the company is able to deliver on time and on budget, investors will be increasingly drawn to Barrick, and plenty of fresh money will pour into the stock. The company also began investing in Russia, a positive move given that Russia's vast resources offer great potential for growth.

In addition to any investments in mining majors, look at junior producers (some of which are listed in the HUI Index) like Canada-based El Dorado Gold (AMEX: EGO), which is focused primarily on Brazil and Turkey. El Dorado's Brazilian mine is operational, producing 82,000 ounces of gold in 2004 at a cash cost of $294 per ounce, a considerably high rate by industry standards. However, El Dorado's new, wholly owned Kisladag Project in Western Turkey is scheduled to deliver 164,000 ounces in the first year, increasing production to an average of 240,000 ounces annually over the ensuing 14 years. Cash costs are estimated to be $165 per ounce due to the open-pit mining operations and the quality of the deposit. The company is also making a move in Western China (Quinghai province) in an effort to be the first North American-domiciled mining company to produce gold from China while at the same time raising gold production to 403,000 ounces by 2007.

Peru-based Buenaventura (NYSE: BVN), a large gold producer that is not part of any major sector indexes in the U.S., also holds a lot of promise. Many Latin American and other foreign mining stocks tend to trade at discounts to their U.S. or Canadian counterparts due to political risks and other considerations that depress valuations of many emerging market gold producers.

Buenaventura operates two growing underground gold mines and the fourth largest silver mine in the world. It also owns a 43.7 percent stake in Yanacocha (Peru), Latin America's largest gold mine and the most profitable in the world. Its partner in that venture is Newmont Mining.

South Africa is synonymous with gold, and yet its stocks underperformed during the metal's initial rally in the 2002-2004 period. Major South African mining stocks like Gold Fields (NYSE: GFI), Harmony (NYSE: HMY), Anglogold Ashanti (NYSE: AU), and Durban Roodepoort Deep (NSDQ: DROOY) have had the incredible experience of seeing their share prices decline (precipitously in some cases) at a time when the price of gold bullion rallied. The reason is the historic rally in the South African rand,[19] which from early lows of 13.86 against the dollar in December 2001 advanced to an incredible 5.60 in December 2004.

South African mining companies saw the highest price for gold in rand terms in December 2001 (see Figure 6-10). Because South African mines pay their costs in rand and sell their gold in U.S. dollars on the international market, they were faced with the double whammy of declining revenues and rising costs. Many of the South African mines have international operations, so the natural response of management was to aggressively expand their foreign operations and slow down their South African production. It was a reflexive, though understandable, response done in the interest of self-preservation.

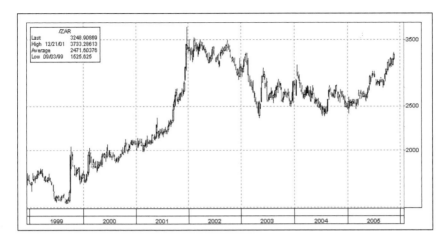

Figure 6-10 Price of gold, per ounce, in rand. (Source: Bloomberg L.P.)

For investors with a long-term view, the selloff in South African stocks may be a welcomed event—it will allow them to establish positions at prices last seen in 2001 and 2002. If gold is in a genuine bull market, the selling in South African mining stocks will prove to be the buying opportunity of a lifetime.

The real bull market in gold will begin when the commodity starts rising in terms of all major currencies, not just against the dollar. So far, gold has behaved as the anti-dollar and an alternative currency, but it has also shown signs that it can perform well as an alternative to all paper money, not just U.S. dollars.

In the end, J.P. Morgan will be proven right, again. The paper-only U.S. currency regime is now entering its fourth decade of existence. This standard has produced numerous macroeconomic imbalances and its record is feeble compared to the 4,000-year history of gold as a tried-and-true store of value.

Endnotes

1. The dollar is the most widely held currency as part of the reserves of foreign central banks, governments, and most international private financial institutions and corporations.

2. Many precious metals enthusiasts believe that the Consumer Price Index is manipulated and the loss of purchasing power is much larger.
3. Although there was no writing at the time, the first golden artifacts can be dated to 4000 B.C. in Europe (Source: Newmont Mining).
4. In Chapter 5, we discussed that by 2010 the current account deficit is likely to top $1 trillion. Within the neighborhood of this number lies a likely target to trigger a dollar crisis, which is likely to cause the start of a debt liquidation cycle in the U.S. economy. Such debt liquidation cycles have happened in Japan after 1990, Asia after the 1997-98 crisis, Russia in 1998, the U.S. in the 1930s, and so on.
5. The U.S. Dollar Index is known to many financial professionals by its quotation symbol DXY; however, unlike stocks, indexes do not have standardized symbols because different quotation systems may use different symbols.
6. In February of 2005, Bank of Japan holdings of U.S. Treasuries reached an all-time high of $702 billion.
7. In 1934, the fixed dollar exchange rate for gold was changed from $20.67 to $35/oz. (Source: *www.gold-eagle.com*).
8. *Gold Bugs* is the term used to indicate investors who hold most of their assets in gold and gold stocks.
9. This method of determining the long-term target for gold isn't the only one. Other calculations have produced a similar target price.
10. Currently, the U.S. dumps onto the world about $2 billion every day; this is the daily rate of the current account deficit that the U.S. economy runs.
11. The Deutsche mark was exchanged into euros at a fixed rate of 1.95583 DEM/EUR and has the highest weight in the euro currency at 20.8 percent. Source: Bloomberg L.P.
12. The possession of gold was sometimes restricted or banned within the United States (1933-1975). President Franklin D. Roosevelt confiscated gold by Executive Order 6102 on April 5, 1933, and President Richard Nixon closed the gold window by which foreign countries could exchange American dollars for gold at a fixed rate, which had been used by the French Government in excessive manner prior to that.
13. For all of the preceding services, the trust charges an expense ratio of only 0.4 percent annually, which is rather reasonable compared to holding actual bullion. For more info, see *www. Streettracksgoldshares.com*.
14. Gold stocks bottomed in November 2000, whereas gold bullion did so later in 2001. The substantial rally in the stocks anticipated the bottom in bullion, as many times is the case.
15. Hedging for gold mining stocks usually involves selling their gold output forward to get a stable price. That removes variability of revenues and profits and allows for better planning in the high-capital intensive business of mining.
16. Early 1997 is as far back as the ratio goes; the HUI index was introduced in late 1996.
17. Oil sand deposits have very high costs for extracting the crude oil, thus making them undesirable when oil prices are low, but very valuable when oil prices are in strong bull market.

18. Return calculated from December 31, 1985 through May 31, 2005 in Canadian dollars. In U.S. dollars, the return is actually closer to 20 percent a year.
19. The rand exchange rate is quoted in number of rands per U.S. dollar, so less rand per dollar is advance in the rand.

Part III

TRENDS OF THE FUTURE

"If a man gives no thought about what is distant,
he will find sorrow near at hand."
— Confucius

7

THE NEW AGRICULTURAL REVOLUTION

I n 1798, Thomas Malthus published his *Essay on Population.* Malthus argued that the world's population was growing far faster than farmers' capacity to produce food. He reasoned that over time, human demand for food would outstrip supply, producing widespread famine, wars to secure dwindling food supplies, and diseases resulting from overcrowding and malnutrition.

Malthus was an Englishman and his dire predictions were based at least partly on Britain's own history. Up until *Essay on Population* was published, Britain's population had never exceeded 5.5 million. The population approached that threshold on at least three occasions between 100 and 1750, but each time crop failures resulted in food shortages and famines, reducing the population to more sustainable levels.[1]

Nevertheless, Malthus' prediction has proven spectacularly incorrect in the two centuries since his *Essay on Population* was published. Although the global population has continued to grow at the geometric, accelerated pace that Malthus projected, food production also rapidly accelerated after 1750 to more than keep up with that growth.

The United Kingdom's population exceeded 17.5 million by 1850 and topped 60 million by the latter part of the 20th century. More importantly, the total world population is at least six times what it was when Malthus penned *Essay on Population*.[2] Not only has the population increased but so, too, has the consumption of food per capita. By the middle of the 19th century, the Industrial Revolution was in full swing in Britain and had begun to spread to other parts of Europe and to the Americas; economic growth in the late 1800s into the 1900s expanded to levels unheard of in prior centuries. That growth gave rise to an ever-larger global middle class that began to demand far more than subsistence-level food consumption. Wealthier consumers have also demanded greater variety in their diets, shunning traditional grain-based subsistence foods in favor of meat, fresh vegetables, and fruits.

In short, demands on global agriculture drastically increased after 1800, at rates far faster than simple population growth would suggest, and faster than Malthus projected. Even worse, as manufacturing began to supplant agriculture as the primary source of income, people began migrating out of rural areas and into cities. Urbanization severely restricted the size of the agricultural workforce.

Yet for most of the world's population, even in poorer countries, food availability has been gradually improving over time. Since the United Nations began compiling such statistics in 1961, availability of grains, meats, and vegetables has improved drastically even in the world's poorest economies.[3] The famines that periodically wreaked havoc on Europe's population throughout the Middle Ages became far less common post-1800, at least in the developed world.

A combination of factors thwarted these Malthusian predictions. Improvement in global agricultural productivity was so dramatic after 1750 that the era has been dubbed the Agricultural Revolution. Malthus could never have predicted the staggering technological and engineering advancements that came to pass.

In the 19th century, Britain's farmers reclaimed land previously thought infertile by draining swamps and fertilizing and cultivating rocky hillsides. Technological advances in fertilizer, crop rotation, and farm machinery drastically increased yields from existing land. In 1850, farmers could get an average of 1.2 tons of wheat from an acre of land. By the end of the 20th century, farmers using nitrogen-based fertilizers could get an average of 8 tons of wheat from an acre of land—a seven-fold increase.[4]

Once again, the global agricultural industry is facing a demand crunch of proportions unseen since the Industrial Revolution of Malthus' day. China, India, and other emerging economies across Asia support a combined population of over three billion, more than half of the global population. And like Britain in the early 19th century, Asians are enjoying growing wealth and incomes.

Just as British farmers of the 19th century adapted new technologies and techniques to feed a growing Europe, Asia will have to undertake its own agricultural revolution to keep up with burgeoning demand for food. This new consumer bloc will have a profound effect on the developed world as Asian consumers start to buy the packaged foods, meat, and other staples Westerners take for granted.

Food Demand Grows

The United Nations predicts that by 2050 the global population will rise from the current six billion to exceed nine billion, with 5.2 billion living in Asia.[5] Clearly, a growing population spells more demand for all sorts of food. But population growth in Asia plays only a tiny role in the boom in demand for food already apparent in the region. A far more important factor is rapidly rising Asian incomes and the emergence of a middle class.

As nations develop and consumers become wealthier, food consumption patterns change. Not only do consumers eat more food, they tend to eat more meat and greater quantities of packaged and processed foods. Income is not the only determinant in these shifts—local tastes, religious practices, and regional supplies certainly have an effect—but it is the primary factor behind differences in food consumption between countries and shifts in diets over time.[6]

Figure 7-1 compares current food consumption patterns among a handful of countries with various income levels. For each country, we've presented the total calories consumed and broken those calories down by food type.

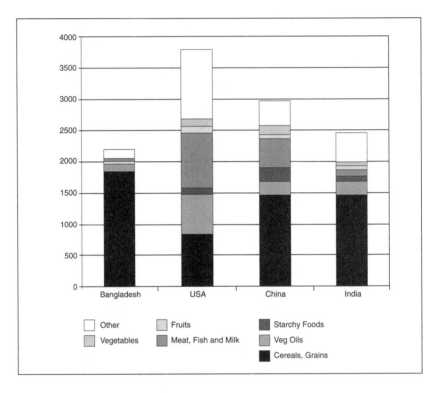

Figure 7-1 Food consumption patterns.
(Source: Food and Agriculture Organization of the United Nations.)

Take a look at Bangladesh's consumption. Bangladesh is one of the poorest economies covered by these statistics. Basic cereals account for more than 80 percent of Bangladeshi food consumption. In fact, rice is by far the most important food product in Bangladesh, accounting for close to three-quarters of total consumption. Meats and other animal products are only a small component of total demand, accounting for barely 3 percent of calories consumed.

This is typical of the world's poorest economies. Poorer countries rely on basic cereals and grains for the vast majority of their food supply. Typically, depending on geographical and climate factors, either rice or wheat is the prime source of caloric intake. There is good reason for that pattern—rice and wheat are relatively easy to grow and, more importantly, are an excellent source of calories. Just a few bowls of rice per day, for example, are sufficient to sustain human life. In poorer countries, the primary consideration is basic subsistence and cereals are the cheapest and most efficient food source.

Meat is expensive to produce. Cattle, pigs, and chickens require considerable land for grazing and roaming. Livestock must consume large amounts of grain as it matures to a size suitable for slaughter and consumption. The average cow consumes between 2.5 and 3 percent of its total body weight in dry feeds every day.[7] A typical 1,200-pound beef steer could consume about 35 pounds of feed per day, or more than 13,000 pounds annually. That's enough grain to feed more than 10 average-sized adults for an entire year. For poorer countries, this is an expensive—and prohibitive—use of resources.

Consumers in more developed economies like the United States have far more varied diets. In the U.S., basic cereals are a relatively minor source of daily calorie intake, accounting for less than a quarter of calories consumed. Meat and animal products, nearly absent in the Bangladeshi diet, are extremely important in the U.S., accounting for nearly 30 percent of calorie intake. Because food is a relatively tiny portion of the average American's budget, most can afford to add a healthy dose of meat to their diets.

China is neither as poor as Bangladesh nor as rich as the U.S.; its consumption patterns lie somewhere between these two extremes. Animal products account for roughly 20 percent of China's calorie intake, whereas cereals are far more important than in the U.S., making up about half the average consumer's diet.

Increased meat consumption is just one consequence of economic growth. Wealthier consumers also tend to drastically boost spending on packaged and prepared foods. Figure 7-2 illustrates this point by comparing annual consumption of sugar and sweeteners, stimulants (mainly tea and coffee), and alcoholic beverages between the U.S. and China.

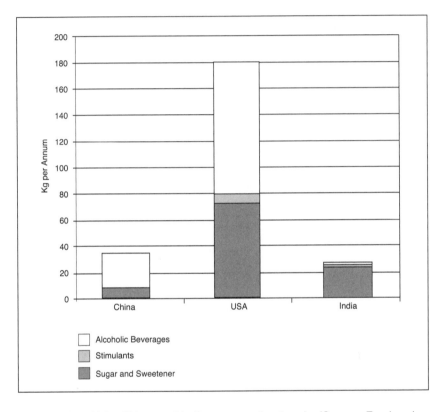

Figure 7-2 U.S., China, and India consumption trends. (Source: Food and Agriculture Organization of the United Nations.)

The average American consumes more than 70 kilograms (155 pounds) of sugars and sweeteners per year, nearly 10 times the amount consumed by the typical Chinese. Much of this sweetener isn't consumed in raw form but as part of packaged products such as cola, candy, or in pre-packaged frozen dinners.

The differences are even more apparent when considering alcoholic beverages: Americans consume nearly four times as much alcohol annually, almost nine times as much wine and five times as much beer.

But this is just a snapshot of global food demand today and will not remain static over time. Even in a developed country like the U.S., there have been significant shifts in consumption over just the past 30 years. Figure 7-3 shows total changes in U.S. consumption for several different food types since 1970. Processed foods like cheese, alcohol, and soft drinks have seen tremendous growth over this period. The same is true of meats, fresh fruits, and vegetables—all items that are relatively expensive to produce and ship from farms to the table.

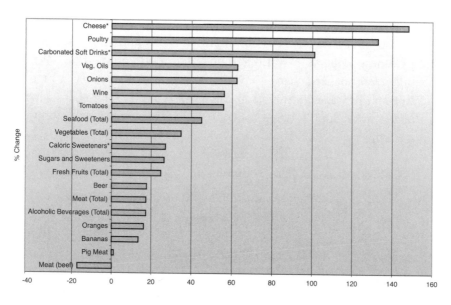

Figure 7-3 Change in consumption 1970-2002. (Source: Food and Agriculture Organization of the United Nations, Economic Research Service [USDA] "Changing Structure of Global Food Consumption and Trade".)

China and the rest of developing Asia are following a similar path. As consumers in the region become wealthier, they're shifting away from subsistence eating of basic cereals to consume ever-greater quantities of high-value processed foods. This is not some pie-in-the-sky prediction—there's already clear evidence of a massive shift in consumption underway across the region.

In an increasingly globalized world food market, these shifts in consumption will happen more rapidly than they did in the United States or Europe. For years, diets among developed economies have been converging. One major reason is the predominance of global brands and restaurant chains. McDonald's and Pizza Hut are ubiquitous brands worldwide, even in relatively poor countries. The Chinese and Indians are becoming as familiar with Coca-Cola as are Americans. Constant exposure to Western foods will accelerate Asian dietary changes in coming years.[8]

The easiest way to measure shifting consumption patterns is to examine global trade data. Because China is the largest agricultural trader in developing Asia, we'll focus our attention there, and more specifically to Chinese imports of various high-value food commodities. We've outlined annualized change in Chinese imports for a variety of higher value and processed products in Table 7-1. A good example of China's dietary upgrading is wine, one of the highest-value commodities on Earth.

Table 7-1 Change in Chinese Dietary Imports* (Source: United Nations Population Division.)

Item	Year 1970	Year 2003
Beef and Veal	156	5412
Beer	400	163170
Beverages Dist. Alcoholic	233	39391
Beverages Non-Alcoholic	0	17167
Breakfast Cereals	0	13481
Canned Meat	0	2903

Item	Year 1970	Year 2003
Canned Mushrooms	0	2762
Cheese and Curd	75	18186
Chicken Meat	0	597955
Chocolate Products	41	25386
Cigarettes	70	25706
Fruit Juice	19	8859
Macaroni	0	2563
Oilseeds	624337	23493429
Olive Oil, Total	1	6471
Pineapples, Canned	0	8611
Total Meat	166	1073598
Wine	13	50476

*Measured in metric tons

In 1970, China imported just 13 metric tons of wine, a number that grew to just over 2,000 tons by 1990. But by 2003, demand in China exploded to over 50,000 metric tons of wine annually; from 1990 to 2003, wine imports into China grew at an annualized pace of nearly 30 percent. The same pattern is obvious for meats, cheeses, and other products.

The U.S. population stands at just under 300 million. Changing U.S. food consumption has had a profound impact on the global commodity markets in recent decades, boosting demand for meat and packaged consumer goods. Imagine how much greater the impact of Asia's development will be. As Asia's more than three billion citizens shift their consumption habits, the economic effects have been and will continue to be far more pronounced.

The Supply Side

Asian farmers are struggling to keep up with rapidly rising demands. Over the past few years, the global markets have seen huge demand from several different parts of Asia. However, China remains the region's largest player in the global agricultural markets, and we will maintain the focus of our attention there.

Between 1980 and 1998, meat production in China grew at an annualized rate of more than 8 percent. That's by far the fastest growth in output of any major meat-producing region of the world but still hasn't been enough to keep up with demand. As a result, China has been an increasingly important importer of agricultural commodities in recent years, including fresh meats such as beef, veal, chicken, and livestock feeds.

Booming Asian demand for complex foodstuffs is having dramatic impacts on the global commodity markets. Huge spikes in soybean prices in 2003 were caused largely by a surge in soybean imports to China. Soybeans are a primary ingredient in most animal feeds. It should come as little surprise that China's rapidly growing meat industry requires ever-greater quantities of beans to meet demand; Chinese soybean imports are already growing at an annualized rate of 47.4 percent since the beginning of 2001.

In absolute terms, China has a great deal of arable land. This is one reason that, until recently, the country has been more or less self-sufficient in food production despite its massive population. As recently as the mid 1990s, in fact, China was a net exporter of meat (mainly to other markets in Asia). It's still a net exporter of many different vegetables, including tomatoes and onions. Although China is increasingly importing larger quantities of processed and packaged western goods, it is still a major producer of a few higher-value prepared products such as beer.

But demands for foods are rising, and the shifts in diet we've outlined are putting huge strains on China's agricultural independence. Products such as meat, where China is seeing particularly rapid consumption growth, require vast quantities of land. To keep pace with rapidly rising demand for agricultural products, Asian agriculture will see major shifts in the coming years and will need to maintain high agricultural efficiency to keep pace.

Exacerbating the issue is China's growing problem of desertification. China has been very aggressive in managing its water supplies, diverting the nation's largest rivers to create hydroelectric power and to supply rapidly growing cities with water. This has led to shortages of water in some parts of the country.

More generally, due to arable land shortages, China has had problems with overuse and overcultivation of marginal lands and reclaimed forests, particularly in the northern part of the country. Every year, 900 square miles of arable land in northern China becomes desert.

Similar to the Dust Bowl that afflicted the Midwest of the U.S. in the early 20th century, plumes of dust blown from Northern China have drifted as far east as the United States mainland. It's estimated that this loss of land costs China as much as $2 to $3 billion annually. China has enacted programs to try to limit land use and stem desertification, but to date there's been only minimal measurable impact. On the margin, this trend will put pressure on China's available land.[9]

China will need to continue boosting yields on limited available arable land to keep pace with higher food demands. Fertilizer is one of the easiest and most effective means of boosting agricultural yields. The data shown in Table 7-2 compares agricultural inputs in the United States, China, and the world.

Table 7-2 Agricultural Production Comparison (Source: FAOSTAT[10])

Production per Hectare of Land:	Unit	China	World	U.S.
Rice	Tons	6.2	3.9	7
Wheat	Tons	3.7	2.7	2.8
Corn	Tons	4.6	4.3	8.6
Soybeans	Tons	1.7	2.2	2.6
Vegetables and Melons	Tons	18.4	15.7	17.1
Fertilizer Consumption per hectare	Kilograms	271	94	111

(continues)

Table 7-2 Agricultural Production Comparison (Source: FAOSTAT[10]) (Continued)

Production per Hectare of Land:	Unit	China	World	U.S.
Farm Workers per 100 hectares	Number	310	82	2
Land irrigated	Percent	40	18	13
Tractors per 1,000 hectares	Number	6	18	27

It's clear that China's fertilizer use is already high, nearly three times the world average and double U.S. averages. This liberal use of fertilizer is partly behind China's superior yields for many crops, including vegetables and wheat. China will have to continue fertilizing its land to maintain agricultural output at levels that can meet new demands.

As China's domestic fertilizer production capacity is limited, it has become a huge importer of fertilizers from abroad. Basic fertilizer minerals include potash (potassium) and phosphate, products that are mined from naturally occurring salt-like deposits in the ground.

China has extremely limited potassium natural resources, and the country's phosphate reserves are difficult and expensive to produce.[11] The United States is a huge exporter of phosphate-based fertilizers, whereas Canada is the world's largest source of potash. China has been opening new mines and plants to reduce import dependence, but China's capability to expand fertilizer production will be limited; look for it to remain among the world's largest importers of potash and phosphate-based fertilizers.

These figures only account for direct fertilizer imports into China. China is also an important indirect importer of fertilizer. As we mentioned previously, China imports massive amounts of soybeans from markets like the United States and Brazil. But soybeans are an extremely fertilizer-intensive crop; countries exporting soybeans to China will be forced to step up their own use of fertilizers.

But no amount of fertilizer will boost China's production of crops far enough to meet all these new demands. China will increasingly focus on crops that offer large yields per acre as a way of conserving precious land. And China has no shortage of labor now, nor will it in the foreseeable future. It will continue to focus on crops that require a great deal of labor to produce—this is where currently its most obvious comparative advantage lies.

The list would include crops like vegetables and fruits where, as Table 7-2 indicates, China already has a considerable yield advantage. China will still have to rely on imports of many basic bulk commodities like soybeans and soy meal; it is not an efficient producer of these crops.

The United States, with a population only a quarter of China's, has more than 30 percent more farmland. Soybeans, a key crop for supporting China's livestock industry, are one of the most land-intensive products around. China will have to continue relying on imports from land-rich economies like Brazil and the U.S. to keep pace with demand.[12]

Even crops that China can domestically produce in large quantities won't totally free the nation from imports. The reason is quality. Traditional Chinese meals such as dumplings and noodles could be prepared with relatively low-quality wheat. And as Table 7-2 shows, China is a fairly efficient producer of wheat. But cakes and breads require wheats higher in gluten, an ingredient that helps breads rise and maintain consistency.

Just as Americans import foreign beef and animal products even though there's sufficient supply at home, the Chinese will increasingly demand higher quality imported wheats to meet demand for new food preparations.

Fortunately, a new agricultural revolution is underway that will allow the global economy to meet these new demands. Vast improvements in transportation and containerized shipping technology allow even perishable items like fruits and vegetables to be transported vast distances at negligible cost. Asia's growing demands for complex items like meats, fresh items, and processed and packaged consumables will be met with exports from other regions such as the United States, Europe, and Latin America. Key companies in these regions producing goods in high demand across Asia are already seeing a massive jump in trade with the region.

The shifting patterns of Asian and global food consumption will have profound effects on global trade. A handful of companies stand to benefit from these changes and investors who understand the changes will profit handsomely in coming years.

Fertilizer Producers

There are several classes of fertilizer traded worldwide. Traditionally, two of the most important are phosphates—in particular, diammonium phosphate (DAP) and potassium (potash). Both of these products are derived from mined rocks.

Phosphate is more widely dispersed around the world. Although North America, in particular, the U.S., is a major, relatively low-cost producer, Asia has been rapidly expanding capacity in recent years with China leading the way. Expanding capacity has meant heavy investment in processing facilities and increased mining activity in China itself. As Figure 7-4 shows, China's imports of phosphates have dropped as China has expanded production. Nevertheless, China is unlikely to become fully independent in DAP and other phosphate-based fertilizers because consumption growth is very strong.

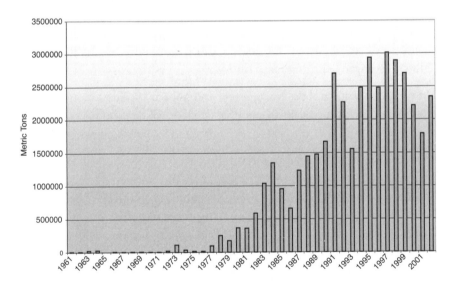

Figure 7-4 China phosphate fertilizer imports. (Source: FAOSTAT.)

More importantly, simply viewing China's own imports and consumption of phosphates is totally misleading. Brazil is a major exporter of crops and agricultural products to China. And although China's direct phosphate imports have been in a steady decline for the past few years, Brazil has been consuming more fertilizer to grow these crops.

Potash is a different story altogether. Asia simply does not have the capacity to expand production of potash-based fertilizers at a rate fast enough to keep pace with demand. It takes about five years and $1 billion capital investment to build new capacity and China simply doesn't have the low-cost sources of mined potash that exist elsewhere in the world.

The same is true for key export markets like Brazil—Brazilian potash consumption and production, illustrated in Figure 7-5, shows that there's been enormous growth in consumption well above the capability of that nation to ramp up production. In fact, according to industry estimates, Latin America accounted for 85 percent of the growth in potash consumption between 1999 and 2003.[13]

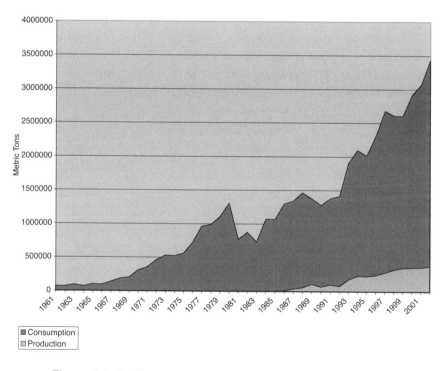

Figure 7-5 Brazilian production and consumption of potash fertilizer. (Source: FAOSTAT.)

There are two major players in the fertilizer business that stand to benefit from Chinese fertilizer demands. U.S.-based Mosaic (NYSE: MOS) is the world's largest producer of phosphate-based fertilizer, most of which comes from mines in the Southeastern U.S.; the company controls about 15 percent of the world's supply of phosphate.

Declines in Asian imports of phosphate have been partly offset by growing exports to regions like Latin America. What's more, Mosaic has been proactive in establishing a physical presence in China and Brazil. In China, Mosaic owns 35 percent of a DAP joint venture that includes three Chinese fertilizer producers. Mosaic also owns several warehouses and blender facilities in the country used to mix fertilizers. In Brazil, Mosaic has several warehouses in strategic locations.

There is likely to be further rationalization of phosphate production capacity in coming years. We suspect that some of the smaller players will exit the market leaving lower cost producers like Mosaic with less competition.

Mosaic is also the world's second-largest potash fertilizer producer with most of that potash coming from low-cost Canadian mines. In fact, Mosaic's Canadian mines are among the lowest-cost producers in the world. About two-thirds of Mosaic's potash is destined for the U.S. agricultural market with the balance exported to primarily China and Brazil. Mosaic estimates that it holds more than 10 percent of the rapidly growing Brazilian market.

Mosaic was formed through the merger of IMC Global and Cargill's crop nutrition unit in late 2004. Privately owned Cargill is one of the most respected names in the agriculture industry and has been operating for years in key growth markets such as Latin America and China. The importance of local knowledge and presence cannot be overestimated in these countries—this gives Mosaic a real advantage over its smaller competitors.

Canada-based Potash Corporation of Saskatchewan (Toronto: POT, NYSE: POT) is the world's largest producer of potash-based fertilizer and a leading producer of phosphate. Mosaic and Potash Corporation are the world's only two potash producers with mining costs under $23 per ton for potash, and Potash Corporation has far more low-cost production capacity than Mosaic—the company has tremendous leverage to higher potash prices.

Potash Corporation is one of the only companies on earth with excess capacity to produce potash. According to the International Fertilizer Industry Association, in 2007, the world's capacity to produce potash will only exceed consumption by about 13 percent, down 4 percentage points from 2003. Potash Corporation will hold much of that excess capacity, and the company will see significant increases in pricing power as a supplier of last resort.

The Processors

Bunge (NYSE: BG) is far and away the world's largest processor of soybeans and other oilseeds and the largest exporter of soybean-based products to Asia. Bunge doesn't actually raise soybeans; rather, it buys soybeans from farmers and processes them to produce a variety of products. Probably the two most important basic products made from soybeans are oil and meal.

Soybean meal is one of the best sources of protein around, and protein is key for raising all sorts of livestock. Therefore, soybean meal is highly prized as the base ingredient for all types of animal feed.

As we pointed out earlier, China, and for that matter the rest of Asia, should continue to see huge demand growth in meat imports as these economies develop and become wealthier. Although meat consumption is rising most rapidly in Asia, it's still a long way from developed Western levels; we see plenty of scope for further gains in demand.

Chinese meat imports have been rising but much of the new demand for meat in China is being met by a rapidly growing domestic meat production industry. As soybeans are a land-intensive crop, China will not be able to increase production enough to feed such rapidly growing demand for animal feed. Imports will fill that gap, and most of those imports will come from the Americas.

Bunge is the largest key supplier of soybean meal to China and operates processing facilities across North and South America. The company has been literally struggling to keep up with demand, especially in Latin

America. In Brazil and Argentina, in particular, transportation infrastructure isn't up to the task of moving all the soybeans from farms to coastal ports. And in periods of particularly strong demand, ships in Latin American ports have been forced to wait for days to be loaded with new cargo. In recent years, Bunge has been spending millions to upgrade transport infrastructure in Latin America, including a port facility in Argentina designed to ship products to Asia.

The second major product that comes from soybeans is oil, a key constituent of the vast majority of vegetable oils and an ingredient in margarines and mayonnaise, among other condiments. As Figure 7-6 shows, Chinese consumption of oils and fats is rising rapidly as the nation becomes wealthier. Also important is the rapid urbanization underway in China. Prepared foods tend to be relatively high in oils and fats, and city dwellers tend to consume more food away from home—this is accelerating the trend toward consumption of more such products.[14]

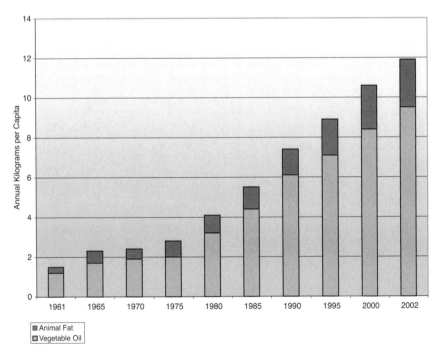

Figure 7-6 Chinese vegetable oils and animal fats. All data in kilos per capita per year. (Source: FAOSTAT.)

Of course, it's not just China—fats and oils are a rapidly growing source of calories for the Indian population as well. In fact, India is the world's largest importer of vegetable oils—this is the most important source of calories except for basic grains.

Bunge is the world's largest producer and bottler of oils. The company has also been very proactive in setting up local facilities. For example, in India, Bunge bought Hindustan Lever's edible oils and fats businesses in 2003 to take advantage of booming demand in this nation. And Bunge has opened processing facilities in North and South America, India, and Europe.

In addition to the soybean meal and oil markets, Bunge has become a very important player in the South American fertilizer market; it's now Brazil's leading retail supplier of fertilizers, especially phosphate-based fertilizers, and it actually produces fertilizer in Brazil. Although still a small part of the overall revenue pie, Bunge will benefit from its key position in Brazil, one of the world's fastest-growing fertilizer markets.

In 2003, soybean-based oils accounted for roughly one quarter of total world demand for fats and oils. Industry estimates suggest that by 2010, world consumption will increase by around 42 percent and that soybean oils will roughly maintain their 25 percent share of the world oil markets.[15] Also in 2003, the second most important source of oil in the world was palm oil, accounting for only slightly less of the world market than soybeans. But by 2010, palm oil is expected to outpace soybeans in importance. The reason: Palm oil is very popular in rapidly growing Asian markets. In India, for example, palm oils satisfy about 70 percent of demand with soybeans making up substantially all of the remainder. Most Asian nations consume relatively high and growing quantities of basic palm oils.

The most interesting way to play this trend is through Belgium-based Sipef (Belgium: SIP). The company has extensive palm-farming capacity in Indonesia, the Ivory Coast, and Papua New Guinea; palm oil accounts for approximately 80 percent of the company's annual revenues. Strong demand from Asian markets has been underpinning palm oil prices in recent years. Sipef has taken steps to facilitate exports into India and elsewhere in Asia. That includes building a major oil storage and export facility in Indonesia, the company's most important producing region for palm oils.

Food Producers

The Americas are truly the world's breadbasket. Although both North and South America consume a lot of the food they produce, these two regions are still major exporters. Latin America, in particular, has considerable arable land suitable for crop production and the raising of farm animals for slaughter.

Although many investors focus on Brazil solely, Argentina remains a huge exporter of grains and crops and, more importantly, beef products. And Cresud (Argentina: CRES; NSDQ: CRESY) is one of the largest agribusiness companies in Latin America. In 2004, Cresud owned more than 400,000 acres of land in Argentina. In total, Cresud produced nearly 75,000 tons of crops, 100,000 head of beef cattle, and more than 6.5 million liters of milk.

Cresud has planned several ways to expand this production even further. One of the primary methods is to improve crop yields at existing properties and start farming more marginal lands owned by the company. In particular, Cresud has spent heavily to buy modern machinery and equipment, improve fertilization, and educate workers on appropriate crop rotation. For marginal lands, better irrigation and more intensive fertilization can make barren land arable. These efforts should lead to even greater production in future years.

We are most interested in Argentina's beef production. The nation remains one of the world's top exporters of beef, and particularly higher-quality beef; in 2002, Argentina exported more than 360,000 metric tons of beef, making it the eighth-largest beef exporter in the world. Although Chinese farming of beef has certainly picked up in recent years, the focus to date has been on pork and poultry—two animals that need less space to roam—so beef imports were nearly 200 million tons in 2002. Cresud is well placed to grab a piece of the Asian beef market.

Of course, all that meat being slaughtered and consumed in Asia needs to be processed and packaged for retail consumption. A fair bet is to focus on companies in the region with established brand names.

Within Asia, the best is Singapore-listed and China-based People's Food Holdings (Singapore: PFH), a leading processor, distributor, and retailer of a variety of meat-based products. People's Food has nine production centers in China capable of processing about 300,000 pigs and 700,000 chickens per month.

People's Food sells unprepared products like frozen and fresh pork as well as frozen whole chickens, and also manufactures about 250 types of sausage, ham, and other processed packaged food products. Most of these processed convenience foods are marketed under the brand name Jinluo and sold by the company's own sales and distribution team. As we discussed at length earlier, these types of convenience foods tend to see rapid acceptance and growth as countries become wealthier. With any retail product, even food-branding is key. By establishing Jinluo as a strong local brand in a growing segment of the food market, People's Food is extremely well placed to take advantage of China's rapid income growth.

We'd be remiss if we failed to mention that some premium Western brands stand to benefit handsomely as India, China, and the rest of Asia become wealthier. Consumer tastes, particularly in urban areas, tend to converge as income levels rise. That's why McDonald's, Yum! Brands, and other traditional American brands have been able to flourish in Asia as well. The best plays are the strongest brands. As Asia grows, consumers will increasingly want to have the same brand name products enjoyed in the West, including premium quality liquor and wines, branded sweets and chocolates, and snack foods. In Chapter 10, "Asia's Evolving Economies," we'll examine a few of these Western icons that will benefit most from Asia's growth.

Endnotes

1. http://www.bbc.co.uk/history/society_culture/industrialisation/agricultural_revolution_04.shtml.
2. http://esa.un.org/unpp/.
3. United Nations Population Division (FAO) Food Supply Data (http://esa.un.org/unpp/) and the United States Department of Agriculture (USDA), "Changing Structure of Global Food Consumption and Trade," edited by Anita Regmi, May 2001.
4. http://uk.encarta.msn.com/encyclopedia_761579911/Agricultural_Revolution.html.

5. United Nations World Population Projects, The 2004 Revision (http://esa.un.org/unpp/p2k0data.asp).
6. United Nations Population Division (FAO) Food Supply Data (http://esa.un.org/unpp/).
7. http://edis.ifas.ufl.edu/AN129.
8. United Nations Population Division (FAO) Food Supply Data.
9. http://news.nationalgeographic.com/news/2001/06/0601_chinadust.html.
10. Gale, Fred. "China at a Glance: A Statistical Overview of China's Food and Agriculture" 1999 page 8; FAO STAT)
11. http://www.buyusa.gov/china/en/agrochemicals.html.
12. Gale, Fred. "China's Food and Agriculture: Issues for the 21st Century," Agricultural Information Bulletin No. 775, USDA.
13. Potash Corporation website (http://www.potashcorp.com/npk_markets/ industry_overview/potash_first_strategy/page_8.zsp).
14. Bunge. "Growth Trends in Agribusiness and Food" (Prudential conference 2004, www.bunge.com).
15. Ibid.

8

FUELING GLOBAL GROWTH

The histories of energy, industrialization, and economic growth are inextricably intertwined.

Steam power produced by burning coal made the Industrial Revolution of the 18th century possible. With the advent of an efficient steam engine in the 1800s, factories no longer needed to be located near natural sources of energy, such as rivers. Mechanized, steam-powered factories proved to be vastly more efficient at producing goods than traditional handmade methods. Coal made it possible for more goods to be produced at cheaper costs, and factories sprung up across the Western world.

Without fossil fuels such as coal or oil, it's difficult and expensive to transport goods. Coal-fired trains sped the development of America's vast western territories in the 19th century. Trains simplified the transportation of manufactured goods from factories to cities and consumers.

In the 20th century, man became ever more reliant on fossil fuels to power economic growth. Oil became the transport fuel of choice, powering cars, trucks, and trains. Electricity produced from coal, oil, natural gas, and uranium lengthened working hours, providing light to the working masses late into the evening.

In short, the modern global economy as we know it could not exist without fossil fuels. The world now consumes nearly 79 million barrels of oil every day, or 3.28 billion gallons per day—roughly 2.5 times the 1965 rate of consumption. Natural gas is no less important as a global power source—more than 250 billion cubic feet of gas is consumed every day, nearly four times the 1965 rate.[1]

Energy consumption is neither a luxury nor a choice; without all that fuel, the economy would grind to a standstill. Global energy demand is now growing at the fastest rate in three decades. Emerging markets, particularly maturing Asian economies, are driving that growth. If history is any guide, Asia's need for energy will only increase in the coming years, putting an even greater strain on global energy supply.

Known supplies of oil and gas are increasingly being exhausted and the search is on for new reserves of fossil fuels that can meet the demands of the future. Meanwhile, new technologies are allowing energy companies to exploit reserves of oil and gas previously thought uneconomical to produce. Alternative fuels such as nuclear energy and wind power hold the potential to power growth while reducing dependence on fossil fuels.

In short, the era of low energy prices is over. The combination of huge demand growth, weak production growth, and rising prices is behind a virtuous cycle for energy companies. It's been more than 30 years since these firms have enjoyed such positive fundamentals. The bull market will continue well into the coming decade and will make a fortune for investors with the foresight to recognize the most profitable trends.

Rising Consumption

Crude oil is by far the most commonly analyzed fossil fuel. That attention obscures the global importance of natural gas, coal, and uranium for nuclear power. But the oil market offers a convenient and accurate model of the coming global energy demand crunch.

Figure 8-1 depicts estimates by the International Energy Agency (IEA) for oil and refined products demand growth over time. The bars represent year-over-year growth in oil demand for the entire world, both OECD (Organization for Economic Co-operation and Development) and non-OECD nations. Throughout the 1990s, oil demand growth was low, averaging just 1.4 percent annually. There were one-off spikes in demand, but nothing sustained in nature. The current decade is a totally different story—oil demand has been consistently higher than the 1990s average. The 2003 and 2004 spikes in oil demand are the largest witnessed since the early 1980s.

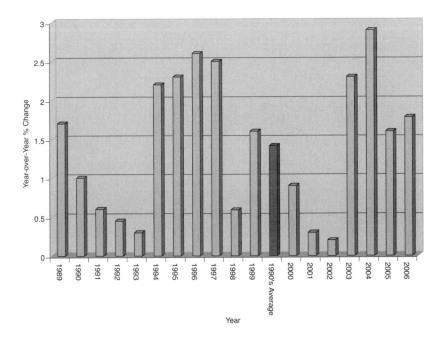

Figure 8-1 Oil demand growth. (Source: International Energy Agency Oil Market Reports, various issues.)

Some of the strongest demand growth of all has come from Asia. Consider, for example, China. As recently as the mid-90s, China was actually a net exporter of crude oil. Figure 8-2 shows that, up until that time, China regularly produced more oil than it consumed.

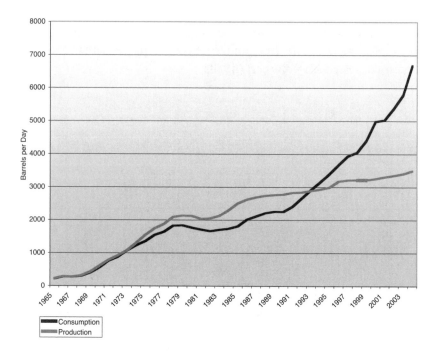

Figure 8-2 China consumption versus production. (Source: BP Statistical Review of World Energy 2005.)

As the Chinese consumer gets wealthier, demand for all sorts of basic consumer items rises, including automobiles. Figure 8-3 depicts the enormous growth since 2000 in vehicle sales in China. As recently as the late 1990s, cars were a vanity. Monthly Chinese vehicle sales roughly quintupled from 2000 to 2005. All that new demand is behind the parabolic jump in China's oil consumption since the mid-90s. Production, especially from offshore China, has also risen since the mid-90s.

However, although demand for oil has risen in parabolic fashion, production has managed growth of only a few percent annually. The yawning gap in Figure 8-2 between production and consumption represents rapidly rising oil imports into China; the Chinese are now importing more than two million barrels of oil and refined products every day.

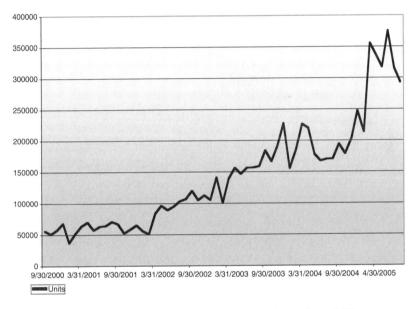

Figure 8-3 China vehicle sales. (Source: Bloomberg L.P.)

If history is any guide, this is only the beginning. Consider the case of Japan, the big economic growth story of the 20th century. In the wake of World War II, Japan's economy lay in shambles, in much worse shape economically than most of Europe. Less than 50 years later, Japan's economy was second only to the U.S. in size. In less than 50 years, brands like Toyota and Sony grew from obscurity to become global household names. But the Japanese economic miracle was built on fossil fuels, as were the British and American economic miracles that preceded it; take a look at Figure 8-4.

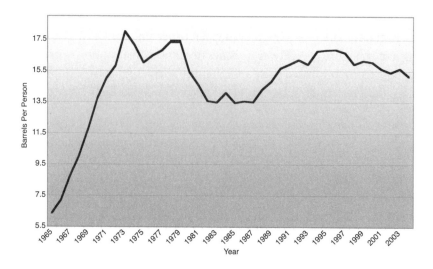

Figure 8-4 Japan oil consumption. (Source: BP Statistical Review of World Energy 2005, United States Census Bureau.)

In 1950, Japan consumed between one and two barrels of oil per person per year. By the mid-60s, as Japan's industrial and manufacturing base began expanding rapidly, so too did oil consumption, to about six barrels annually per person. As the chart shows, growth in annual oil consumption exploded to 15 barrels of oil per capita annually by 2003, around 10 times the 1950 levels. Japan's growing oil consumption was a function of the nation's growth and economic development.[2]

Today, Japan has a population of less than 130 million, up from about 83 million in 1950. Japan's growth resulted in a jump in oil demand of roughly 5 million barrels of oil consumption per day. To put that figure into perspective, the U.S. consumes roughly 20 million barrels of crude oil per day. This represents a large jump in demand. Asia's population exceeds 3 billion, and the local economies are growing much faster than the developed western economies. Imagine if China and India assume a growth path like Japan's in the 1960s and 1970s. If China were to consume just four barrels of oil per capita annually, 15 percent of U.S. totals, the nation would require more than 13 million barrels of oil per day, a number roughly equivalent to the entire European Union's daily consumption.

If that sounds farfetched, think again. Over the past 10 years, China has averaged consumption growth of about 7.5 percent per year. Assuming that growth rate remains constant, China will top 13 million barrels in daily consumption by 2014. And many economists predict that China will consume that amount before 2014.

The emerging economies seeing the most rapid economic growth are also the most oil-intensive in the world. Oil intensity is a measure of how much oil is required to produce one unit of gross domestic product (GDP). Oil intensity tends to drop as economies mature. More mature economies (like the U.S.) rely on service industries—insurance, banking, retail—for an outsized share of their GDP. Manufacturing industries aren't as crucial for these nations. Services require less energy than "heavy" industries like manufacturing.

Countries like China are growing on the back of a rapidly developing manufacturing base and require a lot of oil.

Figure 8-5 shows global oil intensity of the developed OECD countries against that of developing nations like China and Brazil. The contrasts

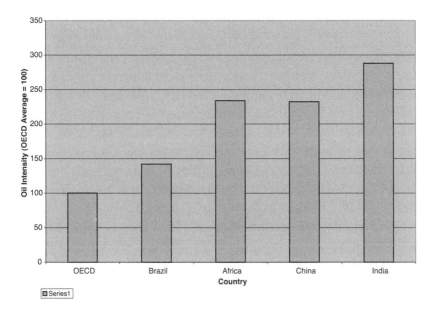

Figure 8-5 Oil intensity index. (Source: International Energy Agency.)

are striking. China's economy, for example, is more than twice as oil intensive as that of the OECD average. China is the world's second-largest consumer of oil and an increasingly significant importer. India was never a big producer of oil, but imports have been growing at a near parabolic pace since the late 1990s as demand rises. India is also one of the most oil-intensive economies in the world, even more so than China.

The Supply Side

The United States remains by far the world's largest consumer and importer of oil. The U.S. once boasted large oil-producing fields in regions including Texas and Alaska, but these reserves have been largely exploited. Despite the discovery of several new fields in the Gulf of Mexico, U.S. oil production peaked in 1972 and has been steadily declining since that time. To make up for that lost production, the U.S. has simply imported ever-larger quantities of oil. Oil imports rose from around six million barrels per day in 1975 to around 13 million barrels of crude and refined products by 2003.

Although the North Sea, Venezuela, and Africa, among other regions, all contributed to available supplies of oil for imports, the major producer by far remains the Middle East. The Middle East—Saudi Arabia, in particular—is the only region with available excess supplies of oil and oil production capacity to meet demand. Vast fields discovered in the Middle East supplied America's burgeoning demand for crude oil in the 1980s and 1990s. Supplies seemed so limitless by the 1990s that oil prices slipped under $10 per barrel. But the emergence of a strong Asian thirst for oil, coupled with continued demand from the West, altered that equation. Suddenly, all that spare capacity in the Middle East began to look woefully inadequate. The big oil companies cut back their exploration and development activities sharply in the 1990s as oil prices fell. There are now fewer new producing fields coming online to make up for lost production from older fields that are largely depleted.

Every year, the big energy companies produce oil and natural gas out of existing reserves. Normally, these companies also explore for new reserves or perform tests to quantify the size of existing yet unproven discoveries. The reserve replacement ratio compares a company's production of oil and gas to growth in proven reserves. If the ratio is 100 percent, that means that for every barrel of oil pumped out of the ground, the company is adding another barrel to proven reserves. Ratios above 100 mean that more oil is being discovered than produced; ratios under 100 are indicative of a drawdown in reserves. The world's largest oil companies have all been sporting low reserve replacement ratios over the past few years, as Table 8-1 indicates. As a consequence of low energy prices, these companies have not been spending money to look for and develop new reserves. The big oil companies are having trouble replacing their reserves, but it's not due to lack of capital. The strong pricing environment for both oil and gas has led to an explosion in profits and cash flow for the industry.

Table 8-1 Reserve Replacement BOE 2004 (Source: Bloomberg L.P.)

Oil Company	Reserve Replacement Ratio
ExxonMobil	-18.48
ConocoPhillips	212.56
Chevron	49.07
Royal Dutch Shell	38.52
Total S.A.	77.58
BP	127.57

Increasingly, some of this cash is being redeployed to explore for and develop new reserves. With debt levels already near historical lows, it's likely the big oil companies will deploy more cash in exploration activities in an attempt to boost anemic reserve replacement ratios. But it takes years to bring major new projects into production. That means it will take a considerable period of time and major investment to reverse the downward trend in reserve replacement ratios and start to meet the increasing global demand for oil. A new multiyear spending cycle is underway in the energy markets, but supplies are likely to remain tight for at least the next five to 10 years.

Rising political tensions add to that supply crunch. Figure 8-6 shows oil production from the U.S., Britain, and Norway as a percentage of total world production. This ratio is a crude metric of political risks in the oil market. The ratio simply compares supplies from the most stable countries to output from the rest of the world (mainly OPEC–Organization of the Petroleum Exporting Countries). Britain and Norway are at the heart of North Sea oil supplies. A boom in supply from this region in the 1980s helped offset declining U.S. production after 1972. As you can see, the ratio actually grew and stabilized at a higher level through most of the 1980s. This helped bring about lower oil prices. In contrast, the period after 1972 through the early 1980s saw OPEC's importance increase, heightening political risk to oil supply, and increasing oil prices.

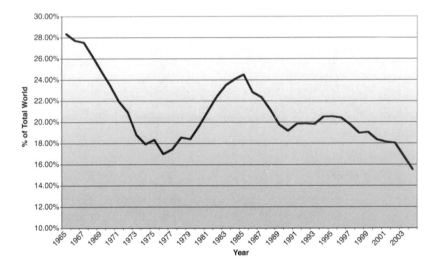

Figure 8-6 U.S., Britain, and Norway oil production. (Source: BP Statistical Review of World Energy 2005.)

But that effect is now reversing. It is clear that North Sea and U.S. oil production is declining relative to OPEC output; the ratio has been hitting new lows in recent years. Based on this simple measure, political risk in the crude market is climbing fast. This factor supports oil prices at levels higher than simple supply and demand suggests. When demand for any commodity increases faster than supply, there's one simple effect: higher prices. Higher prices are the only proven way to ration demand over the long term. Burgeoning Asian demand for oil coupled with slow production increases in the coming years means that the era of low energy prices is over.

The Refining Factor

Consumers often link high gasoline prices with high crude oil prices, but the relationship isn't as direct as most imagine. The missing link ignored by most in the popular press is refining. A shortage of refining capacity is behind much of the jump in gasoline prices in recent years, not a shortage of crude. Major U.S. refiners with the latest technology are in the sweet spot of that trend.

Crude oil is nothing more than a raw material, and, like most raw materials, it must be processed, purified, and altered to be useful. You can't power your car with crude oil; in its raw state, it's not much more flammable than the whale oils and paraffin waxes burned in old-fashioned oil lamps. In fact, the earliest commercial use of crude oil (then known as *rock oil*) was just that, an alternative to scarce whale oil. Nowadays, crude oil is hardly ever used in its raw state. Refiners perform the absolutely critical task of breaking crude oil into useful products like gasoline, kerosene, jet fuel, and even asphalt for covering roadways. Refiners do not make money from high crude prices; pure refining companies do not sell crude oil. In refining parlance, crude oil is known as *feedstock*—the base raw material of the refining business. If a company does not also explore for and produce oil, crude must be purchased on the open market. When crude oil prices rise, so does a refiner's costs.

Refiners do sell gasoline, jet fuel, and other related products, and therefore make money from the relative prices of crude oil and its constituent products. If the price of gasoline rises faster than the price of oil, refiners will see higher profits. A common measure of refining profits is known as the *crack spread*. This measure is determined by examining the futures prices for crude oil and two major refined products: gasoline and heating oil. When the crack spread rises, the prices of heating oil and gasoline are rising faster than the cost of crude. In other words, the value of the products refiners sell is rising faster than their costs, so profit margins are expanding. In recent years, the crack spread has been rising—refining margins are well above the levels seen in the 1990s.

The refining business is booming for one simple reason: Demand for gasoline globally outstrips the capacity to refine crude. Refiners worldwide have been operating at almost full capacity, but have been unable to refine crude fast enough to keep pace with demand. The result: rising prices.

No new refineries have been constructed in the U.S. since 1976. Due to tighter environmental regulations and new standards for mixing gasoline, some older refineries have actually been taken offline. Refining capacity in the U.S. has dropped considerably over the past 30 years. It takes years and billions of dollars to site and build new refineries. In the past, plans to build new refineries in the U.S. have been quashed due to the outrage of local residents. And even if a suitable location were identified, environmental impact studies and myriad bureaucratic hurdles must be overcome. Don't expect any significant new refining capacity in the U.S. until 2008 or later. In Asia, it's easier to get permission to build refineries. But demand is rising so rapidly, it's virtually impossible to construct those refineries fast enough. Existing refineries in the region are less advanced than those in the U.S., making them more expensive to operate.

In past years, the refinery shortage wasn't a problem. If there wasn't enough domestic capacity to refine crude, the U.S. could simply import gasoline from abroad, mainly from Europe. But this is no longer the case. Changes in U.S. environmental regulations mean that it's harder for European refiners to mix gasoline that meets U.S. specifications. Asian demand for gasoline is growing rapidly as economies in the region industrialize; the Asians are now competing with the U.S. for any available supply of refined product.

In coming years, well-placed refiners will enjoy fat, widening profit margins. There's a kicker for the independent refiners in the U.S.: due to U.S. technological superiority in the refining business, domestic refiners are seeing profit margins widen even faster than the crack spread suggests.

Crude oil is not a homogenous product. There are literally thousands of different types of oil—some are thick and black, others less viscous and clearer. Each type has slightly different properties, and those differences are key to understanding profitability in the oil refining business. There are two properties of crude oil that are of paramount importance: sulphur content and density.

Sulphur is a corrosive pollutant. Most governments, even in developing Asia, are forcing ever-stricter environmental regulations on gasoline and diesel fuels. This requires refiners to remove more sulphur each year from fuel oils during processing. Stricter sulphur regulations are slated to come into effect over the next few years as well. The sulphur itself tends to corrode the pipes and holding tanks that are part of a refinery's operations, making it more expensive to refine oils high in the pollutant. Oils with low sulphur content are known as *sweet* oils; crude with high sulphur content is known as *sour* crude.

Gasoline is a relatively light molecule. Very dense oils—known as heavy crudes—tend to be made from large hydrocarbon molecules. These must be broken down into shorter chains to form gasoline, a process that requires special equipment and a major capital investment. Less dense oils known as light crudes are easier and cheaper to refine. Light crude oil trades at a premium to heavy crude oil. Oils with low sulphur content, sweet crudes, tend to be more expensive than sour crudes. The fact that heavy sour crude trades at a discount to light sweet varietals is no mystery. As we explained, the heavy sours are more difficult to refine.

Throughout the 1990s, West Texas Intermediate (WTI)—the light sweet crude oil type most widely quoted on the news—traded at only about a $6 average premium to heavy, sour varietals. The previous high occurred around the time of the first Gulf War, when WTI traded at a $10 premium. But early in the 21st century, light, sweet crude has been trading at much larger premiums, sometimes as much as $20 per barrel above heavy sour.

Asian refiners (at the moment) have little or no capacity to refine heavy or sour crudes, and must import light sweet crudes almost exclusively. At the same time, virtually all oil-producing regions have seen a drop-off in light sweet production in recent years; as wells mature, they tend to produce higher quantities of the heavy stuff. Huge Asian demand for light sweet crude is meeting waning supplies—the price of WTI and other similar oils has risen far more rapidly than that of heavy sours. Asian refineries are forced to buy only the most expensive feedstocks. This is music to the ears of the U.S. refining industry.

U.S. refineries have spent billions upgrading facilities to accept almost any grade of crude. These refineries do not need to buy WTI, but can simply buy cheaper crude oils to keep the cost of feedstock down. However, the gasoline produced is the same regardless of the feedstock used. U.S. refineries employing the latest technology have seen only minimal jumps in costs but have benefited from extraordinarily strong demand for gasoline. As long as light sweet crude continues to trade at a huge premium to heavy sour, profit margins for the U.S. refiners will continue to expand. As it will take years and billions of dollars for Asia to upgrade its refining capacity, this trend will continue for the foreseeable future.

The biggest beneficiaries will be the most advanced refiners, including the largest independent refining company in the U.S., Valero (NYSE: VLO). Valero owned about 15 refineries in the U.S. and across the Caribbean prior to its takeover of Premcor in 2005. Total daily through-put of oil was about 2.5 million barrels per day, roughly 10 percent of total U.S. demand. The takeover added another 0.7 million barrels per day to total capacity. Valero's refineries are among the most complex on the planet. As much as three-quarters of the company's throughput is the cheaper heavy sour crude oils. Valero can buy these oils for a low price and sell gasoline and diesel fuel at full market prices. The company's profitability is exploding.

There is also scope for Valero to vastly expand capacity by adding to existing refineries. Valero can start by upgrading existing Premcor facilities to accept more complex grades of crude. There are even plans to adapt Premcor's facility in Lima, Ohio to accept crude derived from the vast Canadian oil sands. The sands will become an increasingly important source of crude in the U.S. market, and refineries will need to be ready to accept this very heavy crude oil feedstock.

Another emerging story is diesel fuel. New diesel regulations in Europe limit sulphur output for trucks and cars alike. Valero is one of only a handful of refineries globally that can remove the sulphur to meet regulations; the company has actually exported some diesel fuel to EU countries to meet demand as European refining capacity isn't up to the task. Again, profit margins have exploded.

India plans similar sulphur regulations on diesel fuel. Most likely, these will be gradually phased in over the next few years. On the margin, this will continue to increase demand for low-sulphur diesel; the companies that can produce this key fuel will be in the sweet spot of that trend.

Another play on the refining business is Marathon Oil (NYSE: MRO), a hybrid that both produces and refines crude oil. The company's refining arm is capable of just under 1 million barrels of crude oil per day in throughput from a network of seven refineries in the U.S. These refineries, like Valero's, are capable of processing a great deal of heavy sour crude feedstock. On the exploration and production front, Marathon has reserves of a little more than 1.1 billion barrels of crude oil equivalent, a combination of both crude and natural gas reserves. The company is particularly strong off the coast of West Africa, one of the most promising exploration regions in the world today.

Coal

Coal remains king throughout most of the developed and developing world. Coal may no longer be as important as it once was as a source of heat in homes or a transportation fuel for trains, but it still accounts for more than half of the electricity generated in the U.S. and about 40 percent of global electricity generation. It is a particularly important fuel in rapidly developing Asia, accounting for more than 75 percent of electricity generated in both China and India. Although Beijing is trying to diversify the nation's electricity supply, coal will be a key source of energy demand for years to come—China plans to add 171 gigawatts (GW) of new coal-fired power plant capacity to its existing 250 GW over the next 20 years. India also plans major expansions, adding another 57 GW to capacity by 2025, a near doubling of its current capacity.

In addition to electricity, coal has myriad other uses. One of the most important is in the production of iron and steel. As China is by far the world's leading manufacturer of steel, this is particularly important for that nation. *Coking* coal is used to make coke, which is then fed into blast furnaces as part of the steel-making process. The tight supply environment has arisen as China is trying to keep up with steel demand. Until 2003, China was a net exporter of coking coal. But in 2004, it became a net importer and will continue to be for some time.

As a result of coal's use in all these applications, demand will explode over the next 20 years. Coal demand worldwide will grow, driven mostly by demand from China and India. By 2025, these two countries will consume 30 percent more coal than the entire industrialized world.

Coal's detractors say it's an environmentally dirty fuel doomed to extinction. In China, the pollution is particularly damaging. A 1999 World Health Organization (WHO) report detailed the world's 10 most polluted cities—seven of those 10 are located in China. The WHO estimates that corrosive acid rain now falls on nearly a third of China's land area. The main culprit in all this pollution: coal-fired plants. Major pollutants released by coal-fired power plants include sulphur dioxide, a chemical that's been linked to respiratory illness and acid rain. Mercury is a particularly dangerous pollutant released from coal plants. When mercury combines with water, it can accumulate in fish and other marine life; eating such fish has been linked to birth defects and other developmental problems. Coal plants also release carbon dioxide, a gas that many scientists believe is behind the global warming trend.

Coal does have one major advantage: It's widely available (see Figure 8-7). Total world reserves are estimated to be 1,083 billion tons.[3] Some of the world's largest reserves are located in China and India, the very nations that will be the world's biggest consumers over the next 20 years. Based on projected demand for coal in 2025, the world has enough coal resources to last about 150 years, a far longer reserve life than either oil or natural gas.

Coal is not a single commodity. There are actually several different types of coal with unique properties. Coal reserves can be divided into higher-grade bituminous coal, and lower grade lignite, or brown, coal. Higher-grade bituminous coal is suitable for use as coking coal and has higher heat content than lignite coal; it's more efficient as a source of

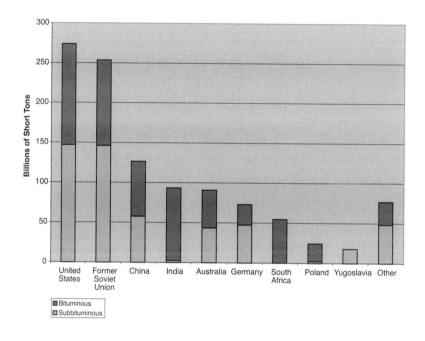

Figure 8-7 Coal reserves by nation. (Source: Energy Information Administration [EIA] International Energy Outlook 2004.)

heat. This coal is the more valuable type and is the source of most world coal trade. The richest three nations for producing bituminous coal, accounting for more than 80 percent of the world's supply, are the U.S., Canada, and Australia. Australian coal, in particular, is becoming an increasingly significant import into developing Asia, a trend that's likely to continue for some time.

Regardless of environmental concerns, coal's widespread availability means it's unlikely to ever be totally supplanted as a power source. With the possible exception of nuclear and hydroelectric power, coal is the cheapest source of power in terms of cost per kilowatt-hour. Modern coal plants in the U.S. and Western Europe release a fraction of the pollution of older power facilities. New clean-coal technologies can drastically release the environmental impact of this cheap and abundant fossil fuel. Companies with the reserves of coal, bituminous coal in particular, will benefit from the increased demand.

Natural Gas

Natural gas has become an increasingly important global power source in recent years. Because gas holds certain advantages over oil, this trend is likely to continue for some time. According to the Energy Information Administration (EIA), natural gas will be the fastest growing source of energy globally between 2005 and 2025. The EIA expects natural gas consumption will rise a total of 70 percent from 90 trillion cubic feet (tcf) in 2001 to more than 150 tcf by 2025 (see Figure 8-8). This is an average annualized growth rate of more than 2.2 percent, higher than the projected 1.9 percent annualized growth in oil use or the 1.6 percent annualized growth for coal.[4]

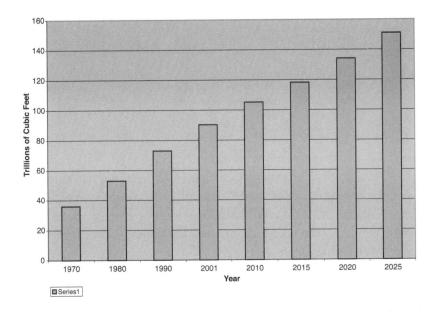

Figure 8-8 World natural gas consumption. (Source: EIA 2004 International Energy Outlook.)

Much of this growth is expected to come from increased use of natural-gas-fired turbines used to generate electricity. The EIA projects a near doubling in global demand for energy to more than 23 trillion kilowatt-hours in 2025 from roughly 13 trillion kilowatt-hours in 2001. Although electricity demand will increase in the U.S. and other industrialized nations, the lion's share of that expansion will be in Asia (see Figure 8-9).

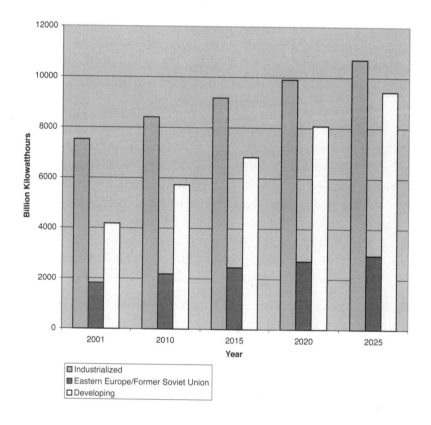

Figure 8-9 Electricity consumption by region. (Source: EIA International Energy Outlook 2004.)

Although China has been growing by leaps and bounds, a good portion of the country still lacks basic electrification. As these areas are finally hooked up to an electric grid, there will be hundreds of millions of new consumers. As cities develop and consumers start buying TVs, refrigerators, air conditioners, and other household appliances, electricity consumption is likely to rise in urban areas as well.

Electricity consumption in the industrialized world is projected to jump about 42 percent between 2001 and 2025. Developing nations are projected to see electricity demand jump more than 125 percent in the same period. By 2025, the developing world will consume nearly as much electricity as the industrialized world.

China is now an increasingly important manufacturing base for the entire world. Just as it took copious quantities of coal to power England's rapidly expanding factories in the 19th century, China needs coal and natural gas to power its own factory base. There's also burgeoning demand for energy at the consumer level.

The EIA estimates that natural gas accounted for about 18 percent of global electricity generation in 2001 and will account for more than 25 percent by 2025. In other words, natural gas will become an ever more important part of world electricity generation, and electricity generation is itself growing rapidly. As previously discussed, gas has several advantages over oil. Most importantly, geologists estimate that there's a lot more gas left to be exploited than crude oil. Gas reserves are more evenly spread from a geographic standpoint—the Middle East simply does not hold the market share in gas as it does in oil.

Figure 8-10 shows global natural gas reserves broken down by region. Estimates put total global gas reserves at more than 6,000 tcf. Based on projected 2025 annual consumption estimates of 150 tcf, that's about 40 years' supply. Russia and the former Soviet republics are key producers of natural gas; reserve estimates in this region have been steadily ticking higher in recent years. Offshore West Africa is another emerging gas production market; exploration activity has stepped up a great deal in this region since the late 1990s.

Another advantage of gas is that it's far cleaner to burn than coal or oil. Industrialized nations are attempting to reduce carbon and greenhouse gas emissions, and increased reliance on gas can reduce emissions of these pollutants. Countries like China and India are currently extremely

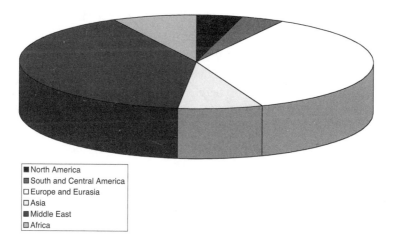

Figure 8-10 Natural gas reserves by region. (Source: EIA.)

Legend:
- North America
- South and Central America
- Europe and Eurasia
- Asia
- Middle East
- Africa

reliant on dirty coal for electricity generation. In the future, China will look to reduce emissions which means more natural gas. Natural gas accounts for just 3 percent of Chinese supply today, but that figure is expected to increase dramatically in the coming years.

Although gas reserves are more abundant than oil, there remains a lot of work to be done to exploit these reserves. Many reserves of gas are of the "stranded" variety, located too far away from existing pipelines to be produced economically. When drilling for oil, natural gas is often found coexisting with oil in a reservoir. Traditionally, much of this gas was simply flared—burned off into the atmosphere—as a useless byproduct because the gas was uneconomical to transport to markets. The big oil companies all have significant reserves of gas left in the ground that are considered stranded.

Liquefied natural gas (LNG) is one solution. Natural gas becomes a liquid when cooled to −162 degrees Celsius (−260 degrees Fahrenheit). When the gas is cooled, it shrinks in size so that LNG takes up about one six-hundredth the space of naturally occurring gas. The advantage here is that gas in stranded reservoirs can be liquefied and transported by tanker ship. Stranded reserves can be exploited. Right now, Japan is the world's largest LNG importer. It has only tiny domestic reserves, so it imports nearly all of its gas requirements. Substantially all of that gas is imported as LNG. Meanwhile, as domestic sources of natural gas in the U.S. become ever more depleted, LNG is expected to gain share, accounting for more than 65 percent of U.S. supply, up from less than 5 percent in 2002. Developing Asia will be another key player in the LNG markets. China's first LNG terminal is scheduled for completion in 2006 in the Guangdong province. A second facility in Fujian is scheduled to begin operations in 2007.

In India, all current gas demand is supplied from domestic sources, mainly from offshore reserves. But the EIA estimates particularly strong growth of roughly 4.8 percent annually through 2025. India is already well aware of its need to start expanding LNG infrastructure and has already negotiated a long-term supply agreement with Rasgas of Qatar, and has built two LNG regasification plants to process those imports.

Two to Own

As natural gas will be one of the fastest-growing energy sources for at least the next 20 years, companies with access to large reserves will be in the catbird's seat. Those that can actually increase production and reserves into a strong market will fare even better.

BG Group PLC (NYSE: BRG), formerly known as British Gas, is one of the "hidden" gems in the energy sector, and a quality pure play on LNG. Once-abandoned gas fields are now viable again because of the simplified transportation process for LNG. Abundant gas supplies in places like Sakhalin Island (on the far east coast of Russia) can now be explored due to advances in LNG technology. The spike in worldwide energy demand has driven LNG growth, a technology pioneered 30 years ago. BG is at the forefront of this developing field. The company has been, historically, a North Sea play, and there are still good reserves in that reservoir. But BG has successfully repositioned its formerly domestic portfolio and now boasts a worldwide collection of high-quality assets, including properties in North America, Africa, and developing regions such as Asia and South America.

For some years, BG has sported the highest reserve replacement ratio in the industry (a function of the company's aggressive expansion plan), a sign that it's building reserves far faster than it's producing them. Based on proved reserves, BG could keep producing at 2004 levels for 13 years even if it never found another cubic foot of natural gas. Probable reserves boost that figure to over 20 years. Management is basing its strategy on the operating principle that gas will become a very important source of energy, and that LNG technology will make it a global commodity.

BG is the largest holder of U.S.-based LNG regasification capacity, making it an important player in the long-term supply of gas to the U.S. market. The company's early-mover status in such an important growth segment will prove to be of great value as competitors try to gain access to LNG.

The colossus of the gas market is Russia, where reserves are estimated at nearly 1,700 trillion cubic feet of gas, or approximately one quarter of the entire world's reserve base. This is also more than any other single country.

Gazprom (US: OGZPF; Russia: GSPBEX) is Russia's largest company and controls more than 90 percent of domestic natural gas supplies. Gazprom is also the largest producer of natural gas in the world. Right now, the company sells nearly two-thirds of its gas to the domestic Russian market. Russian gas prices are controlled, however, so that's a money-losing part of the business. A giant export market more than makes up for the losses at home. Most of the company's gas currently is destined for Western Europe, but that may change in the future. Gazprom is partnering with major international energy companies to help further develop and produce reserves. It also hopes to use the money from these joint ventures to expand elsewhere. In particular, look for more LNG development to open up the U.S. market and pipelines into Asia to supply that fast-growing region.

Nuclear Power

In December 1951, an experimental nuclear reactor in Idaho managed to generate enough electricity to light four 200-watt light bulbs. Nuclear power became a reality.

In the 50 plus years since that first test, nuclear power has grown into a key global source of electricity. Worldwide, there are about 438 commercial nuclear reactors in operation, supplying 16 percent of total global electricity demand. Nuclear power is even more important in the U.S., where 104 reactors produce about 20 percent of the nation's power. Several European countries, including France, Germany, Britain, and Sweden, are even more reliant on nuclear power. France generates nearly 80 percent of its electricity using nuclear power. Despite these successes, nuclear power has been a controversial technology at times. Early promoters suggested that reactors would offer power "too cheap to meter." Apparently, large American utility companies agreed; several hundred plants were commissioned between 1950 and 1974. But construction of plants proved expensive due to regulatory delays, failure to adopt a single standard design for plants, and opposition from antinuclear groups. In the end, less than half of the plants commissioned were built. High profile nuclear accidents like Chernobyl in Russia and Three Mile Island in the U.S. tarnished nuclear power's image still further. No U.S. utility has applied for a new nuclear plant construction permit since the 1979 Three Mile Island accident. By the mid-80s some were already calling nuclear power a failed experiment.

But nuclear power is far from dead. China and India are planning to make nuclear power centerpieces of their respective national electricity policies; these nations are already building new reactors and experimenting with advanced reactor designs. The nuclear option is also back on the table in the U.S. due to high natural gas prices, coupled with the negative environmental impact of coal-fired plants. U.S. utilities are expanding existing facilities and/or considering the construction of new plants.

Nearly 90 percent of the cost of electricity produced from natural gas is attributable to the price of gas itself. In other words, when the price of gas swings wildly, so does the price of electricity produced from gas-fired plants. Figure 8-11 depicts the fuel costs of producing one million BTU of electricity in four different types of power plants: oil-fired plants, coal-fired plants, natural gas turbines, and nuclear plants.

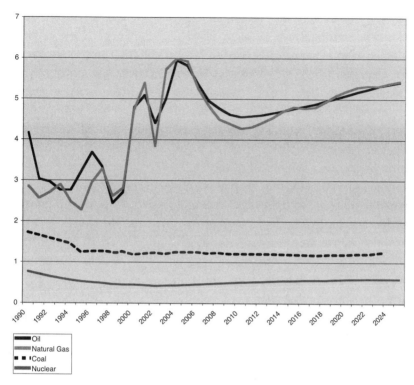

Figure 8-11 Fuel cost comparison of power plants.
(Source: Energy Information Administration.)

Each line on the chart represents average nationwide operating costs for a particular year. The cost of gas-fired power varies a great deal from year-to-year. With natural gas in very tight supply in 2000 and 2001, prices shot up to about five mills per kilowatt-hour. When gas prices collapsed in 2002, electricity prices fell below four mills (mill=1/10 of a cent).

Coal power is much cheaper than gas for most of the years covered by the chart. Coal power prices were also less volatile than gas in the period covered by this data. The price of coal accounts for about three-quarters of the cost of electricity produced in coal-fired plants, so any jump in coal prices feeds directly into costs at the meter. Coal also carries previously discussed environmental concerns.

Nuclear power is the cheapest of all. The cost of electricity from nuclear plants is reasonably stable over time. Note that nuclear prices barely budged even as gas prices soared in 2000 and 2001. There's good reason for that stability: the cost of producing electricity in a nuclear plant stems mainly from plant maintenance and day-to-day operation expenses. The main fuel for nuclear plants is processed uranium. The cost of uranium accounts for only about 3 percent of the price of nuclear power. The costs involved in processing uranium into usable form are another 24 percent of the cost of nuclear-generated electricity. In total, fuel costs for nuclear plants are relatively unimportant as compared to plants powered by conventional fossil fuels. Although uranium is, like gas and oil, a limited resource that must be mined from the ground, high uranium prices do not spell huge spikes in power prices. In addition to being cheap, nuclear power is also environmentally friendly. Nuclear power plants emit no greenhouse gases, mercury, or any other measurable sources of pollution. Repeated studies of nuclear power plants in the U.S. suggest that the amount of radiation emitted from plants is minimal, less than one millerem annually. To put that into perspective, the average American is exposed to about 50 millerems of radiation annually from simple X-rays.

Renewable energies like hydroelectric, wind, and solar are likely to become more important contributors to global electricity supply. Renewable energy is also environmentally friendly. However, the growth in renewable energies is limited; electricity generated from such sources cannot be stored in mass quantities and no renewable energy source is capable of producing power on demand, 24 hours a day, seven days per week. Nuclear power is the only non-polluting fuel suitable for base load generation (minimum power required at a steady, constant rate) available today.

The Japanese government has certainly recognized this fact. Since Japan's adoption of the Kyoto Protocol limiting greenhouse gas emissions, the Japanese government has repeatedly highlighted nuclear energy as the only reliable way to meet the terms of the agreement. Even some prominent environmentalists have embraced nuclear power as a common sense means to reduce greenhouse gas emissions. Over the past 10 years in the U.S. alone, the Nuclear Energy Institute estimates that using nuclear power instead of fossil fuels has resulted in a 6.8 billion ton reduction in carbon dioxide emissions. China and India have also recognized the promise of nuclear energy. China is now planning to construct 40 new nuclear reactors over the next 15 years, one of the most ambitious nuclear expansions since the 1970s. India, with 14 reactors currently in operation, plans to add 8 new reactors to its grid by 2010. The world is rapidly recognizing the myriad advantages of nuclear energy. Far from being a sunset industry, the nuclear industry is entering a period of global growth. This growth is putting a strain on the world's available uranium production capacity.

In 2003, the world's 438 nuclear reactors consumed about 180 million pounds of natural uranium. Only a little more than 50 percent of this uranium was actually mined in 2003; total mining production in 2003 was just 92 million pounds. That 88 million-pound shortfall has been met from a number of different sources. Utilities themselves hold some inventories of uranium for use in their own plants. Over the past few years, these inventories have been drawn down by about 30 to 40 million pounds per year on average. Another 20 million pounds or so came from de-commissioned Russian nuclear warheads. The final chunk likely came from inventories held by a company called Usec; the U.S. government gave Usec 70 million pounds of uranium when it went public in 1997.

This situation is unsustainable even if uranium demand remains constant for the foreseeable future. Utilities' available inventories are already running low; some estimate that commercial inventories of uranium are less than 10 percent of what they were in the mid-80s. Meanwhile, Usec has been a major net seller of uranium since going public, so the company's stocks are rapidly depleting. Even assuming uranium demand remains constant at about 180 million pounds per year, uranium mining activity simply must pick up to meet demand. The spot market for uranium (the market for immediate delivery of yellowcake) only accounts for roughly 12 percent of total supply. Most utilities sign longer-term supply agreements to ensure that there's plenty of uranium on hand to run their plants. Uranium spot prices exceeded $35 per pound in 2005, up from less than $8 per pound in 2001. These spot prices are a good indication of the sort of pricing power uranium mining companies have been seeing over the past few years and will continue to see as utilities step up their buying of uranium.

INVESTING NUCLEAR

The world's nuclear power plants are consuming more uranium than is mined every year. In the future, with new nuclear plants slated for construction in rapidly developing Asia, that supply situation will become even more dire.

Uranium prices are already on the rise, great news for companies that have actual reserves of uranium that can be mined and sold into a strong market. Only a handful of companies have commercially recoverable reserves of uranium. Canada possesses the world's largest reserves of high-grade uranium; its richest reserves are found in Saskatchewan's Athabasca Basin.

With uranium prices on the rise, there has been an explosion in highly speculative uranium mining companies, mainly listed on the Canadian exchanges. Some of these are worthwhile, but one should focus on well-established producing companies with known reserves.

Sitting on some of the largest reserves in the region, Cameco (NYSE: CCJ) controls about 65 percent of the world's total known reserves of natural uranium. Cameco produced 20.7 million pounds of uranium in 2004, more than 20 percent of the total quantity of uranium mined worldwide for that year. For 2005, the company has targeted production of more than 21 million pounds as it expands capacity at its core mines in the Athabasca Basin. Cameco has the potential to drastically expand production over the next five years. The company plans to continue ramping up production capacity at its Cigar Lake mine to a peak production level of nearly 19 million pounds annually.

Cameco is aggressively expanding into Kazakhstan, a country with large reserves of uranium. Its Inkai mine could be a huge asset in future years; the company was planning to start production there by the end of 2005. All told, the management team projects total production growth of approximately 40 percent by the end of this decade.

According to Cameco, in the 1990s, utility companies were signing long-term uranium supply contracts at prices either inline with or at a discount to spot prices. In other words, uranium mining companies were desperate to secure a market for their metal and were willing to sign contracts at discount prices. In recent years, the tables have turned. Cameco has been selling uranium under long-term agreements struck at significant premiums to the spot price of uranium. The reason is simple: Utility companies are willing to pay up to secure long-term supplies. Cameco has suggested that 2008 will be a pivotal year. Up to 2008, it seems that most utilities have some inventories or longer-term supply arrangements to cover immediate uranium requirements. After 2008, however, these companies will be uncovered and will need to scramble to secure adequate supplies. Cameco is enjoying strong pricing in both the spot market and for longer-term contracts. It's also one of only a few companies with the capacity to expand production meaningfully over the next five years.

Another promising uranium company is Denison Mines (US: DNMIF; Canada: DEN), which produces only about 1.4 million pounds of uranium annually. It is a far smaller and more speculative play than Cameco. Denison's production comes mainly from its stake in the McLean Lake mine in Canada, the world's fifth-largest uranium mine. Denison's proven reserves of the metal total approximately 13.5 million pounds.

Several opportunities exist for Denison. The company has other properties on which it's performing exploratory drilling, including additional acreage in the prolific Athabasca Basin. There's significant potential for Denison to boost its reserves through greater exploration activity in the region. Denison also has partnered with uranium giant Cogema on several uranium exploration projects. Cogema is controlled by the French government and is second only to Cameco in annual uranium production. Denison owns 22.5 percent of a uranium mill processing facility near Cigar Lake, one of Athabasca's richest mines. This facility is scheduled to expand production significantly over the next few years. Processing revenues from the mill should be significant.

Renewables and Alternatives

The EIA projects that renewable power sources like wind, solar, and hydroelectric will continue to account for approximately 20 percent of the world's energy needs in coming years. Although some wealthier countries, mainly in Western Europe, are aggressively expanding their renewable energy programs, renewables are never likely to become a significant global source of electricity. A lot of hype surrounds the promise of these technologies, but most of that is simply hyperbole; wind and solar will never replace fossil fuels and nuclear power, no matter how much investment is poured into these technologies.

By far, the most important source of renewable energy worldwide is hydroelectric power. Almost all the growth forecasted over the next two decades is due solely to major hydroelectric power projects in China and elsewhere in the developing world. Excluding hydroelectric power, renewable energy accounts for just 2 percent of global electricity supply. Even hydroelectric power has its problems. Although it can be a cheap and clean source of power, droughts in regions like South America have led to severe power shortages. The construction of major hydroelectric facilities in China has necessitated the relocation of millions of people—hydroelectric dams create large lakes that require moving large numbers of people.

The second most promising renewable power source is wind. Wind power is extremely clean and has become a small component of power generation in the U.S. and several Western European nations, at least on a regional basis. Germany, Spain, and Denmark have been particularly aggressive in adding wind power in recent years. China, too, has planned a major wind power project for Inner Mongolia that could eventually produce some 150MW (megawatts) of power.

The truth of the matter is that existing renewable energies, although important, will never be able to fully supplant fossil fuels as a global power source. It's clear that the scope for hydroelectric power to expand is limited, even in the developing world. And wind and solar power are unsuitable for base load power generation because they're incapable of producing power on a constant basis. Expect solid growth for renewable energies but from a low starting point. Renewables, excluding hydropower, are never likely to account for more than 2 to 4 percent of global electricity demand. That's a marginal contribution, at best.

Far more promising are hydrogen-powered fuel cells. Roughly 70 percent of the oil consumed worldwide is used as a transportation fuel burned directly in cars or trucks. If hydrogen-powered fuel cells could replace gasoline as the world's prime source of transportation fuel, this could greatly ease the world's power shortages. Producing hydrogen in mass quantities is the problem. Hydrogen can be produced from hydrocarbons (oil and natural gas) or by splitting water using electricity. Manufacturing hydrogen from oil and gas doesn't cut reliance on fossil fuels; the most likely source of hydrogen for the future is splitting water, a process that creates only minimal pollution. Unfortunately, burning natural gas or coal to split water actually takes more fossil fuel than hydrogen produced. Nuclear energy is the only logical way to produce mass quantities of hydrogen to power fuel cells.

Asian Energy

Energy companies from all over the world will benefit from rapidly rising Asian energy demand. Many of these firms are located outside Asia itself. But Asia is also an important oil-producing region in its own right; local reserves of oil and gas, located in close proximity to end markets, will be an important source of supply. This is particularly true for natural gas. China, India, Australia, Malaysia, and Indonesia all have significant gas reserves. Gas from all of these areas will need to be explored and produced to meet coming demand from the region.

China National Offshore Oil Company (CNOOC) (NYSE: CEO) is the only company permitted to partner with foreign oil companies in the exploration and development of China's offshore oil and gas reserves. CNOOC was originally designed to be a way of attracting foreign energy companies to invest in the country. The company has well over two billion barrels of oil equivalent reserves and has been expanding rapidly via acquisitions. Its virtual monopoly of the offshore China business provides a number of benefits. First, the company has a lock-hold on its core exploration and production business because all new developments in the nation must go through CNOOC. Second, CNOOC has a long history of working with and acquiring knowledge from advanced foreign partners. In other words, CNOOC has valuable relationships with major energy companies from outside China—already the company has used those relationships to its advantage, grabbing stakes in promising projects around the world.

CNOOC hasn't limited itself to China's offshore waters. It's also among the largest producers in Indonesia and has made significant investments in projects elsewhere around the world. That includes a major investment in a liquefied natural gas (LNG) project in Australia and the purchase of a large stake in a Canadian energy firm with access to the massive Canadian oil sands.

In India, the largest player in the oil and gas production business is Oil and Natural Gas Corporation (ONGC) (BSE: ONGC). This company is still partly owned by the Indian government, and partly traded publicly on the Mumbai Stock Exchange. ONGC contributes more than 80 percent of India's domestic oil and gas production, owns more than 10 percent of the nation's refining capacity, and has an extensive network of pipelines to carry all that oil and gas to end markets in the nation.

ONGC has made some important discoveries domestically. In deepwater offshore India, ONGC is spending big on new exploration projects, including the development of the Krishna-Godavari find in the Bay of Bengal. These are especially rich gas reserves and will help make up for declining production from aging fields onshore.

The real growth engine for ONGC will be the deals it's cutting overseas. Realistically, even with more big finds, India doesn't have the domestic oil and gas reserves necessary to meet its needs. ONGC's offshore arm has been an aggressive acquirer, and the company expects this segment of the business to make up an ever-larger share of the reserve profile. It already has stakes in major projects all over the globe; the list includes a 149-million barrel oil field in Sudan as well as projects in Vietnam, Myanmar, Iran, Qatar, and Australia.

Smaller, but also interesting, is Gail India (BSE: GAIL). Gail, like ONGC, is a partly privatized firm that was originally formed as an arm of the Indian government. The company has some exploration and production assets, including interests in several domestic fields and a foreign gas project in Myanmar. But Gail is most important as a natural gas transmission, marketing, and processing concern. It has more than 4,600 kilometers of natural gas pipeline, by far the largest network in India, and it has seven large gas processing facilities.

Somewhat like oil refineries, gas processing facilities prepare gas for use. Gas in its raw form includes a number of hydrocarbon molecules; gas used in power plants and for residential heating is, in contrast, almost pure methane. Methane can make up anywhere from 70 to 98 percent of the gas produced from a particular well—raw gas composition varies from site to site. Not all gas wells are alike, and neither is the gas produced from the wells. It can exist in wells alone or mixed with oil and other liquid hydrocarbons. It can be found with *condensate*, a valuable hydrocarbon. It's a gas under pressure deep in the reservoir, but becomes a liquid when pressure drops near the surface—gas containing such condensate is known as *wet gas*. Condensate is sometimes called natural gasoline because it is so similar to gasoline in composition. Condensate is usually separated from the gas stream and sold to be mixed with crude oil. It usually trades at a price roughly equivalent to oil.

Raw natural gas usually includes several other compounds. Ethane, propane, and butane often naturally occur with methane. These are all hydrocarbons with unique properties; they are more valuable when removed from methane and sold separately. Together, condensate and these hydrocarbons are called natural gas liquids (NGLs).

There are also several impurities associated with natural gas. Some, like helium, nitrogen, and carbon dioxide, are relatively harmless but have to be separated before the gas enters a long-haul pipeline. Hydrogen sulphide is one of the more dangerous impurities. This highly poisonous and corrosive gas must be removed or it can corrode pipelines and even kill humans. Gas with high sulphur content is known as *sour gas*.

Gail's processing facilities perform the crucial step of removing and selling useful products from natural gas and disposing of harmful pollutants such as sulphur.

With its 87 trillion cubic feet of proven natural gas reserves, Australia is a key supplier of natural gas in Asia. Although Malaysia and Indonesia have higher proven reserves of gas, Australia has the advantage of being politically stable. The country has gone a long way toward investing in advanced energy infrastructure such as liquefied natural gas terminals and pipelines; it is among the best-placed nations in Asia to actually export growing quantities of gas into the rest of the region in the coming years.

Woodside Petroleum (US: WOPEY; Australia: WPL) is Australia's largest publicly traded oil and gas exploration and production company. It's also one of Australia's most aggressive energy concerns, making major investments to both increase proven reserves and develop LNG projects that are the key to exports into major Asian markets like China and India. Woodside is the operator and part owner of the North West Shelf LNG venture; it owns an equal stake in the venture with five other leading energy companies. This $14 billion project is Australia's largest LNG facility and is already a major exporter of gas for the nation. The facility is expected to keep getting larger. A $1.5 billion expansion planned for completion in 2008 will increase capacity at the facility by a third.

Woodside has been negotiating deals with both China and India to supply LNG. The North West Shelf LNG project will be the main supplier for a new LNG regasification facility in Shenzhen, China being built by CNOOC. Woodside, already a supplier of LNG to India, is also working with Gail and the Australian government to build and develop existing LNG infrastructure in India.

Consistently aggressive in expanding reserves, Woodside has set a goal of pumping out nearly twice as much oil and gas in 2008 as it did in 2004. New finds in drilling activity in Australia, the U.S., Libya, and Mauritania put the company well on its way toward that goal.

It's not just oil and gas that China and India need to fuel growth. Coal remains the key energy source across most of the region. In China, Yanzhou Coal Mining Company (NYSE: YZC) is a key supplier to the domestic market. Yanzhou has proven reserves of about two billion metric tons primarily in Eastern China. It's the best domestic China play on coal. For several years, Chinese demand for coal has far outstripped the capability of Chinese coal miners to expand production.

That's led to a general rise in prices since the late 1990s, good news for Yanzhou. Equally important is the company's reserve base and capability to hike production to meet demand and take advantage of higher prices. Yanzhou has made several acquisitions, mainly inside China, and it has also acquired some key high-grade reserves in Australia. These new reserves should help Yanzhou to better meet soaring Chinese demand.

The Integrated Players

Integrated oil companies offer a little bit of everything—refining capacity, exploration, production, and even retail sales of petroleum products. The best in the business are at the forefront of key trends in the energy markets, including LNG, deepwater exploration, and refining capacity.

ExxonMobil (NYSE:XOM) has been a solid company with great leadership for more than 90 years. Some argue that it is the best-run company on earth. Its current incarnation is the result of a 1999 merger; the company has come a long way since John D. Rockefeller formed the Standard Oil trust in 1882.

ExxonMobil has set the benchmark in its industry in terms of financial and operational performance. Its balance sheet is the best in the industry; its cash position greatly exceeds its outstanding debt, giving the company flexibility to make investments in new projects and technologies. It is expected to have ample cash flow from operations and asset sales, allowing it to comfortably meet its investment needs, increase dividends (it has done so for 21 consecutive years), and spend around $15 billion per year in share buybacks. After all this, the company will still have more cash than debt. ExxonMobil also has one of the best-integrated portfolios in the industry, and the largest reserve base among its peers (13.7 billion barrels of oil equivalent).

Despite its leadership status, and given the previously-mentioned bullish expectations for the energy markets, ExxonMobil has been trying to position itself for the future by developing new technologies and investing in new oil and gas projects around the world. It has developed "molecule management" technology to better deal with the lower quality of crude oil increasingly being pumped from the ground. Molecule management involves analyzing the differences in crude types and using that knowledge to increase margins. According to ExxonMobil's research, "Finding out how much nickel, vanadium and salt a certain crude type contains is essential for optimizing the product yield from a refinery." Given the importance of refining in the industry, the company is gaining a long-term advantage over its competition.

ExxonMobil is also focusing more on oil production in emerging markets, and slowly its U.S. and European upstream strongholds will decline in importance because of saturation in older fields. Some of the "new" places oil gains will come from include Angola, Chad, Nigeria, Azerbaijan, Kazakhstan, and Russia.

It is clear that ExxonMobil is moving forward to face the challenges of the future, and given its long-term success, there is no reason to doubt the outcome. Investors should be prepared for setbacks along the way, especially because of the increased exploration and production (E&P) exposure in emerging markets. These efforts are hamstrung to an extent because of the limits of production sharing agreements (PSAs), through which exploration companies and countries divide the proceeds from the oil. PSAs are becoming more and more important given that the majority of the new oil discovered is in emerging economies whose governments demand increasingly higher compensation.

Royal Dutch Shell (NYSE: RDS/A), one of the world's three super-major integrated oil and gas companies (along with ExxonMobil and BP Amoco), has strong global market share in exploration and production, refining and marketing, and chemicals. Since it announced a big reduction in the volume of its global proven oil and gas reserves back in 2004, very few people like Shell. Smart investors stepped in and bought when the stock was trading in the low 40s.

Shell is a turnaround story, one that, if it works out, can return the company to greatness while handsomely rewarding the farsighted investor. Shell today is like Chevron some years ago, and, given time, new management will be able to restore investors' confidence and revitalize operations and corporate structure. Nothing is certain, and the road will be long. Although the company is looking hard into ways to improve its oil operations, the biggest change will come from another part of the business—namely, gas and unconventional oil. Management is seriously contemplating an acquisition. Potential strategic candidates should include Canadian oil sands companies.

A company with a strong position in the LNG sector is another likely acquisition target for Shell. Shell is aggressively expanding the natural gas aspect of its business and aims to dominate the LNG market. The LNG market will be one of the most important energy sectors for years to come. Shell already has one of the largest fleets of purpose-built LNG tankers in the world and a first-class LNG spot trading desk.

Shell is also a leader in gas-to-liquids (GTL) technologies. GTL allows natural gas to be converted into extremely clean, low sulphur fuels. GTL is one way of using reserves of natural gas that are located too far from population centers to be transported by pipeline. And because natural gas derived liquids are so clean, they could well become important fuels of the future.

As the world scrambles to find the energy to grow, a handful of global energy companies stand to benefit. Companies with reserves of oil, natural gas, coal, and uranium will continue to see strong demand for their resources in coming decades. Although recent rises in oil and natural gas prices are well documented, this is only the beginning of a long-term trend. Barring a major and prolonged global recession, oil prices aren't likely to drop below $40 per barrel for the foreseeable future. Eventual oil price spikes to $100 or above are not out of the question given the extraordinary political risks that continue to develop in the oil market. The stronger pricing will benefit the best-placed companies.

Endnotes

1. BP Statistical Review of World Energy 2004.
2. BP Statistical Review of World Energy 2004, U.S. Census Bureau.
3. http://www.eia.doe.gov/oiaf/ieo/coal.html.
4. Department of Energy Information Administration 2004 reports (http://www.eia.doe.gov/oiaf/ieo/index.html).

9

THE LURE OF THE MEGA TREND

T he idea is almost too simple to embrace.

When developing economies need to build their infrastructure to developed world standards, they need a lot of basic materials, or commodities. If those developing economies are small, such needs will not move commodity prices. But as developing economies reach critical mass—as have the economies of China and India—they will exercise greater and greater influence on those prices. Commodity markets today bear the weight of the rapidly expanding Chinese economy, and an increasing number of developing economies will join this competition for resources in coming years.

The simplicity ends here.

The current commodity cycle offers no license to print money, despite bullish long-term fundamentals. China has been growing at breakneck pace for 25 years. Any economic slowdown or policy error in China (or the U.S., for that matter) can cause serious shakeouts in the commodities markets. Though prospects may be bright, the long term is comprised of many short terms—if one mishandles several short terms, it may be very difficult to achieve long-term success.

Why the *caveat emptor*? Not all commodities are created equal. Some commodities are highly economically sensitive. Hard commodities (like metals) are directly correlated to economic activity worldwide. Soft commodities (like certain foods and grains) are a totally different story; affected by crop size, population growth, and such, they are much less economically sensitive.

The last big bull market for metals and mining stocks in the 1970s featured pronounced U.S. dollar weakness. (This issue is also discussed in Chapters 5, "Straws in the Wind," and 6, "The Lost Guarantee.") A weak dollar on the shoulders of rising inflationary pressures was a boon for hard assets, of which metals are an integral part. Most emerging economies are also commodity producers, and they tend to get much higher prices for the particular commodities they export, as a falling U.S. dollar translates into higher dollar prices for their exports.[1]

Because most developing economies' (sometimes exorbitantly high) debt levels are denominated in U.S. dollars, a falling dollar actually creates a double bonus. Debt service costs fall as the local currencies rally, and revenues increase due to the rise in commodity prices. U.S. monetary policy is therefore very important as it affects inflationary pressures, the U.S. dollar, and U.S. interest rates, which serve as a benchmark for new issuance of emerging market bonds.[2] As the dollar's fundamental picture is, based on long-term trade policy, decidedly bearish, and the U.S. is characterized by an extreme lack of financial discipline on both the government and consumer level, the decline in the value of the dollar will continue, significant countertrend rallies notwithstanding.

The bull market in commodities that began in 1999 will be spectacular, possibly much bigger than the last run in the 1970s. But in the midst of the mega trend, there will be vicious corrections for which investors must be prepared. The metals side of the commodity equation would be the most leveraged, both on the upside and downside, in such a situation.

Metals comprise roughly one-third to one-quarter of the major commodity indexes. The Goldman Sachs Commodity International (GSCI) index is the exception: metals comprise only 12 percent (the index is weighted heavily in energy). The major index providers have tried to capture the most important commodities based on their own views of the market. The indexes can differ substantially in their long-term performance due to differences in number of components, weighting, and rebalancing systems.

The Rogers Raw Materials Index (RMI) is the broadest index with a fixed weighting system. Jim Rogers, the legendary hedge fund manager and cofounder of the Quantum fund along with George Soros, started the Rogers RMI. Though it is not widely followed, the Rogers RMI has breadth that many of the more notorious indexes lack. (Rogers competes in this arena with Goldman Sachs, Dow Jones, and Reuters. Index composition and historical performance data is available at www.rogersrawmaterials.com.)

Rogers RMI also has an index-tracking commodity fund that invests in the index via the futures market. Recommending futures funds is beyond the purpose of this book, although those interested should certainly consider the pros and cons of investing in such entities after completing their own due diligence.

Dr. Copper

Copper[3] has been known as "the metal with a Ph.D. in U.S. economics." Because it is so deeply rooted in all economic activity, weakness in copper's price signals a decelerating economy. The reverse is also true: Strength in copper signals economic growth. Investors, focused on the U.S. economy, became leery of copper's capability of the metal to forecast economic deceleration in the last couple of years, threatening its prestigious title. Such contemplation is irrelevant, as it appears copper "earned" a second doctorate in global economics. The metal is now a much better indicator of global economic activity, rather than simple U.S. domestic activity.

Man's fascination with copper dates back more than 10,000 years. The first pure copper artifacts were found in Asia Minor. Later on, copper made possible the Bronze Age, a period of remarkable progress when copper was first used in alloys to produce bronze.[4] Copper has remained popular in modern times due to its extremely high electrical conductivity (see Figure 9-1).[5]

2004 Industry Sector Copper Consumption

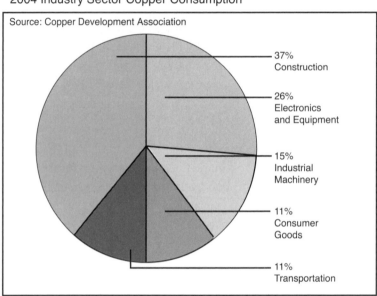

Figure 9-1 2004 industry sector copper consumption. (Source: Phelps Dodge, CDA, www.copper.org.)

China provides one of the best examples of how much copper a rapidly developing economy requires. In 1990, China imported 20,000 metric tons, but now it imports more than 1 million metric tons and is the world's largest consumer of copper. The U.S. consumption rate continues to grow at the fastest pace in the industrialized world, but Japanese and European consumption has been relatively stagnant.

One would assume that such demand would lead to elevated copper prices, and the per-pound rate has roughly doubled in the 2003-05 period. But on an inflation-adjusted basis, copper is trading near its lowest levels of the past 120 years—near its Great Depression lows.

Copper's price peaked at the equivalent of $5 per pound in today's dollars at the outset of the 20th century[6] (see Figure 9-2). As more and more economies reach critical mass and their copper consumption accelerates, $5 copper is conceivable in the not-too-distant future.

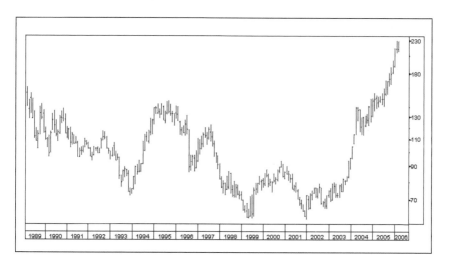

Figure 9-2 Copper futures in cents/pound. (Source: Bloomberg L.P.)

We are not against making leveraged investments in commodities with great long-term potential. We do think it is imprudent for individual investors to be heavily concentrated in such leveraged investments. The next correction (within the context of the current commodity mega trend) will shake out those overexposed investors just before the next leg up. When it comes to holding commodity stocks long term, individuals are always better off with lower volatility alternatives that increase the capability to survive inevitable corrections.

In commodities bull markets, secondary, lower quality stocks tend to have better returns because they see the biggest improvement as commodity prices rise,[7] but the key to long-term success is staying invested in the right stocks. Not too many investors have the stomach to sit though 60 percent to 70 percent selloffs. For every market leader like Nucor Steel (NYSE: NUE), there is a secondary producer like AK Steel (NYSE: AKS); for every market leader like Phelps Dodge (NYSE: PD), there is a Southern Peru Copper (NYSE: PCU). We've focused on the bigger, more established players in the metals markets, and have also diversified across a broad range of commodity stocks.

Anson Phelps and William Dodge founded Phelps Dodge in 1834 to export U.S. goods to England and to import copper, tin, and iron for the rapidly industrializing U.S. economy.[8] A good indicator of the pace of U.S. development at the time is the amount of rail tracks laid: nearly non-existent at the time Phelps Dodge was incorporated, this amount grew to more than 100,000 kilometers when Phelps Dodge entered the mining business in 1881.[9] Railroad length continued on a rapid growth path, along with the roaring U.S. economy, and did not peak until the first part of the 20th century; it then notably declined during the Great Depression.

In the last 20 years, Phelps Dodge has achieved vast geographic diversification throughout North and South America, and has also expanded into resource-rich parts of Africa and Asia. The company's reputation as an innovator in the field of copper mining helps it stay among the lower-cost producers in the world.

Phelps Dodge is an excellent candidate for a long-term holding given how depressed copper prices are in inflation-adjusted terms. The risk is that a global slowdown will depress copper process temporarily, but investors with five- and 10-year outlooks should consider buying on declines.

Nickel Is Worth More Than Five Cents

Nickel, compared to copper, is a relatively new player in human civilization.[10] For centuries, it was mischaracterized as a version of copper and also silver because of its color; the Chinese even called it *white copper* 3,500 years ago. Not until the 18th century did the metal actually get the name *nickel*. The U.S. 5-cent coin is made of a nickel alloy.

Nickel is almost never used in its purest form and its importance as a metal comes from its use in a number of alloys, primarily as a key ingredient of stainless steel. Nickel's versatility and capability to resist corrosion and maintain its mechanical and physical characteristics even under extreme conditions have made it very popular. A number of applications are critically dependent on nickel, including the engineering of jet engines and the processing equipment in the food, drink, oil, chemicals, and pharmaceutical industries (see Figure 9-3).

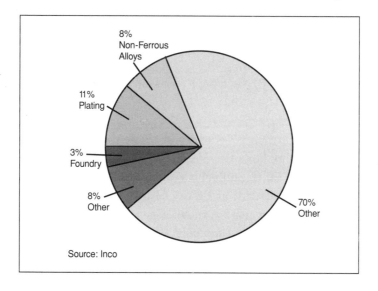

8%
Non-Ferrous
Alloys

11%
Plating

3%
Foundry

8%
Other

70%
Other

Source: Inco

Figure 9-3 2003 world nickel use. (Source: Inco.)

Canada-based Inco (NYSE: N) is the premier nickel producer in the West, accounting for about 20 percent of world production. Initially known as the International Nickel Company, Inco is now known by its popular acronym. The world's largest nickel deposit is located in the Sadsbury region of Ontario, Canada, where Inco started operations a century ago.

Inco's goals are to expand production near existing operations in Canada in a low-cost manner and to partner with other mining concerns worldwide to spread the financial burden of such less predictable and costly endeavors. The two primary expansion projects are in Voisey's Bay, Newfoundland, and Goro, New Caledonia.[11] Those two development projects have the potential to expand Inco's production by 40 percent.

Though it advanced substantially from 2002 to 2005, despite skyrocketing metals demand, Inco stock is selling at mid-90s prices. Due to heavy usage by the steel industry, nickel is heavily cyclical. It's considered an "early cycle" metal, much like copper, with prices rising at the very beginning of the economic cycle before many other metals feel increased demand. The dynamic is also true on the downside: Nickel prices tend to fall before other metals experience decelerating demand.

Buy High, Sell Low... When It Comes to Steel P/Es

A big dilemma for many investors is whether to own steel stocks in a long-term portfolio. For many years, the U.S. steel industry has been plagued by inefficient technology, oversupply, and bankruptcies. Just as oversupply was dealt with using the various (and sometimes crude) mechanisms of the free market, the industry caught the triple whammy of a steel tariff,[12] increased demand from emerging markets (led by China), and economic growth in all major industrialized nations, a confluence of events not seen in 30 years (see Figure 9-4.)

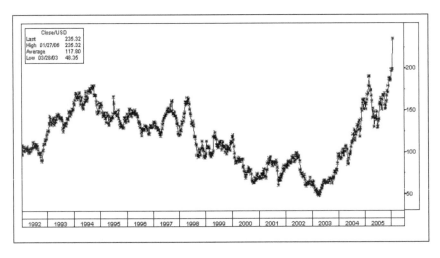

Figure 9-4 Dow Jones U.S. total market steel index. (Source: Bloomberg L.P.)

Steel stocks ran and ran and ran from 2002 lows. Just as other commodity stocks coming off a major bottom, the worse shape the company was in, the higher its stock went. Lower-quality steel stocks increased more than five-fold in some cases, whereas higher quality stocks doubled and tripled.

One rule of thumb when buying commodity stocks—be they steel producers, nickel or copper mines, or any other kind—is to buy them when they look expensive and sell them when they look cheap.

Let us elaborate.

When commodity prices are depressed, commodity stocks have little in the way of earnings. Their P/E ratios (the most popular, but overhyped and sometimes misused, measure of stock value) are very high because of that lack of earnings. This is where the stocks sit at the bottom of the cycle: expensive and hated.

On the other hand, near the top, their earnings have skyrocketed due to the operational leverage of their profit-and-loss statements, their P/E ratios are low, and the stocks are cheap. Investors see nothing but blue skies, forgetting that economies go through cycles. We never bought the idea of a "New Economy"[13] void of cycles. Steel stocks as a group *always* suffer vicious selloffs when the economic cycle peaks. This should help you remember to sell when you have big gains on a steel stock.

One U.S. steel company with a great history of sector outperformance is Nucor (NYSE: NUE). The company traces its roots to the founder of Oldsmobile and experienced many transformations becoming the biggest steel producer in the U.S.[14] Nucor had its problems in the 1960s, but it learned from them and invested heavily in low-cost steel technologies, which allowed it to make money while so many of its archrivals went bankrupt in the 1990s.

Asian steel producers are much closer to the center of the most promising economic region in the world economy today. A standout is Korea-based POSCO (NYSE: PKX); its present name is the acronym for Pohang Iron and Steel, the original name of the company.

POSCO's operations cover the majority of main steel products. But it is also one of the world's most advanced producers, specializing in high-value products like hot-rolled and cold-rolled steel, plates, wire rods, silicon steel sheets, and stainless steel. The value is in the company's cost effectiveness and leverage to the economic development of both India and China. In 2005, POSCO signed a contract for the biggest (not only in the company's history, but also in the history of South Korea) integrated steel production facility to be built in the economically underdeveloped but resource-rich Indian state of Orissa.[15] Although a slowdown in the global economy will undoubtedly affect a global player like POSCO, the inroads the company has made in China and India—as well as its exposure to more profitable higher-end steel products—make it a prime long-term portfolio holding.

Another interesting company is India-based Tata Iron and Steel (India: TISCO). Because the Indian economy is the most domestically oriented in Asia, global economic cycles tend to have a lesser effect on domestic producers. India lags China in infrastructure development, but is likely to catch up fast. Indian steel producers targeting the local economy stand to benefit.

Trying to pick a stock investment in every industrial metal is an exercise in futility; it can be done, but in the end one will end up with too many mining shares for most individual investors' portfolio size. Investors should pay attention to two mining conglomerates that cover a wide spectrum of industrial metals and energy: BHP Billiton (NYSE: BHP) and Rio Tinto (NYSE: RTP).

Every major specialized mining conglomerate like Phelps Dodge or Inco has operations in other metals, most of them due to residual products left from the mining of their primary specialty products. But there is no match in the industrialized world for diversified mining conglomerates like BHP Billiton (see Figure 9-5) and Rio Tinto. The two companies differ enough that they make great choices for coincident exposure to a wide array of industrial metals and energy.

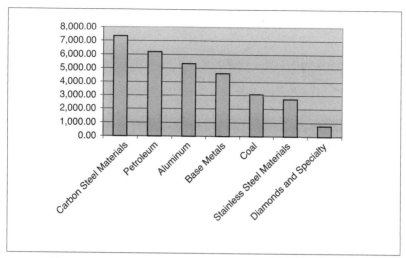

Figure 9-5 BHP: Sum of the parts. (Source: BHP Billiton.)

BHP Billiton is the result of the 1997 merger of UK-based Billiton PLC and Australia's Broken Hill Proprietary. The Billiton side of the company had primarily diversified mining operations, whereas the BHP side had, in addition to the metals, large exposure to oils, natural gas, and coal. BHP Billiton is dual-listed in London and Sydney, with the two companies operating as separate entities but with identical boards of directors and a unified management team. Shareholders in each company have equivalent economic and voting rights in the BHP Billiton Group as a whole. Investors who buy BHP through the NYSE-listed American Depositary Receipt circumvent the complexity of dual shareholding.

Rio Tinto is about half the size of BHP, and it does not have any meaningful oil exposure. For investors already heavily overweight in energy stocks, Rio Tinto may be the better choice. To diversify company-specific risk and gain broad exposure in the metals and mining space, both stocks are recommended. Increased crude oil exposure would only help future performance.

The Fund

One of the best funds in the natural resource arena is RS Global Natural Resources (RSNRX), managed by Andrew Pilara. The fund invests in a diversified basket of commodity producers, with a preference in the energy area. RS Natural Resources invests on a global basis, limiting country risk in the process.

Andrew Pilara has an excellent track record in both good and bad times for commodities, based on his longer-term horizon and good instincts as to when to take on more risk and when to be defensive. Because the commodity bull market over the next decade will have plenty of corrections, a fund with a proven track record of playing defense is the best choice. The fund underperformed other commodity funds in the Asian Crisis years due to heavy oil exposure.

It's likely that RS Global Natural Resources will be more volatile than the average diversified stock fund, but as part of a longer-term portfolio, it's a great way to ride the multiyear bull market in commodities and commodity stocks. In other words, the potential reward is well worth the risk, especially if you're planning to hold the fund for five years or more.

The historical comparisons used throughout this book are important as they aim to illustrate a larger point. The century of rapid U.S. economic development that ended in the 1930s featured many financial and political crises, but the economy continued its rapid pace of development despite the crude interruptions.

There will be many similar shakeouts in this 21st century mega trend, some of them undoubtedly a lot larger than others. For investors who follow a lower volatility approach, there will always be opportunities to pick commodity investments on the cheap—investments that rise from the ashes and continue their remarkable performance until the mega trend runs out.

Endnotes

1. Unless their local currencies appreciate much more than the dollar falls and actually result in lower commodity prices in the local currency. That unfortunate event happened for many South African commodity producers (not only gold mines) when they saw the rand/dollar exchange rate (also quoted, ZAR/USD) go from nearly 14 to the dollar in late 2001 to under 6 in late 2004. A similar, but not as egregious, development occurred with the Brazilian real, which went from 4 to the dollar in 2002 to the low 2 level in early 2005.

2. Emerging market bonds are priced at premium over comparable maturity U.S. Treasury bonds, called a spread. As U.S. interests rise or fall, new emerging market bonds are priced accordingly with the appropriate spread over U.S. Treasuries. In long economic expansion, spreads tend to fall, reflecting the lower risk to hold emerging market bonds. In early 2005, some emerging economies saw their spreads at record low levels, reflecting their substantially improved economic conditions.

3. The word *copper* traces its origin to the Roman Empire as the metal was called *aes Cyprium* because so much of it was mined on the island of Cyprus. Later, the term was simplified to *cuprum*. Copper is a chemical element on Mendeleev's periodic table: symbol Cu, number 29.

4. Bronze is the accepted term for a broad range of alloys of copper, which usually include zinc, tin, and other metals.

5. Under normal room temperature, only silver has higher electrical conductivity, but it is prohibitively expensive.

6. Svedberg, Peter and John E. Tilton. Using indexing from "The Real Real Price Of Nonrenewable Resources: Copper 1870-2000," Institute for International Economic Studies, Stockholm University.

7. This was illustrated with an example in Chapter 6; when high cost gold producers have bigger improvement in the bottom line, they outperform low-cost mines in a rising gold environment.

8. Before China, the previous wildly successful emerging market of proportional magnitude was the United States; Europe was the world's primary developed market.

9. The country's first railroad was 13 miles long in the state of Maryland and began operations in 1830.

10. First uses date back to 3500 B.C. Nickel is a chemical element from Mendeleev's periodic table: symbol Ni, number 28.

11. A French overseas territory.

12. President G.W. Bush imposed a steel tariff of 8 to 30 percent on imported steel in early 2002, which was later lifted on December 8, 2003.

13. New Economy was a term coined in the bubble years to describe the TMT (telecom, media, technology) stocks. A colleague found a baseball hat with "Old Economy" on it and wore it the last days of the bubble as his conservative non-TMT stocks languished and the Nasdaq soared to 5132. He still has that hat with his "Old Economy" stocks at all-time highs while the Nasdaq is down 70 percent.

---

14. Oldsmobile was a prestigious heritage 30 years ago, but the brand is now being phased out by General Motors.
15. Orissa is one of the poorest, but most resource rich states in India. It is also likely to be an arena of concentrated foreign direct investment over the next several decades due to its proximity to the most economically vibrant regions of Asia.

10

ASIA'S EVOLVING ECONOMIES

A rapidly growing and expanding Asian middle class will start to demand many of the same goods and services as their counterparts in developed western economies: This is the idea tying together the geopolitical, economic, and financial issues discussed throughout this book.

Although general economic growth bolsters investment themes identified in previous chapters, the following trends will be the icing on the cake. If the actual outcome approximates our assessment of Asia's economic prospects, the sectors and companies detailed in this chapter will offer investment returns of a lifetime. These specific ideas spring from the continuing integration of Asia's economies into the global financial system.

Asia's enormous middle class will be the largest group of consumers to ever be integrated into the world economy. The experience of the U.S. and Europe in the early 20th century provides a guide showing which industries thrived as consumers became wealthier. Asia's rise will produce an even more dramatic effect.

This growing consumer base will require increasingly advanced financial services—banking services, credit cards, and mortgage loans—to manage growing incomes. Consumers will also want to spend their newfound, hard-earned wealth on clothes, eating out, holidays, and entertainment. The financial and leisure industries in Asia will see tremendous growth in coming years, just as they did in the U.S. and Europe.

Travel and Tourism

One of the most obvious manifestations of a growing economy is growing travel by air, land, or sea. The United States has seen tremendous growth in travel over the past 50 years as measured by *passenger enplanements* (see Figure 10-1).

Passenger enplanements are defined as a single passenger boarding a plane in the U.S., whether that plane is destined to travel domestically or overseas. The data is collected and reported quarterly by the U.S. Bureau of Transportation. As Figure 10-1 shows, passenger enplanements in the U.S. stood at barely 35 million in 1954, but jumped to more than 640 million by 2003, a near 20-fold increase.

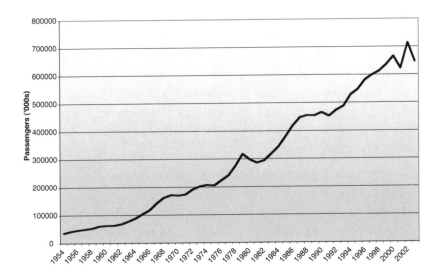

Figure 10-1 U.S. passenger enplanements. (Source: U.S. Bureau of Transportation statistics.)

Enplanements are only one part of the travel story. All those travelers need a place to stay and that means hotels—the stock of hotel rooms in the U.S. has increased dramatically in recent decades, including low-cost hotels as well as more luxurious properties.

A similar pattern is already emerging in Asia. Prior to 1991, India's passenger airline industry was small and tightly regulated; almost all passenger air travel was on expensive, state-owned airliners. But a 1991 economic liberalization plan changed that, opening up the market to low-cost carriers. New budget carriers are springing up across India and consumers who would have been unable to afford the high ticket prices of the pre-1991 era are now traveling.[1] The government is now expanding the domestic air infrastructure by modernizing existing airports, allowing an increase in the number of flights and the use of larger planes.

According to government statistics, the Indian passenger airline market stood at 15 million passengers in 2004, a relatively small number when you consider the sheer size of the population. But the market is growing at about 25 percent annually and is expected to include more than 50 million passengers by the end of the decade.

Chinese travel is also booming. Tourism has actually been limited more by government regulation than economic circumstances in recent years. Hong Kong opened up to Chinese tourists only in the late 1990s with a quota system. In July 1998, that quota was set at 1,142 people per day and all Chinese tourists had to travel in groups. Hong Kong has gradually liberalized those travel restrictions, and now allows individual travel. Chinese visitors to Hong Kong now make up more than 50 percent of the tourist trade—total Chinese visitors jumped from 4.4 million in 2001 to more than 12 million in 2004.[2] Hong Kong's airport handled a total of 34 million passengers in 2004 alone.

There are two primary ways to play the travel trend: the airlines that carry all these new passengers and the hotels with large exposure to these markets.

The big, full-cost U.S. airlines haven't been consistently profitable for years, but the low-cost U.S. carriers like Southwest Airlines have fared much better. Several airlines in the Southwest mold are springing up all over Asia to take advantage of a rapidly growing market.

The best play on the Asian airline business is India-based Jet Airways (India: JET). Naresh Goyal, a former travel agent, founded the company in 1993 with just a few flights. Jet has now grown into India's largest airline with a domestic market share of more than 45 percent, about 50 planes, and close to 2,000 weekly flights both within India and to key foreign markets such as London and Singapore.

In early 2005, Jet became the first of the low-cost carriers to go public. Up to a dozen low-cost carriers will begin offering flights over the next few years. That competition, however, will likely prove a boon to the industry. Falling prices are already accelerating growth in the industry as more Indians conclude they can afford to travel. Competition will simply fuel growth for the industry at large.

The Intercontinental Hotel Group (London: IHG, NYSE: IHG) is the world's largest hotel chain (as measured by number of rooms). Intercontinental has a total of 3,500 hotel properties with more than half a million rooms located in 100 countries around the world. Its flagship brand is InterContinental, a chain of luxury properties, but some investors may be more familiar with Crowne Plaza and Holiday Inn, brands far more common worldwide.

Intercontinental, with a total of more than 40,000 rooms, also has the largest presence in Asia of any major international hotel chain. It's also expanding more rapidly in the region than in any other part of the world. In China, where it has operated for more than 20 years, Intercontinental is planning to more than double the number of hotels it operates or manages from 42 in 2004 to more than 100 over the next few years.

Intercontinental covers all aspects of the Asian market, from luxury properties (such as the InterContinental Hotel in Beijing) to budget hotels (the group introduced the Holiday Inn Express brand to Asia in 2004). This mix caters to all aspects of the hotel market, business travelers and tourists alike.

Hong Kong's Shangri La Asia (Hong Kong: 69, OTC: SHALY) focuses more on the luxury segment of the hotel market. Shangri La owns and manages 36 hotels with a total of about 18,000 rooms and plans to open another 7,000 rooms in 16 hotels between 2006 and 2008. In addition, Shangri La collects royalty fees from an additional eight hotels with nearly 2,500 rooms that it manages.

Shangri La focuses on the promising Hong Kong and mainland China markets. Hong Kong's airport remains one of the busiest in the world and the flow of visitors from China continues to increase. The domestic China market is growing even more rapidly. In addition to those core markets, Shangri La has hotels in Singapore, Malaysia, The Philippines, Thailand, and Indonesia.

Indian Hotels Limited (India: IH), famous for its Taj chain of luxury hotels, is the largest hotel chain in India; holdings include 62 hotels with more than 8,000 rooms located both in and outside of India. Indian Hotels has benefited from a surge in domestic as well as foreign tourism to leisure and resort destinations such as Goa, Kerala, and Rajasthan. Taj brand boasts a market-leading position. The rapid growth in domestic travel is an even more encouraging sign. Taj is popular with domestic tourists, as is IndiOne, a budget chain rolled out in 2004.

India's budget hotel market remains largely unconsolidated. A big company like Indian Hotels is well positioned to enter the market and grab a considerable market share by offering standardized rooms and a centralized reservation system. Indian Hotels is already making plans to expand more aggressively into this market.

The Necessities

For most consumers in Western Europe or North America, products like chewing gum, soft drinks, and bottled water are common household items. As we explained in Chapter 7, "The New Agricultural Revolution," consumption of packaged and prepared foods and beverages has tended to rise over time as consumers became wealthier—consumers in developed markets spend far more on such items compared to consumers in emerging markets.

Staple products have a reputation for slow and reliable growth in the western world. Soft drinks and household cleansers see steady, reliable demand growth regardless of how poorly the economy is performing. But the market for these items is saturated, so growth is slow. In short, consumer staples are the ultimate defensive group.

The same is true, to some extent, of fast food restaurants. The amount that Americans spend on eating food outside the home has dramatically increased in recent decades (see Figure 10-2). Across Europe and the U.S., brands like McDonald's, KFC, and Pizza Hut are ubiquitous. These chains all exhibit modest, reliable growth in the developed world.

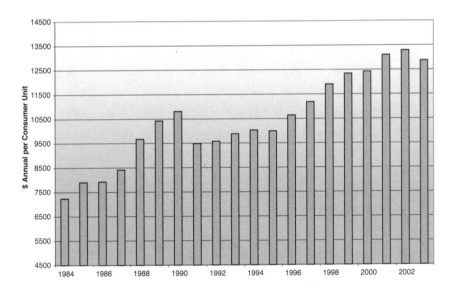

Figure 10-2 Food dollars spent away from home. (Source: U.S. Bureau of Labor Statistics Consumer Expenditure Survey.)

Asia is an altogether different story: Revenue growth in consumer staples reaches well into the double-digits annually in these markets, versus just 1 to 5 percent in the developed world. Coca-Cola, for example, reported sales growth of more than 20 percent in China for 2004 against just 2 percent sales growth worldwide. Restaurant chains with a significant Asian presence (including McDonald's and Yum! Brands) rely upon the region for most of their growth.

Consumer products and staples are one industry where western brands hold a huge advantage over their local domestic counterparts. Global consumer tastes tend to converge as consumers reach equivalent levels of wealth. Thus, local foods and tastes, although important, can give way to global food styles and brands.

Western brands also hold two other major advantages: branding and distribution. Large western companies have the scope to enter Asia with multibillion-dollar advertising budgets; such massive nationwide advertising would be impossible for the majority of local players. Some of the leading global brands have been advertising in markets like China and India for decades. The best global brands tend to attract considerable loyalty in China and India even if they cost more than equivalent local brands. Young Asian consumers also regard western brands as status symbols. While eating at a KFC might not be anything out of the ordinary in the U.S. or Europe, it's a popular chain among younger, upwardly mobile Chinese consumers and their children.

Distribution is another key. Established foreign firms have the scope to set up large distribution centers in markets like China and India. In so doing, they can achieve economies of scale and offer lower-cost sourcing for goods, a huge price advantage in markets that remain rather price sensitive.

Yum! Brands (NYSE: YUM) spun off from Pepsi in the 1990s and is the parent company of five major restaurant chains: Taco Bell, KFC, Pizza Hut, Long John Silver's, and A&W All American Food. Its two key brands in Asia are Pizza Hut and KFC.

China is Yum!'s top growth story right now; it's been operating in this market for more than a decade and has more than 1,250 KFC locations and close to 200 Pizza Hut restaurants. This makes KFC by far the largest fast food restaurant in China with more than twice as many locations as McDonald's, its nearest competitor. Pizza Hut is the market's largest casual dining chain as most such chains in China are one-offs or small local chains. No other major casual dining chain has entered this market.

Yum!'s China-based restaurants generate well over $1 billion in annual revenues and $200 million in operating profits; revenues have been growing at about 20 percent annualized. Yum!'s operations in China are so important that it has separated them into a unique China division that is treated as an operating unit distinct from the rest of the company's international operations.

One of Yum!'s most valuable assets is its distribution chain, painstakingly set up when the company was still part of Pepsi. Yum! distributes its own products and does not rely on third-party players. This large supply chain benefits from significant economies of scale and allows the company to source goods at a fraction of the cost local one-off restaurants pay, one of the key reasons Yum! is capable of out-competing local players.

Beyond China, Yum! has made India a key target market for the future. It already has more than 100 Pizza Hut locations and a handful of KFC restaurants there, and has even developed a KFC menu to cater to India's one-third vegetarian population. Rapid expansion here is facilitated by a franchise system—Yum! plans to open as many as 40 new restaurants each year for the next five years. The benefit of the franchise system is that the operators bear most of the costs associated with starting and running the restaurant. In exchange, Yum! gets a solid, stable royalty stream from new restaurants.

Although McDonald's (NYSE: MCD) is a little behind Yum! in terms of sheer number of locations, the fast-food giant has a stellar brand name and is the number two player in both India (50 locations) and China (more than 600 locations).

McDonald's is benefiting from many of the same factors as Yum! in its key Asian markets. About three-quarters of the company's locations in the Asia-Pacific region are franchised, including the vast majority of its locations in China. This lowers expansion costs and offers the stability of royalties. Because of McDonald's size and global scope, it can better manage supply-chain costs.

McDonald's has been particularly innovative in India. Beef burgers sold in most parts of the world clearly weren't a go in India, where cows are sacred for much of the population. The company created the McCurry

Pan and McAloo Tikka to cater to local tastes. As a result of these innovations, Indian outlets are among its most profitable anywhere in the world, serving an average of 3,000 consumers per day.[3]

On the consumer goods front, chewing gum and confectionary products will become every bit as common and popular in Asia as they are in the West. William Wrigley Jr. Co. (NYSE: WWY) is the world's dominant producer and marketer of chewing gum with more than $3 billion in annual sales, worth nearly half the global market.

Wrigley's, generating 61 percent of its revenue from outside the U.S., is a truly multinational company. The company boasts one of the best high-growth, emerging-markets portfolios. In China, the average consumer chews around 15 to 20 sticks of gum annually—compared to 180 sticks in the U.S.[4] As incomes in China rise and consumption catches up to U.S. levels, companies with the best brand names will enjoy tremendous growth.

Wrigley's has been expanding its presence both organically and via acquisitions. In 2004, Wrigley paid $260 million for the businesses of Joyco Group, a subsidiary of the Spanish food conglomerate Agrolimen. Joyco is a manufacturer of gum products and other candies. Wrigley's paid just over 1 times Joyco's sales, a bargain price given the fact that Joyco has a lot of leading brands in some of the largest and hottest markets in the world. This acquisition has made Wrigley's the number-two player in India and number one in China (almost 60 percent market share).

Innovation and an aggressive push of new products have allowed Wrigley's to offer a balanced portfolio with excellent revenue, earnings, and cash flow growth.

Just as with Yum! and McDonald's, Wrigley's has been able to keep its costs down through more effective sourcing. The company manufactures gum in a dozen countries around the world, and also produces its own flavorings and ingredients. Wrigley's is in good shape to keep costs down because it doesn't rely on third-party suppliers.

Another Western player with a strong global brand is Nestle (OTC: NSRGY), the largest food company on Earth. Most consumers are familiar with the company's iconic brands: Perrier water, Nescafe coffee, Nestea teas, Friskies and Purina pet foods, and, of course, the company's chocolate business, consisting mainly of products sold under the Nestle brand.

For the most part, changes in food consumption can be traced to changes in income levels, but there are some exceptions. One is India and sweets: Indian consumers seem to have a sweet tooth and consume far more sugar than other countries with an equivalent GDP per capita (see Figure 10-3).

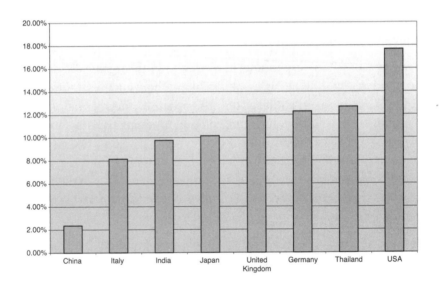

Figure 10-3 Sugars and sweeteners as percent of total calories. (Source: FAOSTAT)

This data from the United Nations compares the number of calories consumed each day by consumers in different markets. Roughly 10 percent of the calories consumed by the average Indian consumer come from sweets and sweeteners. That compares to less than 2.5 percent of the Chinese diet devoted to sweets. Indian sweet consumption is more on a par with Western Europe, though it's still far behind U.S. levels.

It's also likely that China will eventually catch up to levels seen in other Asian countries such as India, Japan, and Thailand as Chinese income rises. The Indian sweet tooth coupled with an opportunity for major consumption growth in China means that Nestle's sugar and confectionary business looks like a long-term winner.

The other likely long-term winner for Nestle in the region is bottled water. Bottled water comprises nearly 40 percent of China's total beverage market compared to just 21 percent for carbonated soft drinks.[5] Nestle's Perrier and San Pellegrino brands are already sold in China. Nestle derives only about 2 percent of its sales there, but those sales are growing at a more than double-digit pace.

Nestle also boasts solid market positions for its core brands in India and has the flexibility to build new brands or change existing brands to fit local tastes. It also has a liquid milk business in India that is expected to be a fast grower.

Although smoking bans and aggressive antismoking advertising have cut down growth across the western world, smoking is still very popular in Asia.

London-based British American Tobacco (BAT) (AMEX: BTI) is behind popular overseas brands Lucky Strike, Dunhill, and Kool. The company produces more than 300 different brands of cigarettes in factories located in 60 countries. BAT currently garners roughly 15 percent of its revenues from the Asia-Pacific region, but that share has been growing in recent quarters. The company's Dunhill brand has a particularly strong position in China and India.

Retail

The consumer's influence is finally reaching critical mass in most of Asia.

Most investors are aware that the American consumer accounts for roughly two-thirds of the U.S. economy. In Asia, however, economic performance has traditionally been based on exporting goods to foreign consumers.

That's changing rapidly. As incomes continue to rise in the region, Asia will develop a culture of consumerism similar to what exists in the western world. Internal consumption is a more stable means of growing an economy than relying on external demand.

In 2004, China's total retail sales were approximately $625 billion, compared to roughly $3.7 trillion in the U.S. In that light, China's retail sales may still seem small, but this represents major growth over the past decade. Ten years ago, U.S. retail sales were more than 10 times Chinese sales.

Traditionally, China's retail sector has been made up of smaller, localized shops and markets. But hypermarts that include a supermarket and a department store rolled into one are growing in popularity. The concept of the big-box discount store (a la Wal-Mart) is spreading.

Traditional western luxury brands (mainly from Europe) have made big inroads into the Chinese market. Contrary to what many investors would expect, China is a huge market for luxury brands despite its still low per capita GDP. Although it accounts for only 4.4 percent of global GDP, China's sales of most luxury-brand goods is more than 10 percent of the global market.

There are two reasons for this. First, Chinese consumers want to obtain western luxury goods to enhance their social image. Second, even though the income disparity is huge and the rich represent a tiny proportion of the total population, there are still enormous raw numbers of wealthy Chinese more than capable of affording luxury merchandise.

Asia's retail space will change dramatically due to the rise of women as key consumers in what is traditionally a male-dominated region. There is a growing population of young, middle-class women in Asian cities, and the spending power of women in general is on the rise in India and China. Asian women are increasingly buying similar items as their western counterparts. Perhaps the most promising segment is cosmetics.

This growth potential has not gone unnoticed at the world's largest retailer, Wal-Mart (NYSE: WMT). Wal-Mart entered the Chinese market in 1996 with a single SuperCenter and Sam's Club location as part of a joint venture with a local company. By 2005, the company had 45 locations, including 40 SuperCenters, three Sam's Clubs, and two small-format Neighborhood Market locations. Wal-Mart is also expanding its footprint in China to enhance its supply chain.

According to the *China Daily*, if Wal-Mart were a separate country, it would be China's eighth-largest trading partner, ahead of Canada and Australia. The company has been expanding its warehouse and supply chain to feed a growing stock of local stores and facilitate the export of Chinese goods to foreign markets.

The other discounter to really tackle the Chinese market is France's Carrefour (Paris: CA; OTC: CRERF), a hypermarket retailer. Carrefour first entered the Asian market in the late 1980s, making it the first western hypermarket retailer to meaningfully expand into the region. Carrefour now operates in eight Asian countries.

Asia is also the company's strongest growth market. About half of all of Carrefour's new store openings are in the region, a testament to the fact that management is concentrating resources on rapid expansion of its operations there.

Carrefour is the largest foreign retailer and the fourth-largest retailer overall in China with more than 200 stores of various formats and scores of new stores scheduled to open over the next few years. The company takes care to adapt its store format to this fast-growing market. Chinese hypermarkets tend to be smaller than in Europe so Carrefour has downsized its stores slightly. The company has increased stocks of vegetables and fresh seafood because Chinese shoppers prefer to see plenty of these items in their stores.

On the luxury goods front, European brands are the key. Switzerland-based Compagnie Financiere Richemont (Geneva: CFR; OTC: RCHMY) owns some of Europe's most venerable luxury-brand names, including Cartier jewelry and watches and Montblanc pens and accessories. The company started a Chinese luxury clothing line, Shanghai Tang, in the mid-90s. The company sells its brands through a network of about 250 retailers. Of those, 60 are brand-specific shops and many of these are for the Cartier brand, the first of Richemont's brands to move into the Chinese market. The company also sells through department stores and other retail outlets. Excluding Japan, mainland China was the company's fifth largest Asian market in 2002, and is soon expected to be the company's second largest behind Hong Kong.

Avon Products (NYSE: AVP) has two main competitive advantages in Asia, its leading brand and its direct sales channel. Avon's brands are second only to L'Oreal's Maybelline in use and recognition in China. And this is a very attractive market in which to have such a competitive position. Less than a fifth of Chinese women use cosmetics at least once a week, compared to about 60 percent of American women. But in households with higher than average incomes, the number is more than 40 percent. This suggests that as Chinese consumers become wealthier, cosmetics-use trends will approximate U.S. averages.[6] Already, the market for cosmetics is growing at around 12 percent annually in China, far above levels seen in more developed nations.

What's even more interesting about Avon is its sales channel. Companies like L'Oreal rely on department stores or other types of retail outlets to sell their products. Avon actually recruits sales agents— women willing to take products to other women and sell to them directly. The Chinese government approved Avon to sell cosmetics in this way in early 2005, the first western company allowed to pioneer a direct sales channel in China. This model will work well in China. About half of Chinese women surveyed by Morgan Stanley indicated an interest in becoming an Avon sales representative.[7] In addition, Avon's direct selling approach will make it easier for the brand to be sold in rural or second-tier cities where retailers selling cosmetics are less common.

Banking and Finance

Credit cards, mortgages, and checking accounts are common services in most western countries. But in parts of Asia, credit, financial, and banking services are relatively new, and much of the population still doesn't have access to these services.

As Asian income levels rise, consumers will need a place to invest their savings and a convenient means of accessing cash. Mortgages and other forms of lending will also make home ownership, automobiles, and other high-ticket consumer goods affordable.

India is our favorite market in Asia when it comes to banking and finance. Although both India and China have seen strong growth in lending and financial services in recent years, that growth is far more sustainable in India. The Indian banking industry is in far better shape than China's. Although China is still a relatively poor country with a GDP of about $1.65 trillion as of 2004, the country's banking industry is actually quite mature. Total loans outstanding in China stand at more than $2.28 trillion, and the country's loan to GDP ratio (total loans outstanding in the economy divided by GDP) stands at nearly 140 percent. That's equivalent to, or higher than, virtually every other economy in Asia, including Korea, Taiwan, Singapore, and Australia.

India's GDP is smaller, less than half of China's at just $649 billion in 2004. But the country had total loans of just $221 billion outstanding in 2004; India's loan to GDP ratio is just 35 percent, a tiny fraction of China's. In other words, China's economy on a per capita basis is a little more than twice the size of India's, but the loans outstanding in the economy are 10 times that of India. India should see substantial growth in GDP and loan penetration as it plays "catch-up" to China.

In 2004, India's banking sector reported a nonperforming loan (NPL) ratio of just 7 percent against close to 13 percent for China. In both countries, bad loans have been falling; in India, this has been due more to growth and prudent management, whereas in China, it's more a matter of government-led bailouts. India has also agreed to adopt the internationally recognized Basel II accounting standard[8] for capital adequacy by the end of 2007.

Robust economic growth and a rising middle class will fuel strong lending growth in both China and India. India is likely to see the faster growth, however. We can divide the plays on growth in Asia's financial services business into two camps: local players with strong positions and foreign companies with scope to expand locally.

HDFC Bank (NYSE: HDB), with more than 300 local branches, offers loan, deposit, investment, and other financial services to both individuals and corporate clients in India. Thanks to strong economic growth in India, HDFC Bank has also been one of Asia's fastest growing banks for years. The company has expanded rapidly into retail lending, including automobile loans and credit and debit cards. The bank already has issued about 350,000 credit cards, mainly to its existing banking customers.

And although the bank's sale of mortgages has been growing strong, there is still plenty of room for HDFC Bank to continue growing as the bank holds only a 3 percent share of India's loan market. The Indian financial services landscape is highly fragmented, leaving room for an ultra-efficient competitor like HDFC Bank to expand via acquisitions.

In addition to growth prospects, HDFC Bank is a well-run, high-quality banking franchise. The company has maintained a focus on credit quality while enjoying strong growth; NPLs fell below 2 percent of loans in 2005, a very low ratio even by western standards.

State Bank of India (Mumbai: SBIN) is the country's largest bank with nearly 10,000 domestic branches and another 60 outside the nation. The company has more than 90 million customers and a total domestic market share of about 25 percent. The company offers personal loans, business loans, and deposit and savings services.

The State Bank of India (as its name implies) was once wholly owned by the Indian government, but was partially privatized and deregulated in the 1990s. One legacy of the Bank's 200-year history as a government body includes handling more than half of all government transactions. It also maintains a strong foothold in all corners of India and has close relationships with most of India's largest corporations.

The largest component of the company's retail loan book is housing loans, a very fast-growing business line. Growth will also come from the company's credit and debit card portfolio, which is by far the largest in India with more than 12 million cards outstanding. Meanwhile, NPLs below 3 percent is very solid.

Outside the banking business, Max India (Mumbai: MAXI) offers life and health insurance products to Indian consumers and businesses through a network of hospitals and doctors offices around the country. A growing cadre of middle class Indians can afford access to the best medical care and want health and life insurance plans to protect them.

The company's life insurance plans are offered as part of a deal with New York Life. New York Life is one of the globe's largest life insurance companies while Max understands the Indian market and can distribute the policies to its existing customer base.

American Express (NYSE: AXP) and Britain's HSBC Bank (NYSE: HBC) are two of the strongest foreign players in Asia. American Express is best known for its iconic credit cards, but the company's business includes travel services, foreign exchange, payment processing, and investment products for retail and institutional clients. Many of the company's services and products will eventually find a market in Asia. American Express' strongest opportunity in the intermediate term is to further expand its credit and payment card business. To that end, American Express signed a deal with China's largest bank, the Industrial and Commercial Bank (ICBC), to issue cards in that nation. With more than 20,000 branches in China, ICBC offers an excellent shot for American Express to distribute its cards.

In India, American Express has signed up for several co-branded cards, including an Indian Airlines card and a card co-issued with Tata Finance Corporation.

American Express also offers the advantage of its own payment-processing network. Unlike Visa or MasterCard, Amex processes its own credit and debit card transactions over its own network, allowing the company to see both the buy and sell side of the transaction. This helps it collect data on card users and target marketing campaigns and new products accordingly.

HSBC is Britain's largest bank and has operations all over the world. The company was actually founded in Hong Kong and Shanghai as Hong Kong Shanghai Banking Corporation in 1865, so it has a long history of operating in Asia. The region remains a very important component of overall operations, accounting for about 28 percent of the company's total global assets.

HSBC operates in China with two brand names: HSBC and Hang Seng Bank. It's the largest bank in Hong Kong and has 12 branches in mainland China. The bank has also invested in major Mainland Chinese financial institutions to increase its footprint there. In 2004, HSBC bought a 19.9 percent stake in China's fifth-largest bank, the Bank of Communications. This was the largest stake ever taken in a Mainland Chinese bank by a foreign institution.

It's worth mentioning a few major players outside Asia's two largest markets. Lippo Bank (Indonesia: LPBN) was Indonesia's first private bank and remains among its largest financial institutions with nearly 3 million customer accounts and 400 branch offices. Indonesia's banking system has even more room for growth than India's. The country's loan-to-GDP ratio stands at just a touch above 20 percent, one of the lowest anywhere in Asia. Deposit growth has been strong, as consumers have retained a very high savings rate. Lippo Bank has been working steadily to lower costs and reduce nonperforming loans; on the loan front, the company has seen solid growth in recent years.

Thailand's largest bank is Bangkok Bank (Bangkok: BBL) with more than 13 million accounts and 650 branch offices across the nation. The company provides a full range of banking services, from lending to commercial banking and even investment banking services. The biggest asset for Bangkok Bank is its huge branch network and customer base that allows the company to cross-sell products and services.

Singapore's United Overseas Bank (OTC: UOVEY; Singapore: UOB) offers good exposure not only on Singapore itself but Malaysia, Thailand, Indonesia, and the Philippines, all markets in which the company has a presence. The company's diversified product offerings include banking, brokerage, and insurance.

Pharmaceuticals and Healthcare

Next to food, water, and shelter, quality healthcare is a basic human need. The enormous and growing Asian population will affect the healthcare sector on both the supply and demand sides.

India's population is growing and remains youthful, but China faces growth and increasing numbers of older citizens. Like older westerners, the aged in China require more drugs. As China and India become wealthier, they'll increasingly demand the same sorts of advanced pharmaceuticals and treatments so common in the West. This spells a whole new source of demand for the global pharmaceutical industry.

What's far more interesting is Asia's emergence as a key player in the supply of drugs. Asia and India, in particular, will be major forces in both the manufacture and development of pharmaceuticals. India is already a world leader in the manufacture and reformulation of existing drugs. Eventually, India will be a major force in drug innovation—actually doing the research, development, and clinical trials required to bring new drugs to the global market.

India benefits from a well-educated, highly skilled population of scientists and doctors with the technical expertise to work in the drug development industry. Skilled doctors and researchers will work for a fraction of the cost of their U.S. counterparts; according to most estimates, salaries are between one-fifth and one-third U.S. levels.[9]

India already has well-developed expertise in the healthcare business. Indian manufacturers account for more than one-third of all filings in the U.S. for generic drug approvals, and the nation has the highest number of FDA-approved manufacturing facilities outside the U.S.

Until recently, Indian drug companies have focused mainly on the manufacture of generic drugs and reformulations of existing drugs. These companies have historically lagged the U.S. in terms of discovering and developing new drugs, due partially to India's intellectual property laws. Up until the beginning of 2005, India's 1970 patent law allowed companies to sell other pharmaceuticals' prescription drugs by simply using a different manufacturing process. This gave rise to fears on the part of some multinationals that Indian drug companies would violate internationally accepted intellectual property laws. But that changed in January of 2005 when the nation adopted the World Trade Organization (WTO) standards for patents.

This change in the law has fostered a new wave of innovation that's set to transform India into a far more important player on the global pharmaceutical market. Indian drug companies realize that they can no longer simply make generic forms of existing drugs or produce pharmaceutical compounds in bulk, but must take the next step and develop their research and development (R&D) capabilities. In this regard, Indian firms have a competitive cost advantage.

The major multinational pharmaceuticals have had considerable trouble developing new drugs in a cost-effective manner. Most estimates place the cost of developing a brand new drug at between $800 million and $1 billion. Some key cost considerations include hiring skilled research staff and conducting expensive human clinical trials and basic molecular work.

India's cost advantage is already starting to alleviate some of these cost concerns. Foreign pharmaceutical players are outsourcing some of their R&D and drug development tasks to India, and Indian companies are moving from copying existing drugs to developing brand new compounds.

Cipla (Mumbai: CIPLA) is India's largest pharmaceutical company and the fourth-largest drug company in the world in terms of bulk pharmaceutical sales. It currently operates in three distinct divisions: formulations, bulk drugs, and technology services. Cipla's largest division, accounting for nearly three-quarters of sales, is formulations. This involves producing generic versions of drugs, including inhaled drugs, pills, and capsules. Drugs produced in this segment are both over-the-counter (OTC) and prescription drugs. The generic drug approval and formulation process involves far more than a few manufacturing facilities that use low-cost labor.

The generics business is not a low-tech, low-skill area. Cipla has a significant competency producing very advanced compounds used in the manufacture of the latest drugs. Generic drug development requires extensive research and testing before FDA approval, and this often requires using new formulations or drug deliveries to manufacture drugs.

The second most important division by sales is bulk drugs, worth about 20 percent of total revenues. Production of bulk drugs involves basic compounds used in the manufacture, testing, and/or delivery of drugs. Many of these bulk drugs are exported abroad to generic and branded drug makers. The technology services group is relatively small, but could be the growth market of the future. This segment involves designing pharmaceutical plants and consulting services for other companies.

Cipla is leveraging its advanced manufacturing and research know-how to partner with major U.S. pharmaceutical companies. The company is developing about 140 drugs on an exclusive basis with major U.S. companies including Ivax, Watson Pharmaceuticals, and Eon Labs.

A handful of foreign companies will benefit from growth in Asia by selling into the market and by sourcing at lower costs in India. Some of these companies' advantages are based on the quality of their product portfolios, whereas others have direct investments in Asia.

One of the first movers in India was GlaxoSmithKline (NYSE: GSK). The company has been running neck-and-neck with Cipla in the Indian market in terms of drug sales with approximately a 6 percent share of the domestic market. That makes India an important market for Glaxo.

Probably because of extended government review and complex manufacturing processes, vaccines are one of the most ignored growth drivers in the pharmaceutical business. Wall Street has ignored this business segment and its potential in favor of drugs. But the vaccine business is worth investors' attention. According to industry sources, sales of vaccines in 2004 were $8 billion, with expectations that this number will grow to $18 billion by 2009. Wyeth's Prevnar (the first billion-dollar vaccine) proved that there is real money to be made in the vaccine area. Expect profit margins to continue to expand in this area.

The most prominent vaccines are those for human papillomavirus (HPV) prevention and rotavirus. HPV vaccines are viewed as an important medical breakthrough and should create solid revenue streams for GSK and Wyeth.

Twenty million people are currently infected with HPV in the U.S., and 5.5 million new cases are diagnosed each year. The virus is the primary cause of cervical cancer, the second-leading cause of cancer deaths in women.

It's estimated that almost all children are infected with rotavirus by the age of five. In the U.S., about one of every 50 children is hospitalized due to dehydration associated with the infection. The problem is more severe abroad—the virus is responsible for about 500,000 deaths annually.

GSK is a major player in the global vaccine business, and recently set up its first plant outside Europe—in India—specifically to produce vaccines. GSK has also started to partner with other drug firms to co-promote their drugs in India, making use of the company's established sales force in the nation. The company is working to leverage its research and development capabilities to conduct clinical trials or handle research on new drugs for multinational firms.

Swiss powerhouse Novartis (NYSE: NVS) also stands to benefit from changing Asian demographics. On the branded drugs front, Novartis has one of the most promising pipelines in the business: Few blockbusters are scheduled to lose patent protection in the near future. (This includes the company's flagship drug, Diovan, used to treat hypertension.) In addition to existing drugs, Novartis has more than a dozen new drugs in late-stage testing, among the most plentiful of the big drug companies.

Novartis is far more than a branded drugs company. It's also one of the top two generics drug manufacturers in the world. Of the so-called Big Pharma players, Novartis is by far the most exposed to the generics industry. Its 51-percent owned subsidiary, Novartis India Limited, focuses on manufacturing generic drugs for consumption in the local Indian market. Given the size of Novartis' generics portfolio, India is likely to become an increasingly important source of low-cost manufacturing and R&D for the parent company.

Switzerland-based oncology and virology expert ($24 billion in sales) Roche (Switzerland: ROG, OTC: RHHBY) is another solid alternative on the global pharmaceutical industry. Roche has a market leading position in cancer treatments and has several new drugs in the pipeline, including one of the most promising cancer drugs to have been developed in many years, Avastin. Roche earns a piece of the royalties from this drug due to its stake in Genentech.

Technology/Outsourcing

China and India are emerging as key centers of technological innovation. In years past, Asian companies were seen as simple manufacturers of electronic and technological products. The products themselves were designed and innovated elsewhere, usually in the United States. But just as Indian drug companies have moved beyond the basic manufacture of generic drugs to actually research and develop new drugs, Asia is also gaining ground as a technology R&D center. The region holds many advantages.

One advantage is education. Europe and the U.S. are producing fewer and fewer university graduates in science and engineering. Meanwhile, such disciplines remain popular in Asia, and there are several highly competitive, world-class universities in China and India supplying workers to the technological industries.

Not every Asian student studies in Asia—the U.S., in particular, has emerged as a key breeding ground for new Asian scientists. Nearly 40 percent of all science and engineering doctorates awarded in the U.S. in 2001 were to foreign students. Of that 40 percent, nearly one-quarter were Chinese. China, India, Taiwan, and South Korea accounted for more than half of all doctorates awarded to foreigners.[10] Many of these graduates remain in the U.S. to work, but a substantial (and growing) number are returning to Asia. These foreign-educated workers are helping to import know-how and innovation into the region.

Another advantage is cost. R&D operations are much cheaper in Asia—this is just as true for science and engineering research as it is for medicine.

General Electric (NYSE: GE) is already taking advantage of Asia's large and highly innovative workforce. The company has constructed a large technology park, The John Welch Technology Center, outside Bangalore, India. Nearly 2,400 scientists and engineers work on new technologies in everything from plastics to aircraft engines. The technology center has been a major success. Scientists at the center have filed for more than 250 patents and received 10. GE is nurturing a top-notch technological research arm at a fraction of what it would cost in the U.S. With several highly competitive Indian universities in the area, there's no shortage of skilled workers to handle research.

One of the leading players in the Asian technology and outsourcing boom is Infosys (NSDQ: INFY). This company, based in Bangalore, employs a small army of software engineers, technology consultants, and call center employees.

Western firms hire Infosys to help them develop software. Due to the time difference between India and the U.S. or Europe, these engineers can be working on code while their western counterparts are asleep. Infosys also handles business process outsourcing functions, including customer service call centers and back office credit cards, checks, or financial exchange trade processing operations. Infosys is also moving up the value chain, offering technology consulting and other high value-added services.

Infosys benefits from the trend toward outsourcing in the short to intermediate term. Over the long term, the company's highly qualified workers will likely get into more innovative and value-added work.

India's I-Flex (Mumbai: IFLEX) is following a similar path. The company caters mainly to the financial services industry with a lineup of technology and outsourcing solutions. The fact that U.S. technology services giant Oracle owns nearly 41 percent of the company is proof of the quality of the company's product suites.

I-Flex's Flexcube includes basic transactions processing and accounting software used by the banking industry. I-Flex also offers software that allows banks to manage client relationships, analyzing customers' transactions to see what sort of products might interest them. The company's product suite also includes software used to manage a financial institution's risk.

Telecom

Asian consumers have embraced the mobile telephone like no other consumers anywhere in the world. Mobile telephony in these countries is simply more practical and reliable than traditional fixed-line telephony.

Most western consumers used a fixed-line telephone system exclusively before cell phones hit the scene in earnest in the early 1990s. The same is not true in Asia. Line telephone systems require major fixed-infrastructure investments: wires, buried telephone cable, microwave towers, and other items. This infrastructure simply didn't exist in parts of Asia, making the telephone system there less reliable.

But mobile systems are far easier to set up—a tower and cell station can cover a fairly wide geographic area reliably with far less investment in buried cable. A whole generation of Asians has skipped over unreliable fixed-line telephony and jumped straight into using cell phones.

There are other motivations. As anyone who has ever lived or traveled in Europe can attest, mobiles are a status symbol. Young consumers everywhere want to have the latest handset designs and features. In India and China, consumers will pay a surprisingly high price relative to their incomes to get the latest technology. As mentioned throughout this book, Asian consumers increasingly demand the same sort of goods as their Western counterparts.

Just to give an idea of the growth of these technologies, consider the case of India. By the end of 2002, the country had a little more than 10 million mobile telephone subscribers. But by 2003, that number had almost tripled to nearly 30 million. By 2004, it had reached more than 60 million. Asia in its entirety accounts for about half of all mobile handset sales on the planet. The beneficiaries of this trend are of two stripes. First are the companies involved in installing and making telecom equipment, and second are the telecoms in Asia that actually provide the service to consumers.

Global telecom equipment giant Ericsson (NSDQ: ERICY) is the market leader in the equipment and systems that are used to make wireless networks function, including wireless antennas, transmitters, and switching gear. As India and China are at the center of new network building, Ericsson is extremely well positioned to profit.

The company has been increasingly focusing on customer satisfaction, market share gains, and exploration of new ideas, while management has been implementing conservative accounting practices in an effort to rebuild Ericsson's balance sheet.

When Ericsson teamed up with Sony in a creative effort to produce a new line of innovative telephones and other handheld communication devices, the critics were easy to find. No one believed that Japanese consumer electronics and European telecommunications were a good fit.

Because of the vast resources of the mother companies, the venture is rapidly becoming one of the frontrunners in the mobile telecommunication/multimedia industry. Ericsson carved out solid positions in the higher end handsets that are so popular in Europe and the cheaper handsets that are big sellers in the emerging markets. If Sony Ericsson continues its strong performance, the venture will contribute between 15 percent and 20 percent to Ericsson's net profits in the next couple of years.

Chunghwa Telecom (NYSE: CHT) is the leading Internet services and wireless telecom services provider in Taiwan. Though the company is by no means a growth story, it's one of the most defensive ways to play the highly profitable Asian telecom market. As the only integrated provider in Taiwan, it has a dominant share in all of all of its key markets, including a 35 percent share of the wireless market. The Taiwanese wireless market boasts one of the highest subscriber penetration rates in the world—more than 90 percent of the population has a cell phone.

Although fixed-line subscribers are falling in number and wireless growth has moderated, cash flows from both segments are strong. This has allowed Chunghwa to continue paying out a very healthy dividend to shareholders.

On the Internet front, Chunghwa also has a dominant share of the nation's broadband subscribers. Broadband Internet penetration is still less than mobile telephones, and the market is growing faster.

Another defensive play is Singapore Telecom (Singapore: ST, OTC: SNGNY), Southeast Asia's largest telecom operator. The company provides all sorts of telecom and Internet services in its home market; these operations throw off solid cash flows and allow Singapore Telecom to offer a solid dividend.

Singapore Telecom is also a growth story. The company has committed some of its prodigious cash flows to other Asian operators, likely to include an investment in the Chinese market, where new government rules allow foreigners to have stakes as large as 49 percent in local operators. The company already holds stakes in India's Bharti Televentures, Globe Telecom in the Philippines, and Advance Info Services of Thailand.

Shipping, Ports, and Transport

If you've shopped at Wal-Mart recently, you know that an increasing number of consumer goods sold in the U.S. markets come from Asia and China, in particular. It's not just the U.S. that's seen vastly increased trade with China since the late 1990s; Europe and other Asian countries are also major recipients of Chinese exports.

Import traffic has increased as well. China exports a lot of manufactured products, but needs to import energy products, food, and metals to fuel its economic engine. Although India's economy is more service-oriented, the nation still has to import oil and other basic commodities to feed its growing economy. This has resulted in an explosion in international trade over the past five years, a trend that shows no signs of abating.

Most of that trade will be made by ship—a whopping 80 percent of global trade. Large container ships carry manufactured goods from China destined for U.S. ports, whereas tankers and dry bulk carriers handle the imports and trade in oil, natural gas, and other basic commodities. Transport by ship is cheaper and easier than transport by plane. Despite all our technological advances, global trade still plies the Seven Seas, just as it did during the 19th century.

China Cosco Shipping (OTC: CSPKF, HK: 1919) is the nation's largest container shipping line. The company owns and operates a fleet of dozens of ships operating on routes between Asian ports and Europe and across the Pacific to America.

The fleet includes standard container ships, special ships designed to carry large cargoes that can't fit in containers, and semi-submersible ships designed to carry particularly heavy cargoes. The company's size and expertise in loading and transporting all sorts of cargoes makes it the premier play on the transport industry in China.

Taiwan is another key port in Southeast Asia. The best play there is Wan Hai Lines (Taiwan: 2615), one of the nation's largest shippers with a fleet of more than 50 container vessels. In addition to providing transport services, Wan Hai also sells and leases ships, operates container freight terminals, and brokers shipping deals for other companies.

The world's largest port operator, Hutchison Whampoa (HK: 13, OTC: HUWHY), has a total of more than 200 berths in 35 ports worldwide. More importantly, the company operates in the world's busiest ports, including one port on each side of the key Panama Canal. One of the busiest shipping ports in the world is Hong Kong, Hutchison's home market. The company owns a controlling stake in the company that controls traffic into the Hong Kong container port.

Hutchison's rapid expansion into China has been facilitated by the fact that the company's senior management has a long history of operating there and has solid connections with the Chinese government. Hutchison has stakes in several of South China's busiest port operations.

Also worth mentioning is Hong-Kong based China Merchants Holdings (HK: 144). The company owns container terminals in Hong Kong and Southern China. Traffic through these ports is expected to double between 2003 and 2008, spelling more revenues for the company. The company also handles cargo logistics and air cargo loading and unloading.

That's Entertainment

Consumers the world over must be entertained. Every year, Americans and Europeans eagerly await the latest blockbuster film out of Hollywood. Across the western world, satellite and cable television make available to consumers an enormous selection of programs.

Asian consumers are no different. India's "Bollywood" films are immensely popular and are probably watched by far more consumers than your average western production. Eighty-five million Indian homes have access to television and 42 million have either cable or satellite access. The number of cable and satellite subscribers is growing at approximately 8 percent annually.

One aspect of all of that is advertising. Whether it's the Sony Ericsson mobile telephone used by a character in a movie, James Bond's latest automobile, or a simple product advertisement on TV, consumers are bombarded with a steady stream of advertising through the media.

The key to the media industry is content. Advertisers will always pay more for eyeballs; in other words, the companies with the best programming will attract the most viewers and the most advertising dollars.

Our favorite play on the Indian media market is Zee Telefilms (Mumbai: Z), India's largest media company and a major producer of films, television series, game shows, and other programs. The company also owns the ZEE TV channel and distributes its own motion pictures.

Zee makes money in two ways, through advertising and via subscription payments for its television network. The company has almost 1 million subscribers worldwide, including subscribers in the core Indian market as well as a large number of expatriates in the United States and Europe.

Zee features a wide range of "must-have" content, including worldwide rights to cricket matches—cricket remains an extremely popular game in India.

As the Asia story unfolds, themes like the ones described here will become more important. This chapter has tried to offer a guideline and can be used as a point of departure by investors interested in the investing opportunities we identified in this book.

As always, success will lay with each individual investor's ability to anticipate change and analyze trends.

Signs of a transformation the world has not seen in ages are appearing. Be a part of it, and enjoy the ride.

Endnotes

1. http://inhome.rediff.com/money/2005/jun/29air.htm.
2. "China Tourism—What Are the Economics" (Morgan Stanley, May 10, 2005).
3. http://www.time.com/time/asia/magazine/article/0,13673,501030901-477977-3,00.html.
4. Morningstar Report. "Wrigley's Future Looks Bright" (May 25, 2005).
5. "China: Non-carb Nation on the Rise" (Morgan Stanley, June 21, 2005).
6. "China Won't Be the Same Opportunity for Everyone" (Morgan Stanley, June 21, 2005).
7. Ibid.
8. The latest (2004) Bank for International Settlements' guideline to international Convergence of Capital Measurement and Capital Standards of banks around the world.
9. "How India Hopes to Reshape the World Drugs Industry" (FT.com, August 17, 2004).
10. Cookson, Clive. "Innovative Asia" (*Financial Times*, June 8, 2005).

EPILOGUE

Globalization and change inspired this book.

We have consciously avoided a discussion of the ethical or existential questions these two phenomena inspire. This is an investment book concerned with particular risks and particular rewards based on what we believe are valid assumptions rooted in historical, economic, and financial understanding.

In identifying catastrophic problems regarding Asia's future economic development, most observers single out AIDS as an ominous, potentially destabilizing force. AIDS could pose a formidable challenge in the future.

But as I write, President Bush is outlining a proposed U.S. response to an avian flu outbreak. Influenza virus could be the biggest challenge the world will face in the near future, possibly the single most important threat to the world's social and economic stability. Although it was initially confined to certain bird species, it has become lethal to humans, too.

According to Laurie Garrett, a senior fellow for Global Health at the Council of Foreign Relations, "if the relentlessly evolving virus becomes capable of human-to-human transmission, develops a power of contagion typical of human influenzas, and maintains its extraordinary virulence, humanity could well face a pandemic unlike any ever witnessed." Of course, there is a possibility that nothing comes of the current scare, but it is impossible to predict.

The results of an avian flu pandemic would devastate the world. No nation—neither developed nor developing—is really prepared. The world cannot produce enough vaccines to cover its current needs efficiently, and no one can say for certain when an outbreak that threatens humans on a global scale will hit. During the 2004 flu scare in the U.S., the country was short of vaccines and it needed help from Canada, Germany, and France. Even then, it took until February of 2005—the end of the flu season—for the U.S. to meet all its needs. During a potential pandemic described earlier, such cooperation among nations is difficult to imagine: Each country will have the needs of its own citizens to address.

That said, reality is marked by rapid change, change that must be understood or accepted sooner or later. This change will eventually allow more than 3 billion people to be incorporated in the global economic system. In a place as diverse as Asia, it is of paramount importance that investors trying to identify new themes for the next decade take into consideration the individual characteristics of the countries to which they direct their capital.

In his book *The Idea of India*, Sunil Khilnani writes, "In fact, no single idea can possibly hope to capture the many energies, angers, and hopes of one billion Indians; nor can any more narrow idea—based on a single trait—fulfill their desires."

The same sentiment could also describe China.

The view here is that consumption (maybe not an "idea" per se, but a very powerful concept nonetheless) appeals usually to a wide variety of people despite differences they may have when it comes to other aspects of life. Many observers forget that the reason for relatively low consumption in some countries is due to lack of access to money. After the financial and institutional foundations necessary to encourage consumption have been established, the outcome is almost always the same: People consume. This is where Asia is heading.

From an economic and investment perspective, this is an important idea to understand, as it can change Asia's economic structure, and therefore the type of opportunities for investors. A stronger and more self-assured Asia is the only chance the world has for strong economic growth in the future—the industrialized market economies have reached their peak.

It is necessary to mention at this point that Asian markets have only recently started to open fully to foreign investors. South Korea and Taiwan, for example, did not become fully accessible to foreign investors (apart from institutions) until 1998 and 2003, respectively. The Asian stock market integration into the global market system is still in its first steps. Expect more investment funds to flow into Asia as these markets open up and investors in richer economies realize that their domestic markets do not—and will not—provide the returns a growing Asia can offer.

Of all the major economies, one that could become Asia's big helper is Japan. A few serious market observers have floated the idea that as Japan's economy is showing signs of emerging from a devastating and prolonged slump (with its banking and corporate sectors being restructured), the rest of Asia will benefit. This rationale is fairly simple and is based on the idea that a strong Japan will invest more abroad as it did in the 1980s and early 1990s. Then, the main beneficiaries were the emerging Asia countries even though they accounted, according to the IMF, for only 26 percent of Japan's total trade. Now, they account for 46 percent.

The idea that Japan is critical to future regional strength has merit. The Japanese seem to be doing the right things to take their economy out of deflation. If this happens, Asia's economic future and consequently future investment returns look even brighter.

The investment thesis presented in this book has a very good chance of materializing. What's important to remember is that, given the challenges ahead, a great deal of cooperation is required for the world to be able to embrace the new economic order and continue to prosper. The overall cooperation among nations in political and economic fronts is the main reason for the extraordinary run the world economy enjoyed since the end of WWII. This cooperation has been in decline since the turn of the century, and it could get worse before getting better.

Economist Paul Seabright wrote a book about the importance of human cooperation, *The Company of Strangers*. In it, he quotes (from Thucydides' *History of the Peloponnesian War*) Pericles's funeral oration to the Athenians: "We throw open our city to the world, and never by alien acts exclude foreigners from any opportunity of learning or observing, although the eyes of an enemy may occasionally profit by our liberality; trusting less in system and policy than to the native spirit of our citizens; while in education, where our rivals from their very cradles by a painful discipline seek after manliness, at Athens we live exactly as we please, and yet are just as ready to encounter every legitimate danger."

And maybe Athens did lose the Peloponnesian War. But the wisdom of freedom and openness that it championed allowed the rest of the world to build the miracle we now call civilization, without which progress— of any kind—would have been impossible.

It is this kind of human cooperation we expect to take center stage again, as people around the world begin to realize that policy inflexibility cannot offer answers to today's complex geopolitical, social, and economic problems. A look at history and humanity's strong learning curve supports our optimism.

INDEX

N

Nasdaq, 82
natural gas, 148, 164-166, 168-169
   Asia, 179
   liquefied natural gas, 167
natural resources, RSNRX, 196
Nayar, Baldev Raj, 63
Nestle, 208-209
New Economy, 197
New York Life, 215
Newmont Mining, 115-116
nickel, 190-192
1929 stock market crash, 82-83
1997 crisis, coming of age, 22-25
non-proliferation treaty, 63
nonperforming loan (NPL), 213
nontradable jobs, 31
nontradable service jobs, 26
North, Douglass C., 52, 55
Novartis, 220
NPL (nonperforming loan), 213
nuclear capability, India, 62-63
nuclear power, 169-172
   investing in, 174-175
Nucor Steel, 189, 193

O

OECD (Organization for Economic
   Co-operation and Development), 149
offshoring, 26-29
oil, 143, 147
   integrated companies, 181
   intensity index, 153
   refining, 157-161
   reserve replacement, 155
   rising consumption of, 148-154
   Saudi Arabia, 154
   supply of, 154-157
   U.S., 154
Oldsmobile, 198
ONGC (Oil and Natural Gas
   Corporation), 178
OPEC (Organization of Petroleum
   Exporting Countries), 156
Orissa, India, 198
   infrastructure, 46
outsourcing, 25-29, 221-222
   China, 27-28
   comparative advantage, 29
   manufacturing share, 28

P

P/E ratios, 86
   steel, 193
Pakistan, United States military aid to,
   64-66
palm oil, 143

paper money, 97-99, 101, 103-105
passenger enplanements, 200
Paul, T.V., 63
People's Food Holdings, 144
personal computers, 11-12
pharmaceutical industry, India, 45
pharmaceuticals, 216-220
Phelps Dodge, 190
Phelps, Anson, 190
Philadelphia Stock Exchange (PHLX),
   Gold and Silver Index (XAU), 112
Phosphates, fertilizer, 138
Pierpont Morgan, J., 97
Pilara, Andrew, 196
Pizza Hut, 205
policy decisions, China, 51
political crisis, currency, 101
pollution, 162
Polo, Marco, 5
Pomeranz, Kenneth, 6
population, 9
   food supply. *See* food supply
   India, 10
POSCO, 193
potash, 139
Potash Corporation of Saskatchewan,
   140-141
PPP (purchasing power parity), 56
precious metals, 98
   gold. *See* gold
preemptive war as U.S. policy, 73
prepared foods, 203
Prevnar, 219
prices, relative prices, 13
*The Principles of Political Economy and
   Taxation*, 25
private sector development, 51-52
productivity, xxiv
property rights, 41, 52
prosperity, wage rates, 30
protectionism, China, 51
PSAs (production sharing
   agreements), 182
purchasing power, 97
purchasing power parity (PPP), 56
Putin, Vladimir, 70

Q-R

Quantum fund, 187
R&D (research and development), 221
Ramachandran, Sudha, 65
real estate bubble (U.S.), 93
refining oil, 157-161
renewable energy, 176-177
research and development (R&D), 221
reserve replacement, oil, 155
restaurants, 204

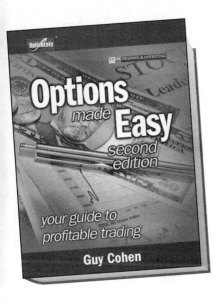

Options Made Easy, Second Edition
Your Guide to Profitable Trading
BY GUY COHEN

Options trading offers unparalleled opportunity for rapid profit, but most options guides are difficult to understand and even harder to use successfully. Not this one. *Options Made Easy* has earned a worldwide reputation for simplicity, clarity, and practical value. In this thoroughly revamped Second Edition, renowned options trader Guy Cohen delivers even more of what makes this book so valuable: better graphics for easy visual learning, updated hands-on examples that walk step by step through real trades, and the clearest plain-English explanations of trading techniques you'll find anywhere.

ISBN 0131871358, © 2006, 368 pp., $27.95

Wealth
Grow It, Protect It, Spend It, and Share It
BY STUART E. LUCAS

FOREWORD BY JOE MANSUETO, CHAIRMAN AND CEO OF MORNINGSTAR, INC.

Here is the first book to integrate all the essential components of wealth management into a coherent whole. Generate higher, more predictable returns...identify, retain, and coordinate the right advisors...get your family to agree on goals and priorities...intelligently manage assets received through inheritances and business sales...and much more. Stuart Lucas draws on 25 years of experience managing wealth. He is CEO of Integrated Wealth Management LLC and Principal and Investment Advisor at Cataumet Partners, his family's investment office. He is also an heir to the Carnation Company fortune after it was sold to Nestlé in 1985.

ISBN 0132366797, © 2006, 304 pp., $25.99